Praise for *The 30-Minute Vegan*

"A host of appealing recipes can be found between the covers of this book, as well as a lot of good information about food and cooking in general, surprisingly realistic approaches to thirty-minute cooking with real food, and more, from glossaries to Web sites."

—Deborah Madison, author of *Vegetarian Cooking for Everyone*

"*The 30 Minute Vegan* has found a permanent home in my kitchen, where its pages will quickly become worn, torn, and stained."

—HungryVegan.com

"*The 30-Minute Vegan* is a fail-safe cookbook designed to save you time and eliminate stress in the kitchen. With a well-planned collection of fast, simple, and healthy recipes, the duo is determined to keep home dining diverse and your diet in tip-top shape."

—*VegNews*

"Any who want to cook vegan food quickly will appreciate *The 30-Minute Vegan*, a user-friendly guide for busy cooks who don't want to spend a lot of time in the kitchen. Nearly 200 simple whole foods involve easy preparation and offer quick cooking charts, raw foods recipes, kid-friendly foods the entire family can enjoy, and extraordinary lunches and snacks."

—Midwest Book Review

"One of the very best vegan cookbooks of all time. Fabulous recipes, healthy food, clear directions, and delicious results!"

—John Robbins, author of *The Food Revolution* and *Diet for a New America*

"*The 30-Minute Vegan* is not only a culinary delight for vegetarians and vegans, it appeals to people who relish a meal that luxuriates the palate and satisfies the spirit."

—Michael Bernard Beckwith, author of *Spiritual Liberation: Fulfilling Your Soul's Potential*

"Don't let a lack of time keep you from making a healthy choice! These quick, delicious recipes will see you through even the busiest mealtimes with good taste and style."

—Jennifer McCann, author of *Vegan Lunch Box* and *Vegan Lunch Box Around the World*

"[A] classic, practical guide to preparing exquisitely tasteful, healthy vegan food that is ideal for busy folks of today. Every home will be enriched by having this book in the kitchen."

—Arthur H. Brownstein, M.D., M.P.H., author of *Healing Back Pain Naturally* and *Extraordinary Healing*

the 30 Minute Vegan's TASTE of the EAST

Also by Mark Reinfeld and Jennifer Murray:

The 30-Minute Vegan

The Complete Idiot's Guide to Eating Raw (with Bo Rinaldi)

Also by Mark Reinfeld:

Vegan Fusion World Cuisine (with Bo Rinaldi)

The 30 Minute Vegan's

TASTE of the EAST

150 Asian-Inspired Recipes—from Soba Noodles to Summer Rolls

Mark Reinfeld and Jennifer Murray

DA CAPO PRESS
A Member of the Perseus Books Group

Except where noted, photography by: Sarah Warfield (www.syawarfield.com) and Sarah Joy Davis (www.sarahjoys-creations.weebly.com)

Designed by Trish Wilkinson
Set in 11-point Minion by the Perseus Books Group

Library of Congress Cataloging-in-Publication Data

Reinfeld, Mark.
The 30-minute vegan's taste of the East : 150 Asian-inspired recipes from soba noodles to summer rolls / Mark Reinfeld and Jennifer Murray.
p. cm.
Includes index.
ISBN 978-0-7382-1382-8 (alk. paper)
1. Vegan cookery. 2. Cookery, Asian. I. Murray, Jennifer. II. Title. III. Title: Vegan's taste of the East.
TX837.R448 2010
641.595—dc22 2010011133

First Da Capo Press edition 2010
ISBN: 978-0-7382-1382-8

Published by Da Capo Press
A Member of the Perseus Books Group
www.dacapopress.com

Note: The information in this book is true and complete to the best of our knowledge. This book is intended only as an informative guide for those wishing to know more about health issues. In no way is this book intended to replace, countermand, or conflict with the advice given to you by your own physician. The ultimate decision concerning care should be made between you and your doctor. We strongly recommend you follow his or her advice. Information in this book is general and is offered with no guarantees on the part of the authors or Da Capo Press. The authors and publisher disclaim all liability in connection with the use of this book. The names and identifying details of people associated with events described in this book have been changed. Any similarity to actual persons is coincidental.

Da Capo Press books are available at special discounts for bulk purchases in the U.S. by corporations, institutions, and other organizations. For more information, please contact the Special Markets Department at the Perseus Books Group, 2300 Chestnut Street, Suite 200, Philadelphia, PA, 19103, or call (800) 810-4145, ext. 5000, or e-mail special.markets@perseusbooks.com.

10 9 8 7 6 5 4 3 2

In gratitude to the vast culinary, cultural, and spiritual contributions of the East

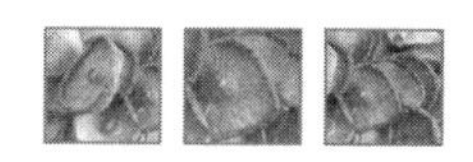

Contents

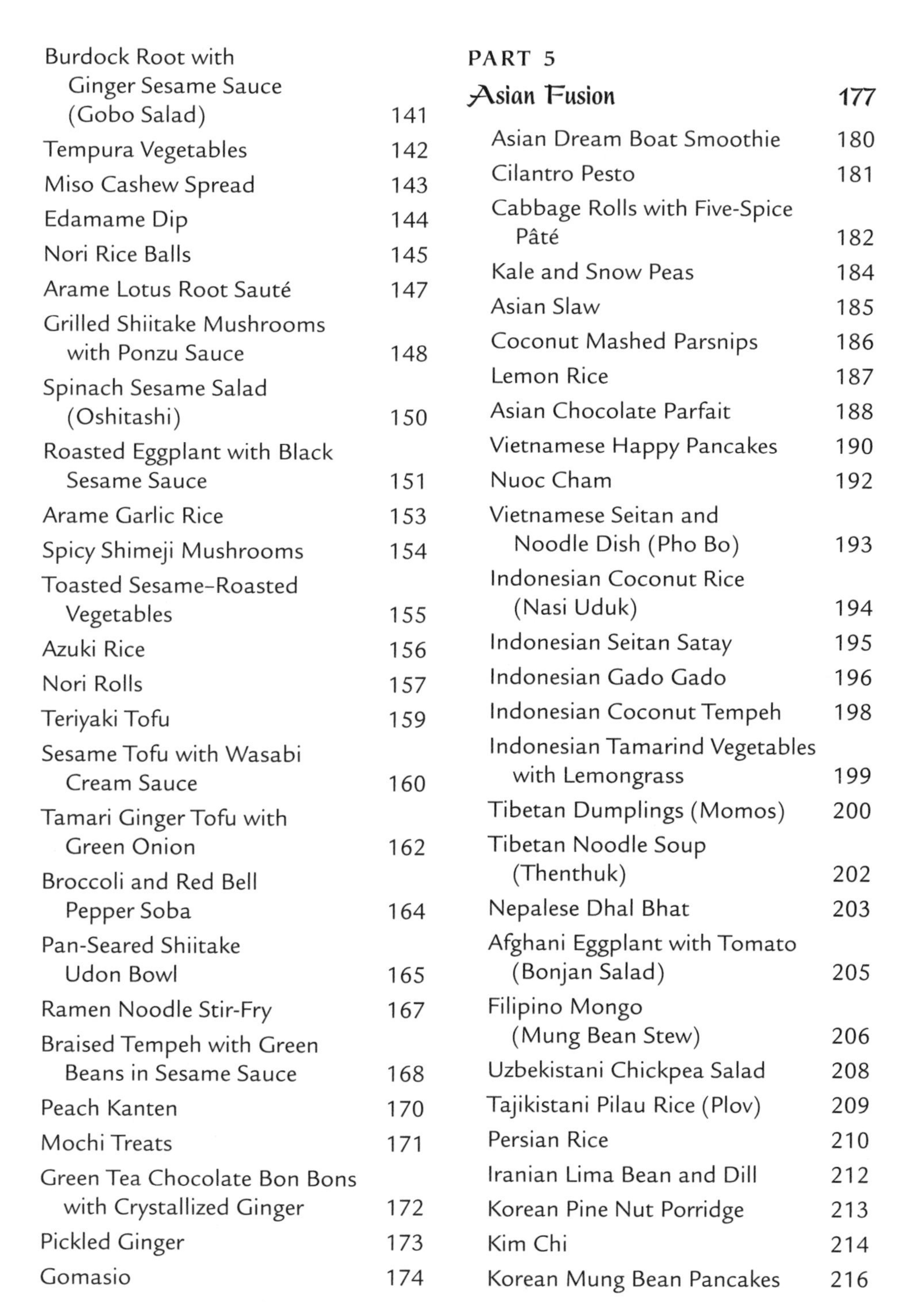

The 30 Minute Vegan's TASTE of the EAST

Photo courtesy Jennifer Murray and Mark Reinfeld.

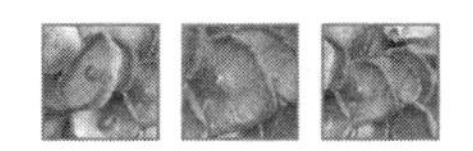

Introduction

We're pleased that you are joining us on our adventure into the rich and bountiful world of Asian vegan cuisine. In the pages of *Taste of the East*, we explore foods from several countries throughout the continent. Our goal is to introduce the distinct flavors of Asia, using ingredients that are accessible here in the West, with recipes that can be completed in 30 minutes or less. Quite a task!

The first four sections explore the cuisines of India, Thailand, China, and Japan. The fifth section is our "Asian Fusion" chapter, in which we share recipes from Korea, Indonesia, Tibet, and Vietnam, in addition to Central Asian countries such as Iran, Afghanistan, and even Uzbekistan. (Yes, you can be the first kid on the block to bring an Uzbekistani dish to your next potluck!)

Our experience with the cuisines is based on our visits to India, Nepal, China, and Thailand, as well as countless dining experiences in New York, San Francisco, and our many other travels. And, with an Asian population of over 40 percent, our home of Hawaii also holds a wealth of Asian culinary traditions in its islands. In some ways, *The Taste of the East* is a culmination of our three prior books. As with *Vegan Fusion World Cuisine* it celebrates international cuisine, like *The 30-Minute Vegan* it provides quick and easy recipes, and like *The Complete Idiot's Guide to Eating Raw* it features some raw food dishes, a growing trend in the culinary world.

We had a lot of fun designing these recipes. Creating this book has been an adventure that opened us up to lots of new ingredients, cooking techniques, and tidbits of folklore. The world is becoming increasingly more interconnected. Learning about the cuisine and culture of Asia is a wonderful window into the lives of billions of others. The deeper our understanding, the more aware we become of our common humanity.

The influence of Asian foods is steadily growing here in the West. Japanese, Chinese, Indian, and Thai foods are continually making their way into our communities through restaurants, farmers' markets, and packaged products in grocery stores. This may be a very healthy trend, for Asians suffer much less from the major common ailments of the West. Many studies have been undertaken to determine which qualities of the Asian diet lead to greater health. Most Asian countries live on diets very low in refined flours, sugar, and processed food as well as a modest amount of sweets.

In addition to world-class cuisine, the West has a lot to learn from the cultural traditions of the East. Important practices like yoga and meditation, practiced in Asia for thousands of years, are making their way into mainstream America. The emphasis on taking it slow, embodied in the Japanese tea ceremony, greatly enhances quality of life, creating balance and harmony. As we introduce you to these international kitchen pantries, we'll share each country's folklore and wisdom.

Choosing the recipes and ingredients has been an exciting balancing act. We go for authentic flavor while being mindful of ingredient availability. If you live in a small town without access to the ethnic markets of many larger cities, most of the ingredients should be available in the Asian section of the larger supermarkets and health food stores. And don't be afraid to ask your grocer to carry certain products—you'll be surprised how accommodating they can be. Otherwise, check out some of the numerous online resources listed in Appendix C. Or, if you are eager to dive in, plan a day trip to an ethnic market in your area.

In general, we chose to create wonderful flavors for our recipes rather than a strict adherence to the culinary traditions. We sprinkle in ingredients from the West that we feel enhance the dining experience. Quinoa is a South American grain that may not be sold at the farmers' market in Shanghai, yet it certainly compliments a stir-fry as much as rice. You will also see maple syrup, or agave nectar, uncommon in Asia, used as sweeteners in our recipes.

We recommend using a minimum of processed and packaged ingredients. This is much better for your health, and the reduction in packaging is good for the planet. Most traditional cultures rely on local ingredients, which are fresh and available. However, when preparing Asian cuisine in the West, many times our only source of ingredients comes in cans or bottles. You can also try asking local Asians where they get their authentic ingredients.

We highly recommend using organic ingredients whenever possible in our recipes. Organic food is grown without the use of chemical fertilizers and pesti-

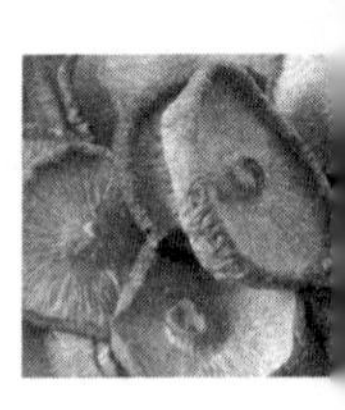

cides, many of which have not been fully tested for their effects on humans. Though people debate whether or not these chemicals are harmful, we know they are not necessary—so we don't take the risk.

Eating locally grown foods whenever possible ensures freshness and saves all of the resources involved in shipping over long distances. Growing foods in your own garden or participating in community-supported agriculture programs (CSAs) is the best option if you have the opportunity. It's very rewarding to see something grow from seed to plant. Farmers' markets are the next best choice. Get to know the people growing your food! Though some of the ingredients may require additional effort, many of the recipes in *Taste of the East* can be adapted to include whatever ingredients are fresh and available.

In addition to creating vegan cookbooks, our company, Vegan Fusion, offers chef training and consulting services, and can assist any food service operation in menu and recipe development with our Innovative Global Cuisine. Our goal is to promote the benefits of vegan foods for our health and for the preservation of our planet. Please visit our Web site, VeganFusion.com, to learn more about us and the vegan lifestyle, and to sign up for our free newsletter.

We encourage you to create an inspiring ambiance when you prepare your meals. Listening to your favorite music and bringing flowers or other objects of beauty into the kitchen will help awaken the creative chef within. May you be inspired by these recipes to prepare more healthy and delicious foods!

With much aloha,
Mark and Jennifer

Photo courtesy Elizabeth Warfield Murray.

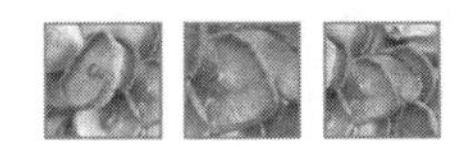

How to Use This Book

Virtually all of the recipes can be completed in less than 30 minutes, including preparation and cooking time. Several recipes do have cooking or baking times that exceed this time frame, but the labor time is kept under 30 minutes. We've also included some of our favorite variations to the recipes, some of which may also take longer than 30 minutes. These are clearly noted.

The clock starts ticking once the ingredients have been gathered and are ready for use. The time doesn't include searching through the cabinets for tools or ingredients. Read through the recipe carefully, perhaps even twice. Make sure you have everything you need and gather it before you begin. Also remember that with practice, everything becomes easier. The more often you make a recipe, the faster you will get.

Within the first four sections, the recipes are listed in the order you might find them on a menu—soups, salads, appetizers, side dishes, entrees, desserts. In one Asian Fusion section, recipes are listed by country of origin. Use these recipes as a starting point for creating your own versions and specialties based on your preferences and whatever ingredients are fresh and available. We are strong believers of creative expression in the kitchen; don't just try to stick to the recipe. Never let one or two missing ingredients stop you from making a recipe. There is always something you can substitute; be creative!

Throughout the book, we introduce many of the techniques of vegan natural food preparation. These techniques are also highlighted in the preparation basics section in Appendix A. For a more thorough exploration, including tips for stocking your kitchen, as well as for an extensive resource guide, please check out *The 30-Minute Vegan.*

To fully dive into the realms of Asian foods we must experience the unique ingredients of each cuisine. Many foods transcend all borders, but some special

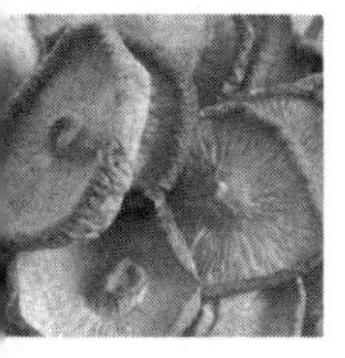

foods have come to be identified with a culinary style. We introduce some of these ingredients in the pantry at the beginning of each section. We encourage you to make the extra effort and stock up on these specialty ingredients to achieve the most authentic flavors in your dishes.

Throughout the pages you will see the following sidebars, which alert you to highlighted features of *Taste of the East:*

Chefs' Tips and Tricks: we share the secrets that make your life in the kitchen easier and more enjoyable

The Asian Pantry: highlights special ingredients of various regions throughout Asia

East Meets West: explores aspects of Asian culture popular in the West

Additionally, we highlight certain recipes with the following symbols:

♥ indicates a **raw food** item, or one that can easily be adapted to a raw recipe. Raw foods are nutrient-rich foods that have not been heated above a certain temperature, thereby preserving many of the food's nutrients.

🕐 **If You Have More Time**: these recipes and variations of recipes take longer than 30 minutes. Give them a try when you have more time to explore them!

Chefs' Tips and Tricks

10 Keys to Success in a 30-Minute Kitchen:
Guidelines for Quickness and Accuracy

Remember that food is an art. These tips will help you have great success in the kitchen and will enable you to enjoy yourself. If you're having a good time, everyone will enjoy the results, no matter what.

1. Read each recipe thoroughly. Look up words and ingredients you are unfamiliar with in our glossary or a dictionary. Understand the process involved. Understand when multitasking is necessary rather than waiting for each step to be complete before moving on to the next step.
2. Before beginning any preparation, create a clean work area. Gather the ingredients in the recipe before you begin. This ensures that you have every-

continues

thing you need, know what you will be using if a substitute is required, and eliminate time spent searching through cabinets. Gather your measuring spoons and cups, tools, and appliances. Preparing food in a clean and organized space is always easier.

3. Having the proper tools is essential to being able to whip food up quickly. Preparation time may be increased if you don't have tools such as a garlic press, zester, citrus juicer, or blender. Work up to a fully stocked kitchen.
4. Though the recipes are designed to taste their best by following the exact measurements, approximations are often acceptable. At some point you will be able to look at ginger and know how much makes a tablespoon. In cases like these, don't worry too much about measuring everything with ultimate precision. With baking, however, measurements need to be precise because leavening is involved.
5. Some herbs, such as parsley, cilantro, or fennel, don't need to be plucked from the thin part of their stems before mincing or chopping. Just keep them bundled together and chop the whole bunch at once. The thin parts of the stems generally have the same flavor and, once minced, basically taste the same.
6. Cut stacks of veggies rather than each individual piece. Don't separate celery stalks when you can cut into the whole bunch at once. Same goes for heads of lettuce and cabbage. Stack tomato, potato, or onion slices and cut them simultaneously.
7. The easiest way to sift flour is with a fine mesh strainer. For accuracy, always sift baking soda, baking powder, cocoa powder, and any spices that have lumps.
8. You don't need to peel carrots, cucumbers, potatoes, zucchini, or beets unless specified; just wash them well. This is not only quicker but also helps preserve the nutritional content of the food.
9. Most blenders have cup and fluid ounce measurements right on the pitcher; no need to dirty more measuring cups.
10. One of the most important tips to help cut down on preparation time is to set aside an hour or so on one of your least busy days for advance prepping. Having prepped ingredients on hand makes it easier to create meals on the go. You can cut vegetables and store them in a glass container in the fridge, and you can cook a squash, grain, or a pot of beans. These foods can then be used in recipes over the next few days. Consider preparing a pot of rice in the morning and using it for the evening meal.

PART ONE

The Cuisine of India

Experiencing India for the first time is like meeting the other half of your mind. There truly are no words to describe the sights, colors, smells, and sounds that flood through you. The Himalayas, the Taj Mahal, the Ganges River—wow! When visiting India, be prepared for adventure. A traffic jam can consist of rickshaws, motorcycles, camels, cows, water buffalo, goats, and even an elephant.

India has a vast history of vegetarian cuisine. Unique culinary traditions have evolved in different regions throughout the country. North Indian cuisine is quite different from that in the South. Even the Northwest (Punjab) is different from the rest of the North. We selected a wide range of recipes to share, including curries, chutneys, rice dishes, soups, and sweets. We encourage you to create an Indian feast that may include Mulligatawny, Rice Pilau, Tempeh Vindaloo, Cucumber Mint Raita, Roasted Garlic Chutney, and a Mango Lassi. Don't forget to save room for the Cardamom Cookies!

The Asian Pantry: India

Asafetida: Also referred to as hing, asafetida has a pungent and relatively unpleasant aroma when raw but imparts the taste of garlic and onion when added to cooked food. It is frequently used by those who avoid onion and garlic in their food. It is also used as a digestive aid.

Chutney: The salsa of India, chutneys are a sauce or relish consisting of fruits, vegetables, herbs, and/or spices that is served as a condiment with Indian meals. Chutneys provide intense flavor. Many are sweet and sour, and spicy hot.

Curry Leaves: Also called sweet neem leaves, curry leaves are used in South Indian cuisine in much the same way bay leaves are used in the West. Despite the name, curry leaves are not a substitute for powdered curry, nor are they generally included in a curry blend. The fresh leaves can be stored in the freezer. They also are available in dried form online and at Asian markets.

Curry Powder: The trademark of the Indian kitchen, curry powder is a ground blend of spices that varies from region to region but generally includes cumin, coriander, and turmeric. It's the turmeric that gives curry its yellow color. For our homemade curry powder recipe, please see page 44.

Dhal (also spelled Dal): One of the most frequent terms you will come across in Indian cuisine, *dhal* refers to a preparation of pulses or legumes that removes the outer shell and splits the husk. It is also the name of the soup or stew that is created by using them, such as mung dhal, chana dhal, and urud dhal.

Garam Masala: This term comes from the Hindi words *garam,* meaning "hot," and *masala*, meaning "spices." In this case the hot refers to pungency, and not necessarily hot as in spicy hot. The ingredients and quantities vary widely throughout different regions in India. Please see page 45 for our garam masala recipe.

Masala: Used often in Indian cuisine, *masala* refers to a blend of spices, either in dried form or a paste.

Tamarind: Indigenous to North Africa, tamarind has been growing in India for so long that it is believed by many to be of Indian origin. The tamarind tree produces a sour and sometimes slightly sweet pod that is used throughout the world in countless culinary ways, including chutneys, jams, sauces, and drinks. If you are unable to find tamarind, you can replace it with an equal amount of lime or lemon juice as well as a minute amount of sweetener. Please see page 13 for our Tamarind Sauce recipe.

Other spices popular in Indian cuisine include cardamom, cumin, turmeric, clove, cinnamon, fennel, fenugreek, and mustard seed.

MULLIGATAWNY

Mulligatawny literally means "pepper water" in Tamil, though peppers are not a common ingredient in this curry-flavored soup. Surprisingly, the origin of Mulligatawny soup, widely considered the national soup of India, is actually of Anglo-Indian origin. There are as many variations of this soup as there are temples in India. Mulligatawny is wonderful when served with Samosas (page 7), rotis (page 17), or dosas (page 21).

SERVES 8

2 tablespoons sesame oil
1½ teaspoons curry powder
1 teaspoon ground cumin
1 cup diced onion
3 large cloves garlic, pressed or minced
6 cups water or vegetable stock (see page 228)
½ cup red lentils
¼ cup white basmati rice
1 small potato, diced (1½ cups)
1 medium apple, peeled and chopped small (1¼ cups)
¾ cup diced celery
1 carrot, diced (¾ cup)
1½ cups soy creamer or coconut milk
2 teaspoons garam masala
Pinch cayenne, or to taste
1 teaspoon tamarind paste, or 2 teaspoons freshly squeezed lemon or lime juice
1 tablespoon soy sauce, optional
2 tablespoons minced fresh cilantro
1 teaspoon sea salt, or to taste
Lemon wedges

1. Place the oil in a large pot over medium high heat. Add the curry and cumin and cook for 1 minute, stirring constantly. Add the onions and garlic and cook for 2 minutes, stirring frequently. Add the water, lentils, and rice and bring to a boil.
2. Lower the heat to medium, add the potato, apple, celery, and carrots, and cook for 20 minutes, stirring occasionally. The rice and lentils should be thoroughly cooked.
3. Add the remaining ingredients, mix well, and garnish with a lemon wedge.

Variations

- You can always add greens! Try adding 2 to 3 cups of kale, collard greens, or Swiss chard, sliced into ½-inch strips.
- Play around with other fresh herbs you may have on hand or in your garden. A quarter cup of minced fresh parsley, and a teaspoon of oregano, thyme, or marjoram would go great in this soup.

TOMATO RASAM

A popular tomato-based soup in Southern India, where it is typically served daily along with idlis or dosas (page 21), and Sambar Curry (page 23).

SERVES 6 TO 8

2 tablespoons sesame oil
1½ tablespoons cumin seeds
1½ tablespoons mustard seeds
1 tablespoon curry powder
3 tablespoons toor dhal or ground yellow split peas (see Chefs' Tips below)
3 cloves garlic, pressed or minced
5 small tomatoes, chopped (3 cups)
4 cups water or vegetable stock (see page 228)
1 hot chile, seeded and diced, or 3 dried red chiles
1 to 2 teaspoons tamarind paste or freshly squeezed lime or lemon juice
½ teaspoon garam masala
½ teaspoon ground coriander
1½ teaspoons sea salt, or to taste
¼ teaspoon ground black pepper
3 tablespoons minced fresh cilantro

1. Place the sesame oil in a large pot over medium heat. Add the cumin seeds, mustard seeds, and curry powder and cook for 2 minutes, stirring constantly. Add the toor dhal and garlic and stir well.
2. Lower the heat to medium, add the tomatoes, water, and remaining ingredients except the cilantro, and cook for 15 minutes, stirring occasionally. Add the cilantro and mix well before serving.

Chefs' Tips and Tricks

If you cannot find any toor dhal (also called red gram dhal) you can substitute them with yellow split peas. Grind them yourself in a strong blender or spice grinder.

INDIAN DHAL

Dhal is a staple of the Indian kitchen. Though chana dhal is the most popular, red lentils are the ingredient of choice for the 30-minute chef. Serve this dish with Coconut Spinach Rice (page 10) and Okra Masala (page 15).

SERVES 8

2 tablespoons sesame oil
1 tablespoon cumin seeds
1 tablespoon mustard seeds
1 cup red lentils
8½ cups water or vegetable stock (see page 228)
1 onion, diced (1½ cups)
3 cloves garlic, pressed or minced
1 tablespoon peeled and minced fresh ginger
1 teaspoon seeded and minced jalapeño or other hot chile
1 large tomato, chopped
2½ teaspoons ground cumin
2 teaspoons ground coriander
2 teaspoons curry powder
1½ teaspoons sea salt, or to taste
¼ teaspoon ground black pepper, or to taste
¼ teaspoon chile powder
Pinch cayenne
3 tablespoons chopped fresh cilantro

1. Place the oil in a large pot over medium-high heat. Add the cumin seeds and mustard seeds and cook for 1 minute, stirring constantly.
2. Add the red lentils and water, and stir well. Add the onion, garlic, ginger, jalapeño, and tomato and cook until the lentils are soft, approximately 20 minutes, stirring occasionally.
3. Add the remaining ingredients and mix well before serving.

Variations

- Try adding a bunch of chopped spinach toward the end of the cooking process.
- You can also add 2 cups of assorted chopped vegetables, such as zucchini, carrots, or parsnips.
- Toast the ground cumin (see page 225).

WOK-TOSSED CABBAGE SALAD

If you have a wok, now is the time to use it. By stir-frying the "dressing" in this recipe you unlock a much deeper taste than the average salad. And tossing the cabbage in the wok for a minute or two gives the cabbage a softer, more munchable texture. This salad is yummers!

SERVES 6 TO 8

1½ teaspoons sesame oil
1 teaspoon brown mustard seeds
10 curry leaves (see Note below)
Pinch asafetida
1 to 2 green chiles, seeds removed and thinly sliced
1½ tablespoons freshly squeezed lemon juice
½ teaspoon sea salt, or to taste
6 cups finely shredded green cabbage
1 cup shredded carrot (about 1 large carrot)
2 tablespoons minced fresh cilantro
½ cup roasted peanuts, optional

1. Heat a wok or pot over medium heat. Add the oil and heat it for 1 minute, then add the brown mustard seeds. When they start to crackle add the curry leaves, asafetida, and chiles. Stir for 1 minute.
2. Add the lemon juice and salt and stir. Add the cabbage and carrot and toss quickly for 1 to 2 minutes, just enough to coat the cabbage and soften it slightly. Turn off the heat and transfer to a serving bowl. Top with the cilantro and peanuts, if using, and serve.

Note: Curry leaves have such a unique flavor that we cannot think of an adequate alternative. Alas, if you cannot find any in your area, you can try online, or simply omit them. Extra curry leaves are stored in the freezer.

SAMOSAS

We wanted to include a samosa recipe here due to popular demand. It would push the limits on a 30-minute meal to cook the potatoes for the filling, wrap the samosas, and bake them. So for your enjoyment, we are starting with a precooked filling. You can look at it as a great way to utilize leftover Curried Potatoes (page 11) or use the Quick Samosa Filling recipe that follows. Serve with Tamarind Sauce, (page 13), chutney (pages 40–42), Cilantro Pesto (page 181), Fabulous Fig Dipping Sauce (page 102), or Mango Ginger Sauce (page 61).

MAKES 8 TO 10 SAMOSAS

9 to 12 phyllo pastry sheets, defrosted (see Chefs' Tips on page 8)

½ to ¾ cup coconut oil, melted vegan butter, or sesame oil

2½ cups Curried Potatoes (page 11) or Quick Samosa Filling (recipe on page 8)

Oil for coating samosas

Sea salt, optional

1. Preheat the oven to 400°F. Place a phyllo sheet on a clean dry cutting board. Brush lightly with oil, using a pastry brush. Place another phyllo sheet on top of the first and brush lightly with oil. Repeat with one more sheet. Cut the sheets lengthwise into three equal strips.
2. Place approximately ¼ cup of potato filling at the bottom of each strip. Traditionally samosas are shaped like triangles, so you want to fold them up as you would fold a flag. To do so, fold the bottom right corner of the strip over to the left side, enclosing the filling. Fold upwards and continue folding until you reach the end of the strip. Brush lightly with oil before placing on a well-oiled or parchment-lined baking sheet. Repeat with the remaining filling.
3. Sprinkle lightly with salt, if using, and bake for 15 minutes, or until golden brown.

QUICK SAMOSA FILLING

MAKES 2½ CUPS

5 small potatoes, chopped small (3 cups)
1 tablespoon cumin seeds
1 tablespoon brown mustard seeds
1 teaspoon curry powder
½ teaspoon sea salt, or to taste
1 tablespoon soy sauce, or to taste
¼ teaspoon ground black pepper

Heat approximately 1 inch of water in a covered pot fitted with a steamer basket over high heat. Place the potatoes in the steamer basket and steam until just soft. Transfer to a bowl along with the remaining ingredients and mash well. (You can use a potato masher or a small and sturdy whisk.)

Chefs' Tips and Tricks

Working with phyllo dough is definitely an art form. Packaged phyllo (sometimes spelled *filo*) is available frozen and must be defrosted completely before using. If you try to unroll it too soon, it will break. It also dries out quickly, so you need to keep it completely covered at all times with a *slightly* damp towel. Replace the towel as soon as you are done peeling off the sheets you need for the recipe.

RICE PILAU

Though similar in many ways to the popular Indian dish biryani (in which the rice is cooked separately), pilaus are cooked with all of the ingredients together in the same pot. By no means are all of these ingredients mandatory. Just use what you have on hand, substituting whatever you like as need be. Pilau is such an easy way to jazz up rice and transform it into a respectable course of its own.

SERVES 6

2 teaspoons brown mustard seeds
2 cups white basmati rice
4 cups water or vegetable stock (see page 228)
1 cup diced yellow onion
2 cups diced assorted vegetables (carrot, celery, zucchini, and/or peas)
2 tablespoons peeled and minced fresh ginger
2 teaspoons curry powder, optional
¼ teaspoon celery seed
8 curry leaves or 2 bay leaves (see Note on page 6)
¼ teaspoon sea salt, or to taste
¼ cup minced fresh parsley

1. Place the mustard seeds in a saucepan over medium heat and toast until they are popping. (If the seeds burn, start over; nobody likes burnt mustard rice.) Immediately add the rice and water.
2. Add all of the other ingredients except the parsley and bring to a boil. Cover and simmer for 15 minutes or until most of the water has been absorbed. Stir in the parsley and serve hot.

Variation

- If you have more time, use brown basmati rice, and cook for 40 minutes in step 2.

COCONUT SPINACH RICE

You can't go wrong with the rice and coconut milk combo. This creamy and flavorful dish can be a meal unto itself. It also nicely compliments many of the dishes in this book, such as Okra Masala (page 15) Tofu Tikka Masala (page 33), and Indian Dhal (page 5).

SERVES 6 TO 8

1 teaspoon ground cumin
2 teaspoons brown mustard seeds
1 teaspoon curry powder
1 teaspoon sea salt, or to taste
½ teaspoon ground black pepper
Pinch cayenne
2 cups white basmati rice
1 (14-ounce) can coconut milk
1½ cups water or vegetable stock (see page 228)
1 (10-ounce) package frozen spinach, defrosted (¾ cup cooked spinach, pressed firmly)
1 (14-ounce) can garbanzo beans, drained, or 1¾ cups cooked beans (see page 230), optional

1. Toast the cumin and mustard seeds in a medium pot for 1 minute over medium-high heat, stirring constantly. Add the curry powder, salt, pepper, cayenne, rice, coconut milk, and water and bring to a boil.
2. Cover, lower the heat to simmer, and cook until the liquid is absorbed, approximately 10 minutes. Turn off the heat and allow the rice to sit for 5 minutes.
3. Add the spinach and garbanzo beans, if using, and gently toss well.

Variations

- Add 2 teaspoons of minced garlic and ¼ cup diced yellow onion along with the spices.
- For a heartier dish, add another 10-ounce package of spinach.
- Add ½ cup chopped roasted cashews along with the spinach.
-  If you have more time, replace the basmati with brown basmati or another brown rice, add an extra cup of water and cook according to instructions on page 231.

CURRIED POTATOES

This recipe comes courtesy of Vi Herbert, our friend and resident expert on Indian cuisine (see page 42). These potatoes are commonly used as the stuffing for Dosas (recipe on page 21). A staple among college students in many countries, these large, heavy wraps burst with spice, flavor, and satisfaction—usually for under $5 apiece. You can serve these habit-forming potatoes with Tofu Tikka Masala (page 33).

SERVES 4 TO 6

MAKES FILLING FOR 4 LARGE DOSA WRAPS OR 6 SMALL WRAPS

4 medium potatoes, red or yellow, chopped small (about 6 cups)
1 tablespoon toasted sesame oil
1 teaspoon brown mustard seeds
½ teaspoon turmeric powder
2 green or red chiles, seeded and diced
1½ tablespoons peeled and minced fresh ginger
3 cloves garlic, pressed or minced
20 curry leaves (see Note on page 6)
1½ teaspoons sea salt
1 yellow onion, sliced into quarter moons
1 tablespoon freshly squeezed lemon juice
¼ cup minced fresh cilantro

1. Heat approximately 1 inch of water in a covered pot fitted with a steamer basket over high heat. Place the potatoes in the basket and steam until a fork can easily pass through, for 10 to 15 minutes.
2. Meanwhile, place a large sauté pan over medium heat. Add the oil, mustard seeds, turmeric, chiles, ginger, garlic, curry leaves, and salt and stir well until the mustard seeds begin to pop.
3. Add the onion and sauté until translucent, for 3 to 5 minutes. Add the steamed potatoes, stir well, then use a fork to mash them up. When most of the potato is mashed, stir until the flavors and colors are distributed. You may want to use a little water to keep the potatoes from sticking to the pan while mashing and stirring.
4. Turn off the heat, add the lemon juice and cilantro, and stir well. The filling can be eaten alone or stuffed into a dosa wrapper.

POTATOES AND SPINACH (ALOO SAAG)

Aloo is potato and *saag* is spinach, and when the two are combined it is simply divine. It's a creative way to include spinach in your diet. The soy milk imparts a creaminess to the dish that melts in your mouth. Serve with Rice Pilau (page 9), roti (page 17), or an entrée such as Tofu Tikka Masala (page 33).

SERVES 4 TO 6

1 large potato, ½-inch cubes (1½ cups)
2 teaspoons fenugreek seeds
2 teaspoons brown mustard seeds
2 teaspoons curry powder
1 teaspoon chile powder
1 tablespoon sesame oil
1 small yellow onion, diced (1 cup)
1 tablespoon minced garlic
1 tablespoon peeled and minced fresh ginger
2 small tomatoes, chopped (1¼ cups)
2 (10-ounce) packages frozen spinach, defrosted and strained (if using fresh spinach, 2 cups cooked spinach)
1 teaspoon ground coriander
1¼ cups soy milk
1 teaspoon sea salt, or to taste
⅛ teaspoon ground black pepper, or to taste

1. Heat approximately 1 inch of water in a covered pot fitted with a steamer basket over high heat. Place the potatoes in the basket and steam until a fork can easily pass through, for 10 to 15 minutes.
2. While the potatoes are steaming, place a large saucepan over medium heat. Add the fenugreek seeds, mustard seeds, curry powder, and chile powder and stir constantly for 1 to 2 minutes. Add the sesame oil, onion, garlic, and ginger, and stir constantly for a few minutes.
3. Add the tomatoes and stir frequently for a few more minutes, adding a small amount of water if necessary to prevent sticking. Lower the heat to simmer, add the spinach and the remaining ingredients except the potatoes, and cook for 10 minutes, stirring occasionally.
4. When the potatoes are done steaming, add to the spinach mixture and gently mix well.

Variations

- Try adding 1 bag of defrosted frozen peas along with the spinach in step 3.
- Add ¼ cup minced fresh cilantro before serving.
- Replace the fenugreek seeds with mustard seeds or cumin seeds.

TAMARIND SWEET POTATOES

Tamarind is a sour and slightly sweet fruit that grows in Asia and North Africa. If you are going to delve into Asian cuisine, purchasing tamarind is a must. Many varieties are available in Asian and specialty markets in the form of pulp, paste, or a puree with a syrupy consistency. Some are sweetened, some aren't. You may need to adjust this recipe based on the type of tamarind you use (see Note). Use this sauce as a dipping sauce for Samosas (page 7) or Tibetan Dumplings (page 200).

SERVES 4 TO 6

3 sweet potatoes or yams, chopped (6 cups)
1 teaspoon sea salt, or to taste

TAMARIND SAUCE

MAKES ABOUT 1½ CUPS

¾ cup water
¼ cup pitted dates (preferably a moist variety, such as Medjool)
2 tablespoons raisins
2 tablespoons tamarind paste
2 teaspoons soy sauce, or to taste
½ teaspoon powdered ginger
¾ teaspoon ground cumin
½ teaspoon garam masala
½ teaspoon chile powder
3 tablespoons agave nectar, organic brown sugar, or sweetener of choice, or to taste

1. Place the sweet potatoes in a steamer basket in a 3-quart pot with an inch of water. Steam until the sweet potatoes are just tender and a knife can easily pass through them, approximately 10 minutes.
2. Meanwhile, prepare the tamarind sauce by combining all of the ingredients in a strong blender and blending until pureed.
3. When the potatoes are cooked, place them in a large bowl with the tamarind sauce, add the salt, and gently mix well.

continues

Variations

- Replace the sweet potatoes with steamed or sautéed veggies of choice—try with broccoli, cauliflower, or carrots.
- Can't find any tamarind sauce and craving sweet potatoes? Try serving the sweet potatoes with the coconut sauce from the Cooked Mixed Vegetables (page 55) or Coconut Mashed Parsnips (page 186). Add 1 teaspoon of curry powder for an Indian flair.

Note: Given the differences in consistency, tanginess, and sweetness of the various tamarind products available on the market, some creative experimentation may be necessary on your part for this recipe. The tamarind paste called for tends to be tangier and more watery than the pulp. If you do use the pulp, add a teaspoon of freshly squeezed lime juice and 2 tablespoons of water to attain the desired result. If you use a sweetened variety of tamarind, adjust the agave nectar to taste.

OKRA MASALA (BHINDI MASALA)

Okra originates in the tropics, and its name is of West African origin. Also called "lady fingers" for its unique shape, okra is one of the most popular veggies in Western India. It has a gelatinous texture that some people require getting used to. Persist beyond this and you will be treated to a true culinary delicacy. As was noted earlier, *masala* is of South Indian origin and refers to a mixture of spices; here we use the curry spices and garam masala (see page 45). Serve as a side dish with Tofu Tikka Masala (page 33), Tempeh Vindaloo (page 28), or Tempeh Vegetable Korma (page 30).

SERVES 4 TO 6

2 tablespoons sesame oil
1 teaspoon ground cumin
1½ teaspoons curry powder
½ teaspoon chile powder
3 cloves garlic, pressed or minced
2 teaspoons peeled and minced fresh ginger
1 large onion, chopped (1½ cups)
4 cups chopped okra, tops removed (½-inch)
1 cup water
1 large tomato, chopped (1 cup)
½ teaspoon garam masala
1 teaspoon sea salt, or to taste
¼ teaspoon ground black pepper, or to taste
Pinch cayenne
2 tablespoons chopped fresh cilantro

1. Place the oil in a large sauté pan over medium-high heat. Add the cumin, curry powder, and chile powder and cook for 1 minute, stirring constantly. Add the garlic and ginger and cook for another minute, stirring constantly. Add the onion and cook for 5 minutes, stirring frequently.
2. Add the okra and water and cook for 5 minutes, stirring frequently. Add the tomato and garam masala and cook until the okra is just tender, approximately 5 minutes. Add more water if necessary to prevent sticking.
3. Add the salt, pepper, cayenne, and cilantro, and gently mix well before serving.

continues

Variations

- Try replacing the okra with chopped zucchini or summer squash.
- Replace 1 cup of the okra with chopped broccoli.
- Add 1 tablespoon of brown mustard seeds or fennel seeds.
- Add 1 teaspoon minced jalapeño pepper.
- For an added crunch and burst of flavor, top with **Masala Nuts** (see Box below).

If You Have More Time: Masala Nuts

Combine the following in a small bowl and stir well: 1 teaspoon fennel seeds, ⅛ teaspoon each turmeric and cayenne, and ¼ teaspoon each ground cumin, ground coriander, chile powder, curry powder, garam masala, and sea salt.

Place 1 teaspoon of sesame oil in a small sauté pan over medium heat. Add the spices and cook for 1 minute, stirring frequently. Add ½ cup chopped cashews or other nuts and cook for 3 minutes, stirring frequently.

ROCKIN' ROTI

If you started making roti at a very young age like girls in India have for centuries, you'd be cranking out perfectly round, moist, and thin rotis by adolescence. Well, there is no time like the present. Using a rolling pin and keeping the dough from sticking to it are the two major hiccups along the road to perfect rotis. But just like that little engine that could, if you persevere, you will find that practice really does make perfect. We believe in you! And the reward is homemade bread, hot off the skillet. You just need to be willing to sacrifice the first few attempts. Then you're in the clear.

MAKES 4 ROTIS

2½ cups spelt flour or whole wheat flour
¼ teaspoon sea salt
½ cup water
Sesame or safflower oil

1. Mix 1½ cups of the flour and the salt together in a bowl with your hands. Add the water slowly, pulling all of the flour into it until you have a soft, moist dough. Knead it for 2 minutes. Divide the dough into four pieces and roll those pieces between your palms to form balls. Lightly oil a bowl or plate to place the dough balls on. Let them sit for 10 to 15 minutes.
2. Place the remaining 1 cup of flour on a plate. Apply a very light coat of oil to the dough balls as well as to a rolling pin. Dip one ball into the flour, making sure that the entire ball is covered. Lay it on a clean, dry surface or cutting board and roll it into a circle about 5 to 6-inches in diameter (about ⅛ inch in thickness). You will most likely want to dip it back into the flour (on both sides) once or twice while you are rolling it out.
3. Heat an iron (or nonstick) skillet and lightly coat it with oil. Place the freshly rolled roti onto it, making sure it lays flat. Within seconds the color will start to change and bubbles will appear. Give it about 25 seconds before flipping. Repeat on the other side.
4. Flip the roti over one more time and press down on it with a flat spatula. Keep moving the roti around and gently press down any air holes that puff up. After you've covered the whole roti a couple of times, flip it over and repeat the process. This time the roti will puff up even more. After you've finished the second side, either serve the roti piping hot with some vegan butter or place it on a plate and cover with a dry towel while you move on to the remaining rotis.

continues

Chefs' Tips and Tricks

Tips for Perfecting Rotis

1. The wetter the dough, the moister the end result. Using your hands for the mixing helps you remember what the perfect consistency feels like.
2. Don't overthink the rolling out process. It doesn't take much rolling and the more flour you use, the drier the end result and the less the roti will puff up when you heat it. Push down firmly on the rolling pin, roll a few times in one direction, dip both sides in the flour, and roll a few times in the opposite direction. With time, your natural hand-eye coordination will lead you in the direction of rounder roti.
3. Use the oil sparingly. This recipe shouldn't use very much oil at all. Coating the dough, rolling pin, and skillet very lightly helps prevent the dough from sticking.
4. Before cooking the roti, make sure the pan is hot by sprinkling it with a couple drops of water; the water should sizzle. Dry the pan with a paper towel before laying down the roti.
5. An alternative cooking method to make the roti puff up involves holding the roti with tongs over an open flame rather than the second round of cooking where you flatten the air out with the spatula: hold the roti over the flame and move it around to cover the entire surface of both sides. The roti will puff up into the shape of a UFO.
6. For time's sake, start heating up the pan before you start rolling the dough. Have your rolling station right next to your stove and roll the next roti while the first one is on its first round of cooking.

Variations

- Add 1 teaspoon of ground cumin or coriander to the flour before adding the water. You may wish to toast the spices.
- Add 2 to 3 tablespoons of diced green onion, chives, or cilantro to the flour before adding the water.

CAULIFLOWER CHICKPEA SUBJI

A popular combination, these two hardy ingredients are commonly used in Indian cooking. Dishes like this prove how easy it is to create robust flavors in a short period of time. Cooking the veggies in the sauce infuses them, leaving them potent and ready to burst with flavor. You can use the same technique with any foods and flavors you enjoy. Serve this dish alongside Coconut Spinach Rice (page 10) or Shahi Paneer (page 26).

SERVES 4

½ small yellow onion
1-inch piece fresh ginger, peeled
2 cloves garlic
½ cup minced fresh cilantro
½ teaspoon ground cardamom
¼ teaspoon ground cinnamon
¼ teaspoon sea salt
¾ cup water
1 tablespoon sesame oil
1 teaspoon brown mustard seeds
¼ teaspoon turmeric powder
½ head cauliflower, chopped
1 (15-ounce) can chickpeas or 1¾ cups cooked (see page 230)
1 medium carrot, thinly sliced

1. Using a blender, combine the onion, ginger, garlic, cilantro, cardamom, cinnamon, salt, and ¼ cup of the water. Blend together for 30 to 40 seconds or until it's a saucy consistency.
2. Heat a sauté pan over medium heat and then add the oil, mustard seeds, and turmeric. Stir frequently until the mustard seeds begin to pop. Add the onion mixture and stir well for 1 to 2 minutes.
3. Add the cauliflower, chickpeas, carrots, and the remaining ½ cup of water. Cover and let cook for 5 to 10 minutes, or until tender. Uncover and stir, allowing to cook for 2 to 3 more minutes to let some of the liquid evaporate. Serve hot.

Variations

- Replace the cauliflower and carrots with veggies of your choosing, such as broccoli, zucchini, eggplant, or squash.
- Replace the chickpeas with kidney beans or cubed tofu or tempeh.

POTATO PEA CURRY (ALOO GOBI)

Rich, bursting with flavor, and satisfying, this dish rocks the house. Though aloo gobi is traditionally served with dishes equally as flavorful, you may be content with a simple Rice Pilau (page 9) and a side salad (page 6). Flavor like this goes a long way. You can take it a step further and add a refreshing chutney (pages 40–42).

SERVES 4 TO 6 AS MAIN DISH OR 6 TO 8 AS SIDE DISH

4 medium-size red potatoes, chopped (about 4 cups)
1 tablespoon safflower or sesame oil
½ yellow onion, finely minced
2 tablespoons peeled and minced fresh ginger
1 teaspoon sea salt, or to taste
2 teaspoons ground coriander
2 teaspoons ground cumin
1 teaspoon turmeric powder
½ teaspoon cayenne, or to taste
1 teaspoon maple syrup or agave nectar
2 cups water
1 (10-ounce) bag frozen peas (about 1¾ cups)
½ teaspoon garam masala
½ lime, juiced
2 tablespoons minced fresh cilantro

1. Place the chopped potatoes in a colander. Rinse under cold water for 30 seconds and let drain.
2. In a large sauté pan or pot, heat the safflower oil over medium heat and add the onion, ginger, and salt. Stir frequently until the onion turns golden, about 6 minutes.
3. Add the potatoes, coriander, cumin, turmeric, cayenne, and maple syrup and stir well. Add 1 cup of the water (or enough water to almost cover the potatoes), cover, and lower the heat to medium-low. Cook for 15 minutes or until a fork can easily pierce the potatoes.
4. Add the peas, garam masala, and the remaining 1 cup of water. Stir well, allowing some of the potato to crumble. Use a fork to mash up some of the potato, making a thicker sauce for the dish (remembering that it will get thicker as it cools). Stir in the lime juice and cilantro and remove from the heat.

DOSA OR IDLI RICE BREAD

A spongy rice bread called *idli* is the everyday breakfast food of the Tamil Nadu region of India. This bread, made from a fermented batter of rice and lentils, is served with extremely flavorful curries such as sambar. The batter that is not used for idlis can later be used to make dosas. Dosas are commonly used as a wrapper for spiced potatoes but can be eaten plain, with vegan garlic butter, or with other vegetables as well. They range in thickness from a pancake to a crepe. Due to the soaking and fermenting process, this dish does go over the 30-minute time frame.

3 cups brown or white rice
1 cup urud dhal or other lentils
1 teaspoon sea salt

1. In separate bowls, cover the rice and lentils with water, leaving 2 to 3 inches of water above the surface of each. Leave on the counter to soak for 4 hours.
2. Heat the oven to 250°F and turn it off when it reaches that temperature (unless you have a very warm place to ferment the batter). Rinse the rice and lentils well by stirring each in clean water and straining about 5 times each. Use a blender to blend the lentils on high speed, adding about ½ cup of water, until a thick batter forms. Blend the rice on high speed, adding as little water as necessary, until a similar but coarser batter forms. Mix both batters together and add the salt.
3. Place the batter in the warmed oven for 12 to 24 hours or until it is doubled in size.
4. To make idli, pour the batter into an oiled or cheesecloth-lined idli pan (see Note) and steam for 12 to 15 minutes. You can also line a bamboo steamer or even a collapsible metal steamer with cheesecloth and pour the batter in using a ⅓ cup measuring cup.
5. To make dosas you may need to add water to the batter. Thicker batter will give you pancake-style dosas. Adding ½ cup or more of water will yield increasingly thinner dosas. The thinner the batter, the easier it is to spread the batter into a circle on the pan.
6. Either use a nonstick pan or brush a regular (heated) pan lightly with oil and place over medium heat. Use a ladle to pour the batter (about ⅓ cup) onto the hot pan and quickly spread the batter around into a large thin circle (or something like a circle) using the bottom of the ladle. Holes in the dosa are fine; these don't need to be perfect and are very sturdy once they are done. Let the dosa cook on both sides for a couple of minutes, until slightly brown. Take care not to overcook these; traditionally dosas are still quite white and, therefore, flexible. Serve hot or keep in a warm oven covered with a damp towel until all the dosas are cooked and you are ready to partake.

Note: An idli pan is essentially a steamer pot with a multilayered insert made just for this purpose. The batter is poured into the rounded indentations, which allow the steam to pass through and cook the batter into perfectly shaped idli.

Variation

- For a **Super Quickie Dosa Batter** simply whisk together 2 cups brown rice flour, 1 teaspoon sifted baking powder, and ½ teaspoon sea salt. Add 2½ cups water and cook according to the instructions in step 6 (though spreading the batter with the ladle will not be necessary). This batter yields about eight large quickie dosas. Adding another ½ cup of water will make them even thinner, which is more authentic but a bit harder to handle.

SAMBAR CURRY

Though this recipe contains a couple of ingredients that most Westerners would consider obscure, sambar curry is eaten daily, and commonly twice or thrice daily, throughout Southern India and Sri Lanka. As early as breakfast this curry is served alongside fresh idli (see page 21), and for lunch or dinner with rice and chutneys. Our friend Vi Herbert from the Tamil Nadu region of India taught us to make this curry, and we are quite grateful to her indeed for that! Sambar powder, a mix of roasted spices and dhals, can be purchased online if you can't find it elsewhere. Any common lentil or dhal can be substituted for the toor dhal. We recommend the red lentils for their quick cooking time. If you simply cannot find sambar powder, use the garam masala substitution. In a pinch you could even use curry powder. It won't be sambar curry anymore, but it will still be delish!

SERVES 6 TO 8

1 cup toor dhal or red lentils
2 cups water
1 tablespoon sesame oil or coconut oil
½ teaspoon brown mustard seeds
¼ teaspoon turmeric powder
Pinch asafetida
½ medium yellow onion, chopped small
10 curry leaves (see Note on page 6)
2 cups chopped vegetables (carrots, cauliflower, radishes, green beans . . .)
½ teaspoon tamarind paste or 1 teaspoon freshly squeezed lemon or lime juice
1 teaspoon sambar powder or ¾ teaspoon garam masala
1 teaspoon sea salt, or to taste
2 medium tomatoes, chopped (about 1½ cups)
3 cups water or vegetable stock (see page 228)
2 tablespoons minced fresh cilantro

1. In a small pot, bring the dhal and water to a boil, lower the heat to low and simmer, uncovered for 20 minutes (about 15 minutes if using red lentils) or until the dhal is soft.
2. Meanwhile, in a large sauté pan or pot, heat the oil and mustard seeds together over medium heat until the seeds crackle. Add the turmeric, asafetida, onion, and curry leaves and sauté for 2 minutes. Add the vegetables and sauté for 3 more minutes.
3. Add the tamarind, sambar powder, salt, tomatoes, water, and the cooked dhal and bring to a boil. Reduce the heat and continue to cook until all of the vegetables are soft, about 5 minutes depending on your choice of vegetables. Add the cilantro, cook for 3 more minutes, and remove from the heat. Optionally, allow it to sit for 10 minutes before serving; the flavors will enhance over time.

TROPICAL COCONUT CURRY

Coconut milk and plantains—ahhh, the taste of the tropics for sure! Feel free to use bananas instead of plantain if necessary. Some people like the sweetness of ripe bananas in this dish. Serve as a side dish with Lemon Rice (page 187) and Cardamom-Scented Tofu (page 32).

SERVES 4 TO 6

¼ teaspoon saffron strands in ¼ cup hot water, optional
2 tablespoons sesame oil
1½ teaspoons brown mustard seeds
1½ teaspoons coriander seeds
1 tablespoon fennel seeds
1 yellow onion, sliced (1½ cups)
1½ tablespoons peeled and minced fresh ginger
1 hot chile, seeded and diced
2 plantains or bananas, sliced (2 cups)
2 zucchini, sliced (2 cups)
1 carrot, thinly sliced
1 (14-ounce) can coconut milk (see page 234 for instructions on making coconut milk at home)
½ cup water
1 teaspoon curry powder
2 tablespoons minced fresh cilantro
¾ teaspoon sea salt, or to taste

1. If using the saffron, place in a small bowl with the hot water and set aside.
2. Place the sesame oil in a large sauté pan over medium-high heat. Add the mustard, coriander, and fennel seeds and stir well. Add the onion, ginger, and hot chile and cook for 3 minutes, stirring frequently. Add the plantain, zucchini, and carrot, and mix well.
3. Lower the heat to low, add the coconut milk, water, and curry powder and cook for 15 minutes, stirring occasionally. Add the saffron and water, if using, cilantro, and salt, and mix well before serving.

Variations

- Substitute vegetables of your choosing, like broccoli, cauliflower, and mushrooms.
- Add roasted tofu or tempeh cubes (see page 227).

Chefs' Tips and Tricks

Not sure what to look for in a plantain? With time you will learn to judge a plantain by its cover. If it is still greenish it is definitely not ready to eat. Wait at least a few days after it turns yellow. Many cultures prefer plantains long after their skins have turned black. In general, the softer, the sweeter. Some firmness for this dish is okay.

MADRAS CURRY

Madras curry is meant to be a powerful combination of hot, red, toasty, sweet, and sour. Using coconut oil adds a smoothness and flavor that is nice, but sesame or any vegetable oil will also do the trick. You can also use any kind of chile powder in place of the cayenne as long as it is a pure chile powder rather than the Spanish-style blends. Other chiles will be less spicy and still impart the classic madras red color (substituting some paprika will also help add redness if the cayenne is too hot for your liking).

SERVES 6

1 tablespoon coriander seeds
2 teaspoons cumin seeds
1 tablespoon brown mustard seeds
2 tablespoons coconut oil (or sesame or other oil)
¼ teaspoon turmeric powder
2 teaspoons ground cayenne, or to taste (see head note)
¼ teaspoon ground allspice or ground anise
1 teaspoon garam masala
¼ teaspoon ground black pepper
2 tablespoons peeled and minced fresh ginger
2 cloves garlic, pressed or minced
1 teaspoon sea salt
2 medium yellow onions, sliced into quarter moons
1 (14-ounce) can coconut milk
2 tablespoons freshly squeezed lime juice or rice vinegar
4 to 6 cups assorted chopped vegetables
(carrots, bell peppers, eggplant, zucchini, etc.)

1. Toast the coriander, cumin, and brown mustard seeds in a large sauté pan or pot over medium heat for 2 minutes or until the mustard seeds are popping. Add the coconut oil, turmeric, cayenne, allspice, garam masala, black pepper, ginger, garlic, and salt and sauté for 1 minute.
2. Add the onion and sauté for 4 to 5 minutes or until the onions turn translucent, then add the coconut milk and lime juice and stir well.
3. Add the remaining vegetables and cook, stirring frequently, until all of the vegetables are soft and you are ready to serve.

TOFU IN TOMATO CREAM SAUCE (SHAHI PANEER)

Paneer is an non-aged farmer cheese that is extremely popular in Indian cuisine. Our veganized version contains firm tofu, which has a similar texture and consistency. For maximum flavor, allow the tofu to marinate for at least an hour. Our cream sauce gets its creaminess from cashews, though you can also use coconut or soy milk. Serve with Coconut Spinach Rice (page 10) and Cauliflower Chickpea Subji (page 19).

SERVES 2 TO 4

TOFU MARINADE

1 (14-ounce) package extra-firm tofu
3 tablespoons freshly squeezed lemon juice
3 tablespoons nutritional yeast
1 tablespoon sesame oil
2 teaspoons raw apple cider vinegar
3 tablespoons water
½ teaspoon sea salt
¼ teaspoon ground black pepper

SAUTÉ

2 tablespoons sesame oil
1 yellow onion, chopped (1½ cups)
3 cloves garlic, pressed or minced
1 tablespoon peeled and minced fresh ginger
2 teaspoons seeded and minced hot chile
3 tomatoes, chopped (2 cups)
2 tablespoons tomato paste
¾ cup water
½ cup cashews, pine nuts, or macadamia nuts, raw or roasted
½ teaspoon ground coriander
¼ teaspoon ground cardamom
½ teaspoon ground cumin
1½ teaspoons garam masala
½ teaspoon chile powder

¼ teaspoon turmeric powder
1¼ teaspoons sea salt, or to taste
2 tablespoons chopped fresh cilantro

1. Preheat the oven or toaster oven to 375°F. Slice the tofu in half lengthwise, forming two cutlets. Slice each cutlet lengthwise three times and then widthwise three times to yield sixteen cubes each (thirty-two cubes total). Place the cubes in a mixing bowl with the remaining marinade ingredients and mix well. Transfer to a baking dish and cook for 15 minutes.
2. Meanwhile, place the sesame oil in a large sauté pan over medium heat. Add the onion, garlic, ginger, and chile pepper, and cook for 3 minutes, stirring occasionally. Lower the heat to low.
3. Place the tomatoes, tomato paste, water, and cashews in a blender and blend until creamy. Transfer to the sauté pan and stir well.
4. Add the tofu and marinade ingredients to the sauté pan and gently stir well. Add the remaining ingredients except the cilantro and cook for 5 minutes, stirring occasionally. Add the cilantro and enjoy!

Variations

- Replace the cashews and water in step 3 with 1¼ cups of coconut or soy milk. This will produce a thinner sauce. Allow it to cook 5 to 10 minutes longer if you want it to be thicker.
- Add ¼ cup vegan yogurt.
- Add 2 cups of chopped vegetables such as carrots, zucchini, or mushrooms along with the onions.

TEMPEH VINDALOO

The name *vindaloo* is actually of Portuguese origin. The dish is popular in Southern India, near the city of Goa, where the Portuguese settlers partied way back when—before the full-moon raves of today. The dish is known for its spiciness, so add as much cayenne as you can! Serve with Rice Pilau (page 9) and Potatoes and Spinach (page 12).

TEMPEH MARINADE

3 tablespoons soy sauce
1 tablespoon sesame oil
3 tablespoons water
¼ teaspoon chile powder
1 pound tempeh

VINDALOO SAUCE

1 tablespoon curry powder
½ teaspoon chile powder
1 teaspoon ground cumin
½ teaspoon garam masala
1 teaspoon paprika
1 teaspoon ground coriander
1 teaspoon fenugreek seeds
1 teaspoon mustard powder
¼ teaspoon cayenne, or to taste
2 tablespoons sesame oil
1 large onion, chopped (1½ cups)
5 cloves garlic, pressed or minced
1½ cups water or vegetable stock (see page 228)
3 tomatoes, chopped (2 cups)
3 tablespoons tomato paste
2 tablespoons raw apple cider vinegar
1½ teaspoons sea salt, or to taste
2 teaspoons agave nectar, or to taste

1. Preheat the oven to 375°F. Place all of the marinade ingredients in a small bowl and whisk well. Slice the tempeh into 1- by 2-inch pieces according to the method on page 27 and place in a casserole dish. Pour the marinade ingredients over the tempeh slices, making sure that all of the pieces are coated. Bake for 15 minutes and remove from the heat.

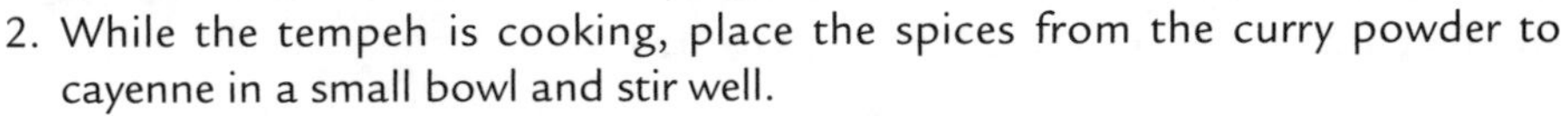

2. While the tempeh is cooking, place the spices from the curry powder to cayenne in a small bowl and stir well.
3. Add the oil in a large sauté pan over medium heat. Add the spices and stir well for 1 minute. Add the onions and garlic and cook for 5 minutes, stirring frequently. Add a little water if necessary to prevent sticking. Lower the heat to medium, and add the tomatoes, tomato paste, vinegar, salt, agave nectar, and the remaining water. Cook for 5 minutes, stirring frequently.
4. When the tempeh is done cooking, add it to the sauté pan along with the marinade and simmer over low heat for 8 to 10 minutes, stirring occasionally. Remember to stir gently to keep the tempeh from breaking apart. Serve with a smile.

Variations

- Feel free to replace the tempeh with tofu, seitan, or portobello mushrooms.
- You may add 2 cups of assorted chopped vegetables such as celery, carrots, and zucchini along with the onions.

TEMPEH VEGETABLE KORMA

Korma is a creamy dish of North Indian/Pakistani origin. *Korma* traditionally refers to a cooking style that involves braising. Nowadays it generally refers to a curry dish with a cream-based sauce or gravy. Our version is a crowd-pleasing and hardy dish, best enjoyed with basmati rice and Okra Masala (page 15).

SERVES 6

8 ounces tempeh, cut into ½-inch cubes
2 tablespoons soy sauce
3 tablespoons sesame oil
¾ cup chopped cashews, raw or roasted
2 cups soy creamer or soy milk
1 teaspoon ground coriander
1 teaspoon ground cumin
½ teaspoon curry powder
1 onion, diced (1¼ cups)
2 large cloves garlic, pressed or minced
2 teaspoons seeded and diced hot chile or ½ teaspoon crushed red pepper flakes
3 cups small cauliflower flowerets
¾ cup water
¼ cup coconut milk or unsweetened vegan yogurt, optional
2 teaspoons poppy seeds
¾ teaspoon garam masala
½ teaspoon chile powder
⅛ teaspoon turmeric powder
Pinch cinnamon
¾ teaspoon sea salt, or to taste
2 tablespoons minced fresh cilantro

1. Preheat the oven or toaster oven to 375°F. Place the tempeh on a small baking sheet. Add the soy sauce and 1 tablespoon of sesame oil and stir well to evenly coat the tempeh. Place in the oven and bake for 10 minutes.
2. Place ½ cup of the cashews and 1 cup of the soy creamer in a blender and blend until creamy.
3. Place the remaining oil in a large sauté pan or wok over medium-high heat. Add the coriander, cumin, and curry powder and cook for 1 minute, stirring constantly. Add the onion, garlic, and chile and cook for 3 minutes, stirring frequently. Lower the heat to medium, add the contents of the blender, as well as the cauliflower, water, and remaining soy creamer, and cook for 10 minutes, stirring occasionally.
4. Add the tempeh, the remaining cashews, and all of the other remaining ingredients except the cilantro and cook for 5 minutes, gently stirring occasionally. Add the cilantro and mix well before serving.

Variations

- Replace the cauliflower with broccoli, cabbage, potatoes, or other vegetables of your choosing.
- You can toast the cashews if you wish (see page 225).
- Replace the tempeh with seitan or roasted tofu cubes (see page 227).

CARDAMOM-SCENTED TOFU

A uniquely flavored dish featuring the exotic spice cardamom, also known as "the queen of spices." For the full effect, allow the tofu to marinate for an hour or longer. Serve with Tropical Coconut Curry (page 124) and Lemon Rice (page 187).

SERVES 4

1 (14-ounce) package extra-firm tofu

MARINADE

1 tablespoon sesame oil
2 cloves garlic, pressed or minced
3 tablespoons water
½ teaspoon ground cardamom
2 tablespoons freshly squeezed lemon juice
½ teaspoon sea salt, or to taste
¼ teaspoon ground black pepper

SAUCE

1¾ cups soy milk
½ teaspoon sea salt, or to taste
½ teaspoon curry powder
½ teaspoon ground cardamom
Pinch cayenne pepper
1 tablespoon spelt flour
1 tablespoon sesame oil
1 tablespoon minced fresh cilantro

1. Preheat the oven to 400°F. Slice the tofu in half lengthwise, forming two cutlets. Slice each cutlet lengthwise three times and then widthwise three times to yield sixteen cubes each (thirty-two cubes total). You can make smaller cubes by cutting the block into three cutlets instead of two. Place the tofu in a mixing bowl with the marinade ingredients and gently mix well.
2. Transfer the tofu and marinade ingredients to a small casserole dish and bake for 20 minutes, stirring occasionally.
3. Meanwhile, place the soy milk in a large sauté pan over medium heat. Add the salt, curry powder, cardamom, and cayenne and gently whisk well. Cook for 5 minutes, stirring occasionally. Combine the flour and oil in a small bowl and mix well. Add to the sauté pan and gently stir well. Lower the heat to low and cook until the sauce thickens slightly.
4. When the tofu is done cooking, add the contents of the casserole dish to the sauté pan and gently mix well. Top with the cilantro and serve while warm.

Variations

- Replace the tofu with tempeh or with vegetables such as eggplant and portobello mushrooms.

TOFU TIKKA MASALA

A fierce battle rages between master chefs in India and a chef in Glasgow, Scotland, of all places. The chef in Glasgow claims to be the first to serve a "masala" sauce with the famed chicken tikka of Indian origin. The chefs in India consider this highly blasphemous as they claim the recipe has been passed down for generations. Not sure where tofu fits in the picture? Give this dish a try and find out! Serve with Coconut Spinach Rice (page 10) and Okra Masala (page 15) for a meal fit for a Raj.

SERVES 2 TO 4

TOFU MARINADE

1 (14-ounce) package extra-firm tofu
1¼ teaspoons ground cumin
¾ teaspoon chile powder
2 tablespoons freshly squeezed lemon juice
½ teaspoon sea salt
¼ teaspoon ground black pepper
1 clove garlic, pressed or minced
1 teaspoon peeled and minced fresh ginger
½ cup vegan yogurt

MASALA SAUCE

¾ cup soy creamer or coconut milk
¼ cup vegan yogurt
1½ tablespoons tomato paste
1 teaspoon freshly squeezed lemon juice
Pinch ground cardamom
Pinch ground cinnamon
¼ teaspoon sea salt, or to taste
1 tablespoon minced fresh cilantro

1. Preheat the oven to 375°F. Slice the tofu in half lengthwise, forming two cutlets. Slice each cutlet lengthwise three times and then widthwise three times to yield sixteen cubes each (thirty-two cubes total). Place cubes in a casserole dish with all of the marinade ingredients except the yogurt and mix well, making sure all of the tofu is covered. Add the yogurt and mix well. Place in the oven and bake for 15 minutes.

continues

2. While the tofu is cooking, place all of the sauce ingredients except the cilantro in a medium sauté pan on medium-low heat and gently whisk well. Cook for 10 minutes, stirring occasionally.
3. When the tofu is done cooking, add it to the sauté pan with all of the contents of the casserole dish, and gently mix well. Allow it to simmer for an additional 5 minutes. Add the cilantro and gently mix well before serving.

The Asian Pantry

Does vegan yogurt sound like an oxymoron to you? Believe it or not, there are several brands, mostly soy based, on the market, with a variety of flavors. Plain works best in these dishes. So Delicious has also put out a coconut-based yogurt that is incredibly flavorful and works well with this dish.

SEMOLINA CASHEW HALVA

Our halva is a slightly sweet, dairy-free version of this traditional Indian dessert, which usually includes lots of butter. There are many versions of halva throughout Asia and the Middle East, some of which are sesame-seed-based. Serve warm or cold. This halva is wonderful on its own and superb when topped with the Coconut Dessert Sauce (page 81).

SERVES 6 TO 8

¼ teaspoon saffron threads, soaked in 2 tablespoons hot water, optional
1 cup semolina flour
⅛ teaspoon sea salt
2½ cups water
¼ cup plus 2 tablespoons vegan butter
¼ to ½ cup chopped cashews, roasted, no salt
¼ cup currants or raisins
¼ teaspoon plus a pinch of ground cardamom
⅛ teaspoon ground cinnamon
½ cup agave nectar, maple syrup, or organic sugar, or to taste

1. If you are using the saffron, place the threads in hot water in a small bowl.
2. Place the semolina flour and salt in a medium saucepan over medium heat. Slowly add the water, stirring constantly until all of the liquid is dissolved and the mixture is thick. Continue to stir for a few minutes longer.
3. Add the remaining ingredients, including the saffron threads and soaking water, if using, and mix well. Continue to stir for another few minutes. Serve in individual dishes or pour into a small casserole dish. Serve warm, or, if you have more time, serve chilled by placing the casserole dish in the refrigerator until the halva is firm (approximately 1 hour), and cut into individual squares, rectangles, triangles, or whatever shape strikes your fancy.

Variations

- Add 1 tablespoon rose water.
- For an even creamier halva, replace 1 cup of water with soy or chocolate soy milk, coconut milk, rice milk, or almond milk (see page 229).
- Go for it and add ¾ cup chocolate chips.
- Replace the cashews with pistachios, macadamia nuts, or your favorite nut.
- Replace the currants with other dried fruit such as chopped dates, apricots, or figs.

CARDAMOM COOKIES

There is a wide range of Indian desserts that, despite their many differences, all wind up looking like a ball covered in powdered sugar. Because many of the ingredients in those desserts are a bit obscure for the Western shopper, we offer up these little gems. Though they are not a traditional cookie, they do have the familiar tastes of India in a similar package.

MAKES 15 TO 18 COOKIES

½ cup shelled raw pistachios, unsalted
½ cup unroasted cashews
½ cup vegan butter (Earth Balance is our favorite)
3 tablespoons agave nectar
1 teaspoon vanilla extract, preferably alcohol-free
½ teaspoon lemon zest, optional
1 cup spelt flour, sifted
1 tablespoon ground cardamom
1 cup powdered sugar

1. Preheat the oven to 300°F.
2. Grind the pistachios and cashews in a food processor fitted with the S-blade for about 30 seconds or until fine.
3. Using a standing mixer with the whisk attachment, a hand mixer, or by hand, whip the butter, agave nectar, vanilla extract, and lemon zest together for 1 to 2 minutes or until creamy and fluffy.
4. Add the flour and cardamom and stir well. Add the ground nuts and mix again. Form the batter into cookie-size balls, place them on a parchment-lined baking tray, and bake for 30 minutes.
5. Let cool for 3 to 5 minutes and then roll them around in the powdered sugar while they are still warm.

East Meets West: Yoga

Yoga has become popular in the West with good reason. It's a practice that can help us cultivate some much-needed peace of mind while staying in shape. There are countless schools of yoga. Many fitness centers and gyms now offer classes, some more intense than others. Some are a gentle workout whereas others are quite vigorous. There also are special yoga techniques for pregnant moms. Visit a local yoga studio near you and check out www.yogawiz.com for an overview of the many forms of yoga and its benefits.

MANGO LASSI

Lassis, both sweet and salty, are a popular yogurt-based drink throughout India. Dairy yogurt lovers frequently find soy-based yogurts to be a far cry from the original. Thankfully, there are coconut-milk-based yogurts that create the epic flavors of this drink. Combined with the tropical mango, this beverage may have you chanting Hare Krishna in no time.

MAKES SIX 8-OUNCE SERVINGS

2 medium-size mangoes, cubed, cold (about 3 cups)
1½ cups vegan coconut-milk yogurt
2 teaspoons freshly squeezed lemon juice
1 cup ice cubes
2 tablespoons agave nectar, optional

1. Place the mango, yogurt, lemon juice, and ice cubes in a blender and blend on high speed for 20 to 30 seconds, until smooth and even.
2. Taste and add agave nectar, if using, as desired. Serve immediately or refrigerate.

Variations

- Not a big fan of yogurt? Try substituting the coconut yogurt with 1¼ cups of coconut milk and ¼ cup of a thickener such as silken tofu, cashews, or coconut butter, being sure to blend well.
- Turn this into a milkshake by replacing the yogurt with vegan vanilla ice cream. (Can you say "yummy?")
- Spice it up by adding ½ teaspoon of ground cardamom!

East Meets West: Ayurveda

Ayurveda is an ancient Indian system of healing and lifestyle that is gaining popularity in the West. Its goal is to create harmony in the body and life through balancing the three substances or doshas–vata, pitta, and kapha. There is a growing number of ayurvedic spas and ayurvedic body care products on the market. Check out the recommended reading section in Appendix C for two wonderful introductions to ayurveda.

VANILLA CARDAMOM ROSE LASSI

Three great tastes that taste great together. This recipe can be used as the base for any kind of lassi you can dream up. Any or all of the three flavor ingredients (cardamom, rose, and vanilla) can be omitted for a plain lassi or exchanged for your desired flavors.

MAKES SIX 8-OUNCE SERVINGS

¾ cup vegan coconut-milk yogurt
1 (12-ounce) package silken tofu
1 teaspoon freshly squeezed lemon juice
¼ cup agave nectar
¾ teaspoon ground cardamom
1 tablespoon rose water
1 tablespoon vanilla extract, preferably alcohol-free
1 cup ice cubes
¼ to ½ cup ice water, if necessary

1. Place all of the ingredients except the ice water in a blender and blend on high speed for 20 to 30 seconds, or until smooth and even.
2. Taste and, if desired, add ice water to thin the mixture. Serve immediately or refrigerate.

Variations

- Not a big fan of yogurt? Try substituting the coconut yogurt with ¾ cup of coconut milk and ¼ cup of a thickener such as cashews, macadamia nuts, or coconut butter, being sure to blend well.
- Turn this into a milkshake by replacing the yogurt with vegan vanilla ice cream.
- Omit the cardamom and rose water and replace the vanilla with one teaspoon of another extract, such as almond, butterscotch, or even cherry!
- Make a Limetastic Lassi by omitting the cardamom, vanilla, rose water, and lemon juice and adding ¼ cup of freshly squeezed lime juice and ½ teaspoon of lime zest.

WARM CARDAMOM MILK

You can make even quicker work of this recipe by using 4 cups of store-bought rice milk instead of making your own as in this recipe. But if you enjoy this beverage as much as we do, you'll save a lot of packaging and have a fresher product by following the recipe as it is. Either way is a win for you! Warm cardamom milk is such a soothing, nurturing, warming way to end a busy day.

MAKES 32 OUNCES

1 cup uncooked brown rice

4 cups water

30 green cardamom pods, shells removed (about 2 teaspoons cardamom seeds)

2 tablespoons to ¼ cup sweetener of choice (try maple syrup, brown rice syrup, or agave nectar)

1. In a blender on high speed, blend the rice and water for 40 to 60 seconds or until a white liquid forms. Note: If you have a powerful blender, be sure not to overblend. If the rice is ground too fine it will not strain out and the milk will turn out very thick.
2. Strain the liquid through a fine mesh strainer or cheesecloth, into a pot. Place the pot on the stove over low heat. Add the cardamom seeds and allow the mixture to heat for 10 to 15 minutes or until the flavor of the cardamom has been well released, stirring occasionally.
3. Whisk in your desired sweetener and serve warm. If you prefer, you may strain out the cardamom seeds, but it is not necessary to do so.

Assorted Chutneys

For our chutney recipes, we consulted with our friend and resident Indian food expert, Vi Herbert (see inset on page 42). Chutneys are the condiment of choice in India. They are exceedingly flavorful and typically spicy. Here we provide a few different versions for your culinary enjoyment. Try them alongside any of the Indian dishes in this section. They go particularly well with Samosas (page 7) and dosas (page 21).

MINT CILANTRO CHUTNEY

MAKES 2 CUPS

1 bunch fresh mint (about ½ cup)
2 bunches fresh cilantro, chopped (about 2 cups)
1 green chile
3 cloves garlic
1 tablespoon peeled and minced fresh ginger
1 cup chopped red onion
Pinch chile powder
1 teaspoon freshly squeezed lime juice or ½ teaspoon tamarind paste
1 small tomato, chopped (about 1 cup)
¼ teaspoon garam masala
½ teaspoon sea salt

Remove the mint leaves from the stems. Place the leaves in a blender or food processor with the remaining ingredients. Process until smooth. Store in a glass container in a refrigerator for up to 3 days.

TOMATO CHUTNEY

MAKES 2 CUPS

3 cups chopped tomatoes
1½ tablespoons sesame oil
½ teaspoon brown mustard seeds
⅛ teaspoon turmeric powder
½ cup chopped yellow onion
5 curry leaves (see Note on page 6)
3 cloves garlic, pressed or minced
1½ teaspoons peeled and minced fresh ginger
1 green chile pepper, seeded
½ teaspoon sea salt, or to taste
⅛ teaspoon garam masala
¼ cup coconut milk
1 tablespoon minced fresh cilantro

1. Place the tomatoes in a blender and blend until pureed.
2. Heat the oil in a sauté pan over medium heat. Add the mustard seeds and cook for 1 minute, stirring constantly until they pop. Add the turmeric and onion and sauté for 3 more minutes, stirring frequently.
3. Add the curry leaves, garlic, ginger, chile, salt, and garam masala and sauté for 3 more minutes, stirring frequently. Add the tomato puree, cover, and cook for 5 minutes.
4. Add the coconut milk and cilantro, lower the heat to low, and cook for 2 minutes.

ROASTED GARLIC CHUTNEY

MAKES 2 CUPS

2 tablespoons sesame oil
1 red onion, chopped
1 cup garlic cloves
½ cup shredded coconut
½ cup coconut milk
3 tablespoons coriander seeds
3 dried red chiles
1 teaspoon tamarind paste, or 2 teaspoons freshly squeezed lime or lemon juice
Sea salt to taste

1. Place the sesame oil in a large sauté pan over medium heat. Add the onions and garlic, and cook for 10 minutes, stirring frequently. Add the shredded coconut and coconut milk, stir well, and remove from the heat.
2. In another pan, dry-roast the coriander seeds and dried chile over low heat for 2 minutes, until a pleasant aroma is released. Remove from the heat. Grind in a spice grinder or blender.
3. Place everything together in a food processor or blender and pulse chop until you have a chunky and well combined chutney. Optionally, you can puree it smooth.

Outreach Programs

Vi Herbert runs a nonprofit called the Kolam Charitable Foundation (www.kolam.info). It helps women and children in developing countries achieve economic independence. The organization is currently supporting a free rural area school in southern India in Tamil Nadu. Please visit the foundation's Web site to learn more about its outreach programs.

CUCUMBER MINT RAITA

Raita is a yogurt-based sauce that is served as a condiment with Indian meals. It has a cooling effect on the palate and is the perfect balance to the spiciness of curries and other favorite Indian dishes. Add a small dollop to your feast, which may include Mulligatawny (page 3), Cauliflower Chickpea Subji (page 19), Tempeh Vindaloo (page 28), and Rice Pilau (page 9).

MAKES APPROXIMATELY 3½ CUPS

1 teaspoon ground cumin
½ teaspoon ground coriander
2 cups plain vegan yogurt
1 medium cucumber, peeled, seeded, and thinly sliced (about 3 cups)
3 tablespoons loosely packed, julienned fresh mint
1 lime, juiced
½ teaspoon sea salt, or to taste
⅛ teaspoon ground black pepper, or to taste

1. Place the cumin and coriander in a small sauté pan over high heat. Stir constantly for about a minute or until the cumin turns golden brown and a pleasant aroma is released.
2. Add to a large bowl with the remaining ingredients and mix well.

Indian Spice Blends

Why not impress yourself and create your own spice blends for the freshest flavors? Here are two of the more popular blends we use throughout the India section. These recipes create just over 1/3 cup each. Feel free to double or triple the recipe depending on how fast you plan to go through them. Store in a glass jar. For maximum freshness, use within a month.

CURRY SPICE BLEND

Here is a simple base recipe for curry powder. Create your own blends by experimenting with the variations and altering the quantities.

3 tablespoons ground coriander
2 tablespoons ground cumin
1 teaspoon ground cloves
1 teaspoon turmeric powder
1 teaspoon ground black pepper
½ teaspoon mustard powder
½ teaspoon cayenne pepper

Whisk all of the ingredients together and store in a glass container.

Variations

- You can add 1 teaspoon each of ground fenugreek and fennel.
- Another variation is achieved by adding 1 teaspoon ground cardamom, 1 teaspoon ground cinnamon, and ¾ teaspoon ground nutmeg.
- If you want to start with the whole seed, grind all of the seeds separately in a spice grinder and combine in a bowl. Use mustard seeds instead of powder and dried red chiles instead of cayenne. You can toast the spices well in a large sauté pan, preferably cast iron. Try toasting each one individually before blending in the spice blender (see page 225).

GARAM MASALA BLEND

There are more variations of garam masala than there are rickshaw drivers in New Delhi. And there are a lot of rickshaw drivers in New Delhi! Try altering the spices and quantities to come up with your own signature blend.

2 tablespoons ground coriander
1 tablespoon ground cumin
1 tablespoon ground black pepper
1 tablespoon powdered ginger
1 teaspoon ground cardamom
1 teaspoon ground cinnamon
1 teaspoon ground cloves
1 teaspoon ground nutmeg
¼ teaspoon turmeric powder, optional

Whisk all of the ingredients together and store in a glass container.

Variations

- You can add ½ teaspoon cayenne to spice it up.
- Try adding 1 tablespoon ground fennel seeds.
- Grate the nutmeg fresh with a nutmeg grater—a wonderful kitchen gadget!
- You can toast the coriander, cumin, black pepper, and cloves before grinding (see the toasting variation in curry powder on page 44).

PART TWO

The Cuisine of Thailand

When you remember Thailand, images of crystalline seas, verdant hillsides, and lavish palaces linger in the background of your mind, overshadowed by some of the best food on the planet. Even if you only have a layover in Bangkok, you simply must get into town and eat the food. You can become a raw foodist when you get home. But when you're there, eat green curry. Eat it as often as you can, order it for breakfast, and when you think it would be silly to eat any more, eat one more for us.

Thai food has power-packed flavor in every mouthful. Whether it's brothy Galangal Lemongrass Soup or coconut-milk–based Massaman Curry, Thai food never fails in flavor. And if you are an intense spice lover, you will meet your match in Thailand. Seemingly everything from the luscious Green Papaya Salad to the scintillating Red Curry leaps off the plate with chile pepper goodness. Thankfully, in your own kitchen, you can easily control the spice level of each dish.

Once your kitchen is stocked with the component flavors of Thai cuisine, you can create a fusion of your own devising with seasonal produce and your unique culinary style. We've combined the best of both worlds in this chapter with healthy, delicious renditions of authentic Thai classics such as Thai Basil Eggplant and Thom Kha Pak (Thai Coconut Vegetable Soup) alongside our own inventions like the Kaffir Lemongrass Tofu Cutlets and Funky Thai Salsa. Use these recipes to re-create the taste of Thailand and then sit back, relax, and enjoy yourself in true Thai fashion.

The Asian Pantry: Thailand

Coconut Milk: Made from the meat of mature coconuts, this sweet, milky white liquid is used throughout Asia, frequently as the base for curries. Coconut milk is different than coconut water or juice, which is the clear liquid found inside the coconut. See page 234 for our homemade Coconut Milk recipe.

Fish-Free Sauce: The use of fish sauce is extremely popular in Thai cuisine. Our version on page 85 uses the sea vegetable arame to create the flavor of the sea. We also use Bragg's Liquid Aminos as a substitute. The liquid aminos are a soy-based salt substitute that contains the essential amino acids.

Galangal (Thai Ginger): This is a large knobby rhizome with a unique earthy flavor. If you cannot find fresh galangal, substitute regular fresh ginger. Do not use the dried and powdered versions of galangal, which just are not the same.

Green Papaya: Green papaya is immature papaya rather than unripe papaya. Unripe papaya will still look slightly orange or pinkish inside. Immature papaya is whitish with a touch of green. The papaya is picked at a young age when the enzyme levels are at their peak, making green papaya a highly nutritious antioxidant.

Jasmine Rice: An aromatic long-grain white rice with a distinct floral note, jasmine rice is commonly cultivated and eaten across Thailand. See page 230 for cooking instructions.

Kaffir Lime Leaf: If your neighbor doesn't have a kaffir lime tree, you can find the leaves, fresh and dried, in specialty markets or ask your grocer to order some for you. The zest from regular limes makes a fine substitute. In general, you can replace each kaffir lime leaf with ½ teaspoon lime zest.

Lemongrass: A tall grass that provides a wonderful burst of lemon flavor, fresh lemongrass is more available than the kaffir lime leaf, and it's very easy to grow. It can be stored frozen to have around when not in season. When lemongrass is called for in recipes, trim the very bottom off, remove the outer layer, and use the white part only.

Palm Sugar: Thais frequently add a little sugar to their food. In the past, palm sugar, a brownish sugar with a deep rich flavor, was the sweetener of choice. These days, white sugar is most commonly available although there is a growing specialty market for palm sugar made the old-fashioned (and therefore pricier) way. We like to replace the more typical white sugar with agave nectar, which also doesn't interfere with the color of the dish.

Sriracha Sauce: Sriracha is a chile sauce typically made with Thai red peppers. It is frequently used to spice up everything from green papaya salad to Pad Thai. Sriracha can usually be found in the Asian food section of grocery stores or see page 86 for our homemade Sriracha sauce.

Sticky Rice: Also known as sweet rice or glutinous rice, this short-grain rice is particularly sticky when cooked. The stickiness does not come from any gluten but rather from starches. It is traditionally steamed in a banana leaf. We use it in our Thai desserts.

Thai Basil: With smaller leaves and a purple stem, this variety of basil has a strong and slightly licorice flavor. Thai basil is used in Vietnamese as well as Thai cuisine.

BANANA PANCAKES

In a country short on Western-style breakfast foods, these pancakes really hit the spot! Usually served as big as the plate and sprinkled with a touch of powdered sugar, they are enough to power you up for a good long morning of sight-seeing. Keep the heat low to cook all the way through the pancake without burning the bananas. Serve as they are, with maple syrup, or topped with a dab of vegan butter and a sprinkling of powdered sugar.

MAKES EIGHT 4-INCH FLAPJACKS

½ cup spelt flour
½ cup brown rice flour
2 teaspoons baking powder
½ teaspoon sea salt
½ teaspoon ground cinnamon, optional
2 cups thinly sliced banana (about 3 medium bananas)
1¼ cups water
1 tablespoon safflower, coconut, or other oil or melted Earth Balance vegan butter, plus more for cooking
2 tablespoons maple syrup
½ teaspoon vanilla extract, preferably alcohol-free
1 teaspoon granulated organic sugar, optional

1. Sift the spelt flour, rice flour, baking powder, salt, and cinnamon, if using, into a large mixing bowl. Whisk together well, making sure there are no lumps.
2. Using a standing mixer with the whisk attachment or a hand mixer, whip ½ cup of the bananas for 20 seconds or until well blended and a little bit fluffy. Add the water, oil, maple syrup, and vanilla and continue to whisk until creamy and well blended.
3. Turn the heat under a griddle or other pan to low and allow the pan to heat up while you proceed with the batter. You may need to lightly oil the pan. Add the wet ingredients to the flour mixture and use a spoon or rubber spatula to stir until the batter is uniform. Be careful not to overmix the batter.
4. When the griddle or skillet is very hot, use a ¼ cup measuring cup to form as many pancakes as room allows. Working quickly, cover the tops of the pancakes with the remaining banana slices. You can push the slices in just a little, which will spread the batter out some. If you like, sprinkle the bananas with a little of the sugar.
5. Flip the pancakes when there are bubbles on top and they smell toasty. (Note that there won't be as much bubbling as there is with regular pancakes. The smell and perhaps a tiny bit of smoke will be the best way to tell if they are ready to flip.) Continue to cook on the banana side for about 2 minutes. Repeat with the remaining batter. Serve immediately.

GALANGAL LEMONGRASS SOUP

Though all soups benefit from spending hours simmering on the stovetop to allow the full flavors of the dish to sing in perfect harmony, those of us short on time can also choose to increase the flavor ingredients for a similar effect. In this case, using a larger than normal amount of lemongrass, kaffir lime leaves, and galangal counteracts the limited cooking time while providing you that symphonic splendor you deserve. Served with rice noodles, this dish can be a satisfying light meal.

SERVES 4 TO 6

8 cups water or vegetable stock (see page 228)
3 stalks lemongrass, bottoms and outer stalks removed
4 kaffir lime leaves, thinly sliced, or 2 teaspoons lime zest
2-inch piece galangal, thinly sliced, or 2 tablespoons peeled and minced fresh ginger
4 cloves garlic, pressed or minced
1 red chile, seeded and diced
1 cup thinly sliced carrot
1 (15-ounce) can straw mushrooms, or 1½ cups sliced cremini mushrooms
1 handful green beans or snow peas, thinly sliced (about ½ cup)
8 to 10 cherry tomatoes, quartered (about 1 cup)
¼ cup Bragg's Liquid Aminos, soy sauce, or a combination
1 lemon or lime, juiced
¼ cup thinly sliced green onion
2 tablespoons minced fresh cilantro

1. Place the water in a large pot and begin heating over medium heat. Slice the lemongrass in half lengthwise and crush it by lightly pounding with a wooden spoon or other heavy object. Add to the pot with the lime leaves, galangal, garlic, and chile pepper. Cover and cook for 10 minutes.
2. Add the carrot, mushrooms, green beans, and tomatoes and cook for at least 5 minutes more, or until the carrots are soft.
3. Remove from the heat and add the Bragg's, lemon juice, green onion, and cilantro. Stir well and remove the lemongrass before serving hot.

THAI COCONUT VEGETABLE SOUP (THOM KHA PAK)

Simple and satisfying, this soup will have your guests *oohhing* and *aahhing.* If you aren't serving all of this soup immediately, you may want to leave the cabbage on the side. Portion out some shredded cabbage to each bowl (it will shrink down quite a bit when it gets hot), add the soup, and stir.

SERVES 8

6 cups water or vegetable stock (see page 228)
1 stalk lemongrass, bottoms and outer stalks removed
2 (14-ounce) cans coconut milk
2-inch piece fresh ginger, peeled
2 kaffir lime leaves, or 1 teaspoon lime zest
4 cups assorted chopped vegetables (carrots, zucchini, broccoli, eggplant, mushrooms)
1 cup yellow onion, sliced into quarter moons
2 red or green chiles, seeded and diced
1 lime, juiced
¼ cup Bragg's Liquid Aminos
1 teaspoon sea salt, or to taste
¼ cup minced fresh cilantro
4 cups shredded napa cabbage, lightly packed
1 cup mung bean sprouts, optional garnish

1. Place the water in a large pot over medium heat. Slice the lemongrass in half lengthwise and crush it by lightly pounding with a wooden spoon or other heavy object, and add it to the pot. Using a blender, combine about half of the coconut milk with the ginger, and lime leaves on high speed for 20 seconds or until there are no chunks. Add the remaining coconut milk and blend for 5 to 10 seconds to incorporate. Pour this mixture into the water and continue cooking over medium heat while you prepare the vegetables.
2. Place each vegetable into the soup pot as you go, starting with the hardest, longest-cooking veggies. Add the onion and chiles, cover, and heat for 10 minutes or until all the veggies are tender.
3. Add the lime juice, Bragg's, and salt, and stir. Cook for 2 more minutes and taste. If you think the soup needs more lemongrass, ginger, or kaffir lime, blend more now with ½ cup of the broth. Otherwise, add the cilantro and cabbage, stir well, and remove the lemongrass stalks. Serve immediately, garnished with mung bean sprouts, if using.

GREEN PAPAYA SALAD

As we noted earlier in this section, you may want to ask your grocer if the papaya is immature papaya or just unripe. If you simply cannot find immature papaya, go for the unripe papaya as the next best choice. Rather than grating the papaya you can use a mandoline, which yields longer, thicker julienne strips. They take longer to absorb the dressing, but they do not get as soggy as the grated papaya does over time. Using a spice or coffee grinder to grind the lime leaves works best, but a mortar and pestle are the time-honored tradition. Serve this refreshing salad with Thai Summer Rolls (page 59), Red Curry vegetables (page 70), or Pad Thai (page 66).

SERVES 4 TO 6

4 cups shredded or coarsely grated green papaya (about ½ of a large green papaya)
1 lime, juiced
1 cup shredded carrots
2 kaffir lime leaves, ground, or 1 teaspoon lime zest
2 cloves garlic, pressed or minced
¼ cup minced fresh cilantro
1 tablespoon agave nectar
1 teaspoon Bragg's Liquid Aminos, or soy sauce
½ teaspoon crushed red pepper flakes or ½ hot red chile pepper, diced
½ teaspoon sea salt
4 cherry tomatoes, quartered
½ cup chopped cashews or peanuts, toasted (see page 225), optional

1. Place the green papaya in a mixing bowl and cover with the juice of ½ of the lime. Toss well to coat the papaya.
2. Add the carrots, ground lime leaves, garlic, cilantro, agave, Bragg's, crushed red pepper, sea salt, and the remaining lime juice and toss well.
3. Serve on individual plates topped with a tomato and cashews.

Variation

- Replace the papaya with jicama for a unique twist.

CUCUMBER SALAD WITH PEANUTS AND CHILE

This salad is a simple and sublime palette cleanser. The playfulness of the mint, chile pepper, vinegar, and agave makes this salad dance in your mouth. Serve alongside very flavorful curries such as Massaman Curry (page 78) or Madras Curry (page 25), or simply serve this salad over lettuce.

SERVES 6

2 large cucumbers, peeled
2 tablespoons rice vinegar or freshly squeezed lime juice
1 teaspoon agave nectar
1 tablespoon mirin
1 tablespoon red chile pepper, seeded and diced or ½ teaspoon crushed red pepper flakes
¼ cup chopped roasted peanuts
1 tablespoon minced fresh cilantro
1 teaspoon minced fresh mint
½ teaspoon sea salt

1. Cut the peeled cucumbers in half. Use a small spoon to scoop out the seeds, then cut them into ¼-inch slices.
2. Add the remaining ingredients and stir well. Serve immediately or store in an airtight container in the fridge until ready to serve.

COOKED MIXED VEGETABLES (YUM TAVOY)

This is quite a decadent way to enjoy your veggies—they melt in your mouth with the creamy coconut sauce. Feel free to replace the galangal with ginger and to replace the Thai basil with sweet basil or your favorite herb. Serve as a side dish with Pad Thai (page 66) or Kaffir Lemongrass Tofu Cutlets (page 73).

SERVES 6

1 (14-ounce) can coconut milk
½ cup diced shallots or onions
1 inch sliced galangal or peeled and minced fresh ginger
2 lemongrass stalks, crushed, optional
3 kaffir lime leaves, optional
4 cups broccoli or cauliflower flowerets, or a combination
2 cups sliced carrots
1 hot chile pepper, seeded and diced
1 tablespoon Fish-Free Sauce (page 85) or Bragg's Liquid Aminos or soy sauce, or to taste
1 teaspoon Sriracha (page 86) or a pinch of cayenne
½ teaspoon sea salt, or to taste
Pinch white or ground black pepper
2 tablespoons minced fresh Thai basil

1. Place the coconut milk in a large sauté pan on medium-low heat. Add the remaining ingredients except the basil, and cook until the broccoli and carrots are just tender, for 8 to 10 minutes, gently stirring frequently.
2. Remove the lemongrass and kaffir lime leaves, if using. Add the Thai basil and gently stir well before serving.

Variations

- This dish works well with any vegetable. Replace the broccoli and carrots with asparagus, bok choy, thinly sliced yams, or a combination of all three.
- You can add roasted tofu or tempeh (see page 227).
- Replace the galangal with 2 cloves of garlic, pressed or minced.

TOMATO MUNG BEAN SALAD

This is a simple and light salad that makes use of common ingredients in a Thai kitchen. If you have time, allow this dish to sit in the fridge for 20 minutes; the flavor enhances with time. Enjoy as a side dish when served with Kaffir Lemongrass Tofu Cutlets (page 73) or Pad Thai (page 66).

SERVES 6

3 large tomatoes, chopped (5 cups)
1 clove garlic, pressed or minced
1½ cups mung sprouts
½ cup sliced green onions
2 tablespoons minced fresh cilantro
1 hot chile pepper, seeded and diced, or to taste
1 tablespoon minced fresh mint
1 tablespoon soy sauce
2 tablespoons freshly squeezed lime juice
2 tablespoons sesame oil
1 tablespoon rice vinegar
1 teaspoon Sriracha (page 86) or cayenne pepper to taste
½ teaspoon sea salt, or to taste
¼ teaspoon ground black pepper, or to taste

Combine all of the ingredients in a large mixing bowl and gently mix well.

THAI VINAIGRETTE

Add the tastes of Thailand to your salads with this simple and zesty dressing.

MAKES 1½ CUPS

½ cup water
½ cup sesame oil
¼ cup rice vinegar
1 tablespoon minced galangal or peeled fresh ginger
2 kaffir lime leaves or ½ teaspoon lime zest
1 tablespoon freshly squeezed lime juice
1 tablespoon agave nectar
1 tablespoon minced fresh cilantro
2 tablespoons minced lemongrass, white part only, outer stalk removed
1 tablespoon plus 1 teaspoon soy sauce
2 teaspoons seeded and diced hot chile pepper
¼ cup coconut milk, optional
Pinch of sea salt, or to taste

Combine all of the ingredients in a strong blender and blend until liquefied. Store in a glass container in the refrigerator for up to 4 days.

Variations

- Replace the sesame oil with mildly flavored oils such as safflower.
- Replace the cilantro with any herb of your choosing, such as dill, basil, or parsley.
- Add an extra tablespoon of minced fresh cilantro.
- Replace the rice vinegar with another vinegar of your choice.
- For a ❤ raw version, omit the coconut milk and substitute cold-pressed olive oil for the sesame oil.

FUNKY THAI SALSA

This salsa combines traditional Thai flavors with a Mexican American favorite. Why not? It's fun to surprise people with bold new flavors. Though you can certainly use this salsa with Thai Summer Rolls (page 59), in wraps, or as a topping on Rice Pilau (page 9), it makes a fun dip for chips or cucumber slices.

MAKES 3 CUPS

1¼ cups cherry tomatoes, chopped small
1 medium mango, chopped small (about 1¼ cups)
1 medium avocado, chopped small
2 tablespoons diced red onion
2 teaspoons freshly squeezed lime juice
1 kaffir lime leaf
1 tablespoon lemongrass, chopped small, white part only (about one small stalk)
2 teaspoons Bragg's Liquid Aminos
2 tablespoons minced fresh cilantro
¼ teaspoon sea salt, or to taste

1. Place ¼ cup of the tomatoes and ¼ cup of the mango into a blender. Place the remaining tomatoes and mango together with the avocado and red onion in a mixing bowl. Cover with the lime juice and stir well to keep the avocado from browning.
2. Add the kaffir lime leaf, lemongrass, and Bragg's to the blender and blend starting on low speed and increasing to high speed for 15 seconds or until the lime leaf and lemongrass are finely blended. Pour over the tomato mixture, scraping the sides of the blender to get all of the goods out.
3. Add the cilantro, sprinkle with salt, and stir. Serve immediately or refrigerate for up to two days.

Variations

- Replace the mango with papaya or pineapple.
- Add ½ teaspoon chile powder for a subtle twist.

THAI SUMMER ROLLS

Summer rolls make a pretty package out of all manner of fresh summer vegetables and fruits as well as noodles, rice, or tofu. Once you get the hang of the technique used here, the sky's the limit as far as what you can stuff into these rolls. Serve with peanut sauce (page 64), Mango Ginger Sauce (page 61), Dim Sum Dipping Sauce (page 101), Nuoc Cham (page 192), or Funky Thai Salsa (page 58).

MAKES 8 ROLLS

½ (14-ounce) package extra-firm tofu
1 tablespoon soy sauce
2 ounces bean thread noodles
1 cucumber, peeled, seeded, and sliced into thin strips
2 cups shredded lettuce
1 large carrot, shredded
1 red bell pepper, seeded and cut into thin strips
1 cup mung sprouts, optional
¼ cup minced fresh cilantro
16 leaves basil or Thai basil
16 to 24 fresh mint leaves
16 rice paper wrappers
Soy sauce for dipping

1. Preheat the oven or toaster oven to 350°F. Slice the tofu into six rectangles about 4 to 5 inches long. Place in a baking dish, pour the soy sauce over the top and roll them around a bit to coat them in the soy sauce. Place in the oven and bake for 10 to 15 minutes. Set them aside and allow them to cool.
2. Boil water in a pot or tea kettle. Place the noodles in a bowl, cover with the boiling water, and stir them occasionally for 5 to 8 minutes while you prepare the other veggies. Strain and allow them to cool.
3. After all of the filling ingredients are prepared, add warm water to a large bowl or casserole dish large enough to fit the rice paper wrappers. Dip one of the wrappers in the water to soak and lay it on a clean work surface. Lay another soaked wrap above the first one, overlapping by a couple of inches into an eight formation. Arrange a small amount (about one-eighth) of each of the filling ingredients on the first rice paper.

continues

4. When the rice paper is soft and flexible, fold up the end of the wrapper that is closest to you, then fold in the sides. Continue to roll and tuck in the sides until the whole thing is sealed together in a happy little roll. Be sure to press firmly as you roll in order to keep the roll tightly packed. This way they will slice in half without spilling their insides and are easier to eat. Slice and serve immediately or cover with a damp cloth in the refrigerator for up to 2 days.

Chefs' Tips and Tricks

If you have enough counter or table space, lay out all of your wrappers at the same time. This is the most time-efficient way to go. And by the time you are done adding all of the fillings, the rice paper is the perfect rolling consistency—damp and sticky.

It's easy and economical to bake the tofu strips in a toaster oven. Alternatively, you could sauté the tofu in a bit of toasted sesame oil.

TEMPEH LETTUCE WRAPS WITH MANGO GINGER SAUCE

The handheld wrap is a popular item throughout Asia, with many cultures adding their own favorite ingredients. Here we use roasted or grilled tempeh as the main component. The mango ginger sauce can also be served as a dipping sauce for Nori Rolls (page 157), Tempura Vegetables (page 142), or Samosas (page 7).

MAKES 6 ROLLS

MARINATED TEMPEH

8 ounces tempeh
2 tablespoons soy sauce
2 tablespoons water
1 tablespoon sesame oil
1 teaspoon agave nectar, maple syrup, or organic sugar, optional

FIXINGS

6 large lettuce leaves or 12 small leaves
½ cucumber, seeded and sliced
1 tomato, small wedges
12 fresh mint leaves, optional

MANGO GINGER SAUCE

MAKES ½ CUP SAUCE

½ small mango, chopped (½ cup)
1 tablespoon peeled and minced fresh ginger
Pinch of crushed red pepper flakes or
½ teaspoon seeded and minced hot chile pepper
1 tablespoon water, or more for desired consistency
1½ teaspoons freshly squeezed lime juice
¼ teaspoon soy sauce or to taste
Maple syrup or agave nectar to taste

continues

1. Preheat the oven to 350°F. Slice the tempeh into twelve ½-inch slices. Place the remaining marinade ingredients in a small casserole dish and whisk well. Add the tempeh and flip over once or twice. Place in the oven and bake for 15 minutes.
2. While the tempeh is cooking, prepare the mango ginger sauce by placing all of the ingredients in a blender or food processor and blending until smooth. Adjust the quantity of red pepper flakes to your desired spiciness. Pour into a small bowl and set aside.
3. Prepare the fixings and place them on a platter. When the tempeh is done cooking, place it alongside the fixings or on a serving plate of its own. Have fun as everyone takes a lettuce leaf, tops it with some tempeh and fillings, rolls it up, and dips it into the sauce.

Variations

- Replace the tempeh with tofu or even grilled seitan from Indonesian Seitan Satay (see page 195).
- Get creative with your fixings. Add avocado slices and sprouts. Try adding some grilled vegetables like zucchini, red bell pepper, or portobello mushrooms. You can even marinate them in the tempeh marinade above.

THAI BASIL EGGPLANT

Though abundant in flavor, this dish is light enough to accompany heavier dishes such as Pad Thai (page 66), or simply served over rice or quinoa. It also makes an innovative filling for a wrap, hot or cold. Use regular basil if the Thai variety is not available to you.

SERVES 3 TO 4 AS A MAIN DISH

1 tablespoon sesame or safflower oil
4 cloves garlic, pressed or minced
1 to 2 red chile peppers, minced, optional
2 medium eggplant, chopped medium (about 6 cups) (see Box below)
1½ cups water
1 tablespoon agave nectar
2 tablespoons Bragg's Liquid Aminos or soy sauce
¼ to ½ cup Thai basil leaves

1. Sauté the oil, garlic, and chile pepper over medium heat for 1 minute or until the garlic starts to brown, stirring frequently.
2. Add the eggplant and water, cover and simmer for 8 minutes or until the eggplant is very soft. Add the agave and Bragg's and stir. Continue cooking for a couple of minutes until the eggplant is that perfect edible consistency. Add the basil, stir well, and remove from the heat.

Chefs' Tips and Tricks

An old tip for cooking with eggplant is to cut it in irregular shapes of the same size. This makes them easier to turn and helps the eggplant not stick to the pan. Many people prefer to "sweat" the eggplant first, believing this lends a softer, more chewable eggplant. First slice the eggplant, lay the pieces out on a baking tray, and sprinkle with sea salt (kosher if you have it). Let it sit for 15 minutes or longer, then rinse before using in a recipe.

SPICY SESAME PEANUT NOODLES

This dish makes a great appetizer or side dish but can also come through as an entrée simply by adding some steamed vegetables such as broccoli, bok choy, carrots, or kale. If you aren't familiar with peanut sauce, this dish makes a great intro course. Serve before Loving Jungle Princess (page 72) with Spicy Asparagus (page 65).

SERVES 4 TO 6

8 ounces vermicelli or angel hair pasta
1 teaspoon toasted sesame oil
2 cloves garlic, pressed or minced
2 tablespoons peeled and minced fresh ginger
½ cup peanut butter
1 tablespoon soy sauce or Bragg's Liquid Aminos, or to taste
½ cup water (or more if needed to stir)
2 tablespoons rice vinegar or freshly squeezed lime juice
2 tablespoons agave nectar
1 teaspoon crushed red pepper flakes or fresh minced chile pepper
1 tablespoon toasted sesame seeds
1 large carrot, shredded (about 1 cup)
2 tablespoons minced fresh cilantro
1 stalk green onion, green and white parts, thinly sliced

1. Prepare the noodles according to the package's instructions. Once strained, toss with the oil and set aside.
2. Blend or whisk together the remaining ingredients except the carrot, cilantro, and green onion to make your peanut sauce. When you are ready to serve, toss the peanut sauce with the noodles, carrot, cilantro, and green onion. If the dish sits around (for even a short period of time) you will need to add a tablespoon or two of water to stir it up again.

The Asian Pantry

Peanut butter is surprisingly uncommon outside of the United States but works great in re-creating an authentic peanut sauce in dishes such as this one. It also saves you the time of harvesting peanuts, roasting them, and simmering them into a savory sauce. *Phew*! But if you ever come across raw peanuts at an Asian market, you should definitely check them out. The flavor might surprise you—more subtle and juicier than packaged peanuts. Here in Hawaii, boiled peanuts are frequently served, still inside their shells, at Polynesian events and luaus. Also look for sprouted peanuts at your local farmers' market—truly a treat!

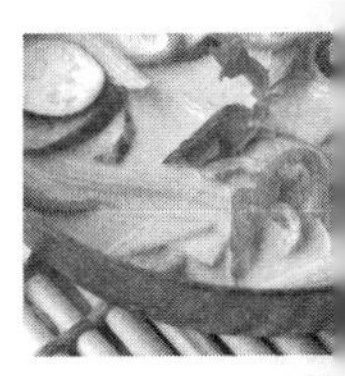

SPICY ASPARAGUS

This is the sort of fun-loving creation you can whip up once your kitchen is stocked with wonderfully authentic Thai ingredients like kaffir lime leaf. Try serving it along with Thai Coconut Vegetable Soup (page 52) and Pad Siew (page 75).

SERVES 4 TO 6

2 teaspoons sesame oil
2 cloves garlic, pressed or minced
1 teaspoon peeled and grated fresh ginger
2 green onions, white part only, thinly sliced (about 2 tablespoons)
1 teaspoon diced red chile pepper or crushed red pepper flakes
4 kaffir lime leaves, thinly sliced, or 2 teaspoons lime zest
1 pound asparagus, stem ends trimmed
1 medium red bell pepper, sliced, optional
¾ cup water
1 tablespoon soy sauce or Bragg's Liquid Aminos
¼ cup thinly sliced fresh basil

1. In a sauté pan over medium heat, sauté the oil, garlic, ginger, green onion, chile, and kaffir lime leaves for 2 minutes.
2. Add the asparagus and the red bell pepper, if using, and sauté for 2 more minutes. Add the water and continue to cook for 5 more minutes or until the asparagus is soft, but still bright green, and most of the water is evaporated.
3. Add the soy sauce and basil, stir, and remove from the heat.

PAD THAI

Pad Thai is the quintessential Thai dish, and yet no two Pad Thais are alike. It's another one of those dishes where each region has developed its own style. Many variations use egg; ours uses tofu. If you have the time to make the Fish-Free Sauce (page 85) and the Sriracha (page 86), you will experience the full flavors of the dish. Serve with Cucumber Salad (page 54) or Thai Summer Rolls (page 59).

SERVES 4 TO 6

1 (14-ounce) package Pad Thai noodles (thin and flat, like linguini)
2 tablespoons soy sauce
3 tablespoons sesame or peanut oil
1 (14-ounce) package extra-firm tofu
1 batch Pad Thai Sauce (recipe follows)
1 cup minced shallots or onion
3 large cloves garlic, pressed or minced
½ cup thinly sliced green onion
¼ cup minced fresh cilantro
1 cup mung bean sprouts
½ cup roasted unsalted peanuts
Lime wedges

PAD THAI SAUCE

¼ cup freshly squeezed lime juice
1 teaspoon lime zest
2 tablespoons peanut or sesame oil
1 tablespoon agave nectar or organic sugar
1 tablespoon rice vinegar
2 tablespoons soy sauce
3 tablespoons Fish-Free Sauce (page 85), or add extra soy sauce or Bragg's Liquid Aminos to taste
1 clove garlic, minced
1 teaspoon tamarind paste, optional
2 teaspoons Sriracha (page 86) or ½ teaspoon crushed red pepper flakes, or to taste

1. Preheat the oven to 375°F. Cook the noodles according to the instructions on the package. Strain into a colander and set aside.
2. Place the soy sauce and 1 tablespoon of the sesame oil on a small baking sheet. Slice the tofu into ½-inch cutlets. Slice each cutlet into 2 inch by ½-inch strips and place on the baking sheet. Flip the tofu to ensure even coating. Place in the oven and bake for 15 minutes.
3. Prepare the Pad Thai Sauce by combining all of the ingredients in a bowl and whisking well.
4. Place 2 tablespoons of the sesame oil in a large sauté pan or wok over medium-high heat. Add the shallots and garlic and cook for 3 minutes, stirring constantly. Lower the heat to low. Add the cooked noodles and Pad Thai Sauce and cook for 3 minutes, gently stirring well. Add the tofu and gently stir well.
5. Garnish each serving with green onion, cilantro, sprouts, peanuts, and lime wedges.

The Asian Pantry

Rice pasta is God's gift to the gluten intolerant. Check out the Asian section in your supermarket or visit an Asian grocer to discover the selection available to you. Our favorite natural-foodstore brand is Tinkyada, which offers a wide variety of shapes and sizes to choose from.

GREEN CURRY

Green curry has to be one of Thailand's greatest contributions to the culinary experience. Served at breakfast, lunch, and dinner, this dish is smooth, comforting, and oh-so-pleasing. Prepare the veggies for this dish while you are waiting for the curry paste ingredients to roast. Serve with Green Papaya Salad (page 53) or Thai Summer Rolls (page 59) and finish the meal off with some Sticky Rice and Mango Slice (page 80).

SERVES 6

GREEN CURRY PASTE

5 to 10 green chiles, halved and seeded, to taste (see Note on page 69)
1½ tablespoons coriander seeds
1½ stalks lemongrass, chopped into ½-inch pieces, white part only (about 6 tablespoons)
2 tablespoons diced galangal or peeled fresh ginger
½ medium green bell pepper, seeds removed
4 kaffir lime leaves, or 2 teaspoons lime zest
½ cup packed basil leaves
1 teaspoon sea salt

GREEN CURRY

1 tablespoon sesame oil
2 (14-ounce) cans coconut milk
6 to 8 cups assorted chopped vegetables (eggplant, onions, carrots, zucchini, cabbage, green beans, bamboo shoots, oyster mushrooms, baby corn, water chestnuts, etc.)
1 tablespoon soy sauce or Bragg's Liquid Aminos, or to taste
1 teaspoon agave nectar, or to taste
½ cup minced fresh sweet basil and/or cilantro

1. Place the chiles in a sauté pan with the coriander seeds, lemongrass, galangal, and green bell pepper. Roast over medium-low heat for 8 to 10 minutes or until everything looks a little browned, stirring occasionally.
2. Transfer to a blender, add the kaffir lime leaves, basil, and salt, and blend until a thick paste forms, for 20 to 30 seconds. You may need to add a bit of the coconut milk to the blender to get the ingredients moving and well blended. Start with ¼ cup and work your way up as needed.
3. In a large sauté pan or pot over medium heat, add the sesame oil and allow it to heat for 30 seconds. Add the curry paste and sauté over medium heat until aromatic, about 2 minutes. Add the coconut milk and cook over medium-low heat, bringing the mixture to a low boil. Add the vegetables, starting with the hardest veggies that will take the longest to cook.
4. When all of the veggies are just soft, add the soy sauce and agave nectar and stir well. Cook for 2 minutes, add the minced basil, and remove from the heat. Serve immediately.

Variations

- Protein lovers can follow the directions on page 227 for adding marinated, roasted tofu or tempeh to this dish.
- Go even greener by adding 2 tablespoons minced fresh parsley to the curry paste and 2 cups kale, collard greens, or Swiss chard cut into strips in step three, a couple of minutes before removing from the heat.

Note: Many recipes in this chapter call for chile peppers. The quantity of chiles that you use will entirely depend upon the particular chile's level of spiciness. This will vary greatly from pepper to pepper and largely depend on the season as well as many other factors. The seeds inside the peppers are particularly hot and should always be removed unless you are looking for a fire-hot dish. If you aren't sure how hot your pepper is, slice off a tiny strip at the end with no seeds on it and taste it. If jalapeño is the only green pepper you can buy, for example, you may only want to use one rather than the five to ten called for in the Green Curry recipe.

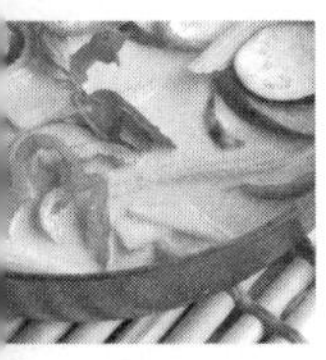

RED CURRY

This beloved sister of green curry takes a bit less time to make because the curry paste ingredients are not roasted. What is the most fun here is that you can really start to get a sense of how the different chiles taste. Red curry is generally hotter than green curry, and the flavors are a little brighter. When we sit down at a Thai restaurant, our question is always the same: Red curry, or green? What are you in the mood for? As most things do, this dish goes great with Green Papaya Salad (page 53), Cucumber Salad (page 54), or Tempeh Lettuce Wraps (page 61).

SERVES 6

RED CURRY PASTE

5 to 10 red chiles, halved and seeded, to taste (see Note on page 69)

1½ stalks lemongrass, chopped in ½-inch pieces, white part only (about 6 tablespoons)

2 tablespoons diced galangal or peeled fresh ginger

3 cloves garlic

4 kaffir lime leaves, or 2 teaspoons lime zest

1 teaspoon sea salt

RED CURRY

2 (14-ounce) cans coconut milk

6 to 8 cups assorted chopped vegetables (eggplant, onions, carrots, zucchini, cabbage, green beans, bamboo shoots, oyster mushrooms, baby corn, water chestnuts, etc.)

1 tablespoon soy sauce or Bragg's Liquid Aminos, or to taste

1 teaspoon agave nectar, or to taste

1. Place the chiles in a blender with the lemongrass, galangal, garlic, kaffir lime leaves, and salt. Blend on high speed for 20 to 30 seconds or until you have a thoroughly blended thick paste. You may need to add a bit of the coconut milk to the blender to get the ingredients moving and well blended. Start with ¼ cup and work your way up as needed.

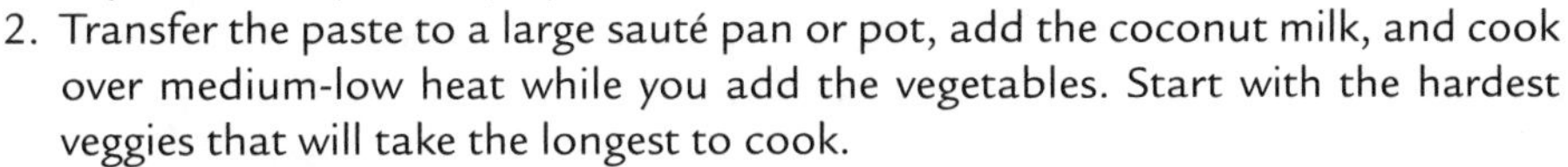

2. Transfer the paste to a large sauté pan or pot, add the coconut milk, and cook over medium-low heat while you add the vegetables. Start with the hardest veggies that will take the longest to cook.
3. When all of the veggies are just soft, add the soy sauce and agave nectar and stir well. Cook for 2 more minutes. Serve immediately.

Variations

- Protein lovers can follow the directions on page 227 for adding marinated, roasted tofu or tempeh to this dish.
- Add a bit of green to your red with 2 tablespoons of thinly sliced Thai basil (add just before removing the curry from the heat).

Chefs' Tips and Tricks

Though some recipes offer several suggestions of foods you can use as "assorted vegetables," the fewer you choose, the less time the dish will take you to prepare. Choosing two or three veggies is a good start. As your speed and skills develop, adding more variety and special ingredients becomes easier, faster, and more gratifying.

LOVING JUNGLE PRINCESS

We always feel a little funny about ordering a dish called Evil Jungle Prince. It just sounds so . . . severe. Why is he evil? Was he banished to the jungle? At our restaurant, the Blossoming Lotus, we would call this dish Curry by Murray in a Hurry. The Loving Jungle Princess is the gentle speed-dial version of the other more elaborate curries. Serve with brown rice, Green Papaya Salad (page 53), and Black Rice Pudding (page 81) for a Thai feast.

SERVES 6

CURRY PASTE

4 red chiles, halved and seeded, to taste (see Note on page 69)

1 stalk lemongrass, cut in ½-inch pieces, white part only (2 tablespoons chopped)

4 kaffir lime leaves or 2 teaspoons lime zest

3 cloves garlic

¾ teaspoon sea salt

CURRY

2 (14-ounce) cans coconut milk

6 cups chopped mixed vegetables (carrots, zucchini, green beans, onions, eggplant, bamboo shoots, oyster mushrooms, baby corn, water chestnuts, bean sprouts, etc.)

1 tablespoon soy sauce or Bragg's Liquid Aminos, optional

1 teaspoon agave nectar or organic sugar, optional

¼ cup thinly sliced basil

6 cups shredded cabbage

1. Place the chiles in a blender with the lemongrass, kaffir lime leaves, garlic, and salt. Blend on high speed for 20 to 30 seconds or until you have a thoroughly blended thick paste. You may need to add a bit of the coconut milk to the blender to get the ingredients moving and well blended. Start with ¼ cup and work your way up as needed.
2. Transfer the mixture to a large sauté pan or pot, add the coconut milk, and cook over medium-low heat while you add the vegetables. Start with the hardest veggies that will take the longest to cook.
3. When all of the veggies are just soft, add the soy sauce, if using, and the agave nectar, if using, and stir well. Add the basil, stir it in, and remove from the heat. Serve hot over the shredded cabbage.

Variation

- You can bump up the flavor profile by adding 1 tablespoon curry powder. Or try adding 2 teaspoons each of toasted ground coriander and toasted ground cumin (see page 225).

KAFFIR LEMONGRASS TOFU CUTLETS

Transform average everyday tofu in a jiff. Because your Thai pantry is already so well stocked from making all of these other dishes, you should have what it takes to elevate ordinary tofu into the sensation that's rocking the nation. Serve these succulent cutlets with Green Papaya Salad (page 53), on top of a green salad, in a wrap, or sliced and used as a filling inside Thai Summer Rolls (page 59).

MAKES 6 CUTLETS

1 (14-ounce) package extra-firm tofu
2 tablespoons soy sauce
2 teaspoons maple syrup or agave nectar
2 kaffir lime leaves, or 1 teaspoon lime zest
2 stalks lemongrass, white part only
1 teaspoon lemon or lime zest
1 teaspoon peeled and grated fresh ginger

1. Preheat the oven to 350°F. Slice the tofu into thirds widthwise and then cut the thirds in half diagonally to make six triangles. Mix together the soy sauce and maple syrup. Place the tofu in a baking dish, drizzle with the soy sauce mixture and flip to ensure even coating. Allow it to marinate while the oven heats up, flipping the tofu after a few minutes. Place in the oven to bake for 15 minutes while you proceed to step two. If using a toaster oven, add 2 tablespoons of water to the baking tray.
2. In a spice grinder or using a mortar and pestle, grind the lime leaves, lemongrass, lemon zest, and ginger to a fine paste. When the 15 minutes is up, remove the tofu from the oven, flip it over, top each of the tofu cutlets with an equal portion of the paste, and put it back in the oven for 5 to 8 more minutes, or until the topping has dried out a little. Serve hot or chilled.

Variations

- Replace the tofu with tempeh, or use veggies such as portobello mushrooms, thick zucchini slices, or eggplant.

COCONUT PUMPKIN CURRY

The inherent richness and creaminess of pumpkin makes it an irresistible base for curry. This warm and comforting meal has a beautiful presentation as well. The orange pumpkin, red chile pepper, and green basil make music for your eyes that melts in your mouth. Serve with Cucumber Salad (page 54), Green Papaya Salad (page 53), and Mango Custard Pudding (page 130).

SERVES 4 TO 6

- 6 cups ½-inch pumpkin cubes (about ½ pumpkin, seeds and skin removed)
- ¼ teaspoon turmeric powder
- 2 cups water or vegetable stock (see page 228)
- 1 tablespoon coriander seeds
- 1 teaspoon fennel seeds
- 1 stalk lemongrass, chopped, white part only (about 2 tablespoons)
- 4 kaffir lime leaves, or 2 teaspoons lime zest
- 2 tablespoons chopped galangal
- 1 (14-ounce) can coconut milk
- ½ medium yellow onion, sliced
- 1 teaspoon sea salt
- 1 teaspoon crushed red pepper flakes or minced fresh hot red chile pepper
- 1 teaspoon agave nectar
- 1½ tablespoons soy sauce, or to taste
- ¼ cup thinly sliced basil

1. In a pot over medium-high heat, boil the pumpkin, turmeric, and water until the pumpkin is soft, about 8 minutes.
2. Meanwhile, place the coriander, fennel, lemongrass, kaffir lime leaves, and galangal in a blender and blend together on high speed for 30 seconds or until a thick paste forms. You may need to add a bit of the coconut milk to get the mixture thoroughly blended. Start with ¼ cup and work your way up as needed.
3. Add the contents of the blender to the pot along with the coconut milk, onion, and salt and cook until the onion is soft. Add the crushed red pepper, agave, and soy sauce and cook for 2 minutes. Add the basil, stir, and remove from the heat. Serve immediately or allow it to cool completely before refrigerating.

Variations

- Replace the pumpkin with squash—butternut, buttercup, acorn, or your favorite.
- Substitute ¼ cup of orange juice for the agave nectar and add ½ teaspoon of orange zest along with the crushed red pepper in step three.
- Add or substitute carrots, yellow bell pepper, cherry tomatoes, kale . . . you get the idea!
- For a lower-fat version, substitute ½ cup of water for the coconut milk and blend about 2 cups of the final curry in step three for 20 seconds or so until creamy. Add it back to the curry and enjoy!

SWEET SOYBEAN SAUCE WITH NOODLES (PAD SIEW)

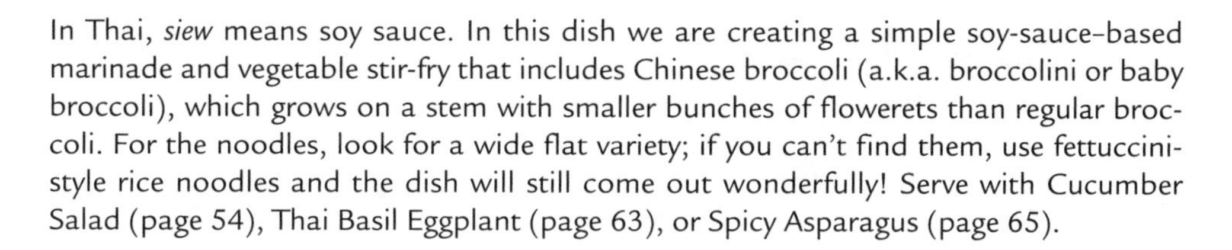

In Thai, *siew* means soy sauce. In this dish we are creating a simple soy-sauce-based marinade and vegetable stir-fry that includes Chinese broccoli (a.k.a. broccolini or baby broccoli), which grows on a stem with smaller bunches of flowerets than regular broccoli. For the noodles, look for a wide flat variety; if you can't find them, use fettuccini-style rice noodles and the dish will still come out wonderfully! Serve with Cucumber Salad (page 54), Thai Basil Eggplant (page 63), or Spicy Asparagus (page 65).

SERVES 4 TO 6

1 (14-ounce) package noodles
2 tablespoons sesame oil
1 cup diced shallots
2 tablespoons peeled and minced fresh ginger
3 cloves garlic, pressed or minced
1 tablespoon seeded and diced hot chile pepper
2 large heads Chinese broccoli or 1 large regular broccoli, stems and flowerets (see Box on page 76) (6 cups)
1 cup thinly sliced shiitake mushrooms
1 cup thinly sliced carrots
2 cups water
¼ cup plus 2 tablespoons soy sauce
3 tablespoons agave nectar or sweetener of choice to taste
2 tablespoons freshly squeezed lime juice
2 tablespoons Fish-Free Sauce (page 85), optional
1 tablespoon Sriracha (page 86) or other hot sauce, optional
¾ teaspoon sea salt, or to taste
1 tablespoon arrowroot dissolved in ¾ cup water
½ cup sliced green onion
1 tablespoon each white and black sesame seeds

continues

1. Cook the noodles according to the package instructions. Pour into a colander, drain, rinse well, and drain again.
2. Meanwhile, place the oil in a large sauté pan over medium-high heat. Add the shallots, ginger, garlic, and chile pepper, and cook for 3 minutes, stirring frequently. Add the Chinese broccoli, mushrooms, and carrots and cook for 2 minutes, stirring frequently and adding a small amount of water if necessary to prevent sticking.
3. Lower the heat to medium. Add 1½ cups of water, soy sauce, agave nectar, lime juice, Fish-Free Sauce, if using, and Sriracha, if using, and mix well. Cook for 5 minutes, stirring occasionally. Add the salt and the arrowroot-water mixture, and gently stir until sauce thickens, approximately 3 minutes. Add the noodles and gently mix well. Garnish each serving with sliced green onion and sesame seeds.

Variation

- If you have more time, add Marinated and Roasted Tofu (see page 227).

Chefs' Tips and Tricks

Don't toss that thick stem on the broccoli. Use a peeler or paring knife to remove the thick outside layer, then chop the stem. The result is a crunchy, slightly sweet, and tender delight. The Chinese broccoli stem is thin and does not need to be peeled. Just cut off the very bottom.

PANANG CURRY

Similar to the red curry with the addition of toasted cumin and coriander, this dish holds solid space on Thai food menus across America. Consider serving with Green Papaya Salad (page 53) or Spicy Tomato Mung Salad (page 56), and it never hurts to top off the meal with a little Creamy Tapioca Pudding (page 79).

SERVES 6

PANANG CURRY PASTE

5 to 10 red chiles, halved and seeded, to taste (see Note on page 69)

1½ stalks lemongrass, chopped into ½-inch pieces, white part only (about 6 tablespoons)

2 tablespoons diced galangal or peeled fresh ginger

3 cloves garlic

4 kaffir lime leaves

1 tablespoon toasted cumin seeds (see page 225)

1 tablespoon toasted coriander seeds (see page 225)

1 teaspoon sea salt

PANANG CURRY

2 (14-ounce) cans coconut milk

2 cups chopped long beans or green beans

2 cups cubed eggplant

4 cups napa cabbage, ½-inch strips

1 tablespoon soy sauce, or Bragg's Liquid Aminos, or to taste

1 to 2 teaspoons agave nectar, or to taste

2 tablespoons thinly sliced sweet basil

1. Place the chiles in a blender with the lemongrass, galangal, garlic, kaffir lime leaves, cumin, coriander, and salt. Blend on high speed for 20 to 30 seconds or until you have a thoroughly blended thick paste. You may need to add a bit of the coconut milk to the blender to get the ingredients moving and well blended. Start with ¼ cup and work your way up as needed.
2. Transfer the paste to a large sauté pan or pot, add the coconut milk, and cook over medium-low heat while you add the vegetables. Start with the hardest veggies that will take the longest to cook and add them into the pot as you go.
3. When all of the veggies are just soft, add the soy sauce and agave nectar and stir well. Cook for 2 minutes. Serve immediately, topped with the sliced basil leaves.

Variations

- Replace the long beans and eggplant with carrots, mushrooms, potatoes, or your favorite vegetables.
- Replace the napa cabbage with bok choy or kale.

MASSAMAN CURRY

This unique curry is a little bit salty, peanutty, and not so spicy. If you like pineapple, definitely give this curry a whirl—pineapple transitions nicely into the savory side of food. Serve over brown rice and with Tomato Mung Bean Salad (page 56).

SERVES 4 TO 6

2 to 4 red chiles, halved and seeded, to taste (see Note on page 69)
6 cardamom pods, shells removed (about ½ teaspoon cardamom seeds)
2 teaspoons coriander seeds
1 teaspoon cumin seeds
1 tablespoon ground star anise
4 cloves garlic, skins removed
1 stalk lemongrass, ½-inch pieces, white part only
¼ cup chopped galangal or peeled fresh ginger
½ teaspoon ground cinnamon
1 teaspoon sea salt
2 (14-ounce) cans coconut milk
3½ cups russet potatoes, ½-inch cubes (about 2 medium potatoes)
1 cup pineapple, ½-inch cubes
¼ cup roasted unsalted peanuts
1 tablespoon agave nectar or organic sugar
1 tablespoon soy sauce
½ cup water

1. In either a sauté pan over low heat or a toaster oven set to 200°F, roast the chile peppers, cardamom seeds, coriander, cumin, anise, garlic, lemongrass, and galangal for 10 minutes or until the garlic is starting to brown and the spices smell toasty.
2. Transfer to a blender and add the cinnamon and salt. Blend until a thick paste forms. You may need to add a bit of the coconut milk to get the mixture thoroughly blended. Start with ¼ cup and work your way up as needed. Once blended, transfer to a large sauté pan or pot and add the coconut milk. Bring to a low boil over medium heat.
3. Add the potatoes and allow them to cook until the potatoes are soft, approximately 10 minutes. Add the pineapple, peanuts, agave nectar, soy sauce, and water and cook for 2 minutes. Remove from the heat and serve immediately, or allow it to cool completely before refrigerating.

CREAMY TAPIOCA PUDDING

Tapioca is the starch from the cassava plant, a sweet root originally from South America and highly cultivated in tropical climates. This thick, custardy dessert will change your perspective on tapioca. Though you need to soak the tapioca for an hour, the rest of the process takes less than 30 minutes.

SERVES 4

1 (14-ounce) can coconut milk
¼ cup small tapioca pearls
1 tablespoon vegan butter (Earth Balance is our favorite)
¼ teaspoon sea salt
¼ cup agave nectar
1 tablespoon vanilla extract, preferably alcohol-free

1. Fill the bottom of a double boiler with 2 to 3 inches of water. In the top, soak the coconut milk with the tapioca pearls for one hour at room temperature.
2. Turn the heat to medium and stir occasionally for about 15 minutes, until the pearls begin to turn translucent in the center. Add the vegan butter, salt, and agave nectar, and continue to stir frequently for 10 to 15 minutes more or until the pearls are completely translucent and soft. Add the vanilla, stir, and serve warm.

STICKY RICE AND MANGO SLICE

Sticky rice, or glutinous rice, is a mainstay in Thailand and other Asian countries. Generally it is steamed rather than boiled in water. The resulting sticky, clumpy rice is easy to scoop up with your hands. Coconut milk raises the decadence bar, and you're on your way to a satiating end of the day. This recipe does go over the 30-minute time frame if you include the soaking time.

SERVES 4 TO 6

1 cup sticky rice
water
1 (14-ounce) can coconut milk
¼ cup agave nectar
2 tablespoons maple syrup, optional
¼ teaspoon sea salt
1 medium mango, peeled and sliced

1. Soak the rice in water for at least 1 hour. Strain well.
2. Fill the bottom of a steamer pot with approximately 1 inch of water (do not let the water come above the steamer holes). Lay cheesecloth over the bottom of the steamer basket and place the rice evenly over the top. Bring the water to a boil, turn the heat to medium, cover the pot, and steam for 20 minutes or until the rice is soft.
3. Meanwhile, whisk the coconut milk, agave nectar, maple syrup, if using, and sea salt together in a small pot over medium-low heat for 5 to 10 minutes, until the mixture thickens slightly.
4. When the rice is finished, transfer it to a bowl and add half to three-fourths of the coconut milk mixture. Allow it to sit for 5 to 10 minutes as the rice absorbs the coconut milk. Serve hot with cold mango slices and top with the remaining coconut milk mixture. Simply divine!

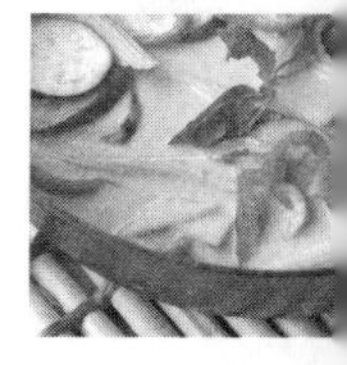

BLACK RICE PUDDING

With a unique color and flavor, black rice is also high in nutrients. This delicacy is frequently served in Thai restaurants, where the sweet and slightly salty flavor of the dish is sure to wow. With rice cooking time, this recipe does go slightly over the 30-minute time frame.

MAKES 3½ CUPS

¾ cup black rice
2 cups water
¼ teaspoon sea salt, or to taste
A few pinches cinnamon
¼ cup dried unsweetened coconut, toasted (see page 225)

COCONUT DESSERT SAUCE

1 (14-ounce) can coconut milk
¼ cup agave nectar, organic sugar, or sweetener of choice to taste
1 tablespoon maple syrup or organic brown sugar
2 teaspoons mirin, optional

1. Place the rice, water, and sea salt in a medium pot over medium-high heat. Bring to a boil. Lower the heat, cover, and simmer until all the liquid is absorbed, approximately 30 minutes.
2. After the rice has been cooking for 20 minutes, prepare the Coconut Dessert Sauce by placing the coconut milk, agave nectar, maple syrup, and mirin, if using, in a small pot over low heat. Gently simmer, stirring occasionally, until the rice is cooked but do not let the coconut milk come to a boil.
3. Scoop the rice into individual serving bowls and top with the sauce. Garnish with a pinch of cinnamon and a sprinkle of toasted coconut.

Variations

- Serve with sliced mangos—yum!
- You can also add the coconut milk, agave nectar, and mirin to the rice after it has cooked and stir well before serving. This will create a lighter-colored dish.
- For added flavor, try adding a sliced banana to the pot along with the rice in step 1.

continues

The Asian Pantry

Black rice is an heirloom grain that actually turns a shade of purple when cooked. It has a rich, slightly nutty flavor. The most commonly available black rice is called "forbidden" rice. It is rumored that forbidden black rice comes from China, where it was only served to the emperor and his family. There is also a black sticky rice, if you can find it, that works well in this dish.

If You Have More Time

Try soaking the rice for a few hours before cooking. This will speed up the actual cooking time.

East Meets West: Meditation

Meditation, which has been bringing peace to the people for thousands of years, is a vast topic. Definitions vary depending upon who you ask, and there are many different forms. In general, meditation involves awareness, concentration, and the calming of restless thoughts. A simple form of meditation is to become aware of your breath and return to it when you find your thoughts wandering. Other forms involve singing, dancing, or chanting. Check out your local holistic magazine or inquire at a yoga studio near you to learn about the meditation scene in your area.

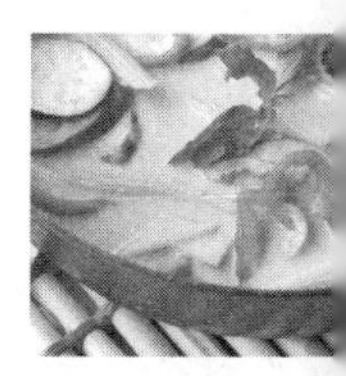

COCONUT ICE CREAM

Creamy and decadent, and whipped up in just minutes, this quick and easy dessert actually takes quite a bit of time to freeze, but it's so worth it. Plan ahead and prepare it the night before you wish to enjoy it. If your kitchen is not equipped with an ice-cream maker, check out Appendix C for a Web site where you can order one. Enjoy this ice cream on its own, with some fresh berries, topped with Mango Custard Pudding (page 130), or served alongside Halva (page 35) or Black Rice Pudding (page 81).

MAKES APPROXIMATELY 1 QUART

2 (14-ounce) cans coconut milk
1 cup mashed bananas
½ cup agave nectar, or sweetener of choice to taste
2 teaspoons vanilla extract, preferably alcohol-free
Fresh berries, optional

1. Place all of the ingredients except the berries in a blender and blend on high speed for 30 seconds or until the mixture is completely smooth.
2. Either prepare according to the ice-cream maker's instructions or if you are without an ice-cream maker, pour the mixture into a glass container and freeze until solid, approximately 6 hours or overnight. Remove from the freezer, transfer to a food processor, and process on high speed until creamy. You can enjoy it now as a soft-serve consistency or return it to the freezer for 2 hours for more of an ice-cream consistency. Serve topped with fresh berries, if desired.

Variations

- For a fruitier version, blend the coconut milk, agave nectar, and vanilla with 2 cups of fresh mango, papaya, berries, or banana until smooth. Prepare according to the ice-cream maker's instructions.
- Add ½ teaspoon ground cinnamon, ¼ teaspoon ground cardamom, and ¼ teaspoon of ground nutmeg or allspice to the ice cream base, then prepare according to the ice-cream maker's instructions.

THAI ICED TEA

Though tea and coconut milk may be plentiful in Thailand, a constant supply of wasteful to-go packaging is not. Therefore, do not be surprised if the street vendor hands you your iced tea in a plastic bag. Yep, a small clear plastic bag filled with ice, sweetened condensed milk, and red Thai tea. You can find Thai tea online and in some supermarkets, but we have found that plain black tea also works well and still gives that classic orange color when combined with the coconut milk.

MAKES FOUR 12-OUNCE GLASSES

4 cups water
10 tea bags of black tea or red Thai tea
1 cup chilled coconut milk
¼ cup agave nectar

1. Boil the water in a pot or tea kettle. Remove from the heat and add the tea. Steep for 10 minutes and remove the tea bags. Whisk in the agave nectar and place in the freezer until chilled thoroughly, approximately 20 minutes.
2. To serve, fill the glasses with ice and add 1 cup of the tea. Slowly pour the coconut milk over the ice to achieve a layered effect. Stir with a spoon or straw before drinking.

FISH-FREE SAUCE

Fish sauce is used in just about everything in Thailand, and just like kaffir lime and galangal ginger, it adds a flavor that distinguishes itself as Thai. This fish-free sauce is less complicated to prepare than traditional fermented fish sauce (*nam pla*), which involves placing fish in a jar for nine months to a year! Here we use the sea vegetable arame to create the flavor of the sea. Adding a couple of tablespoons of this sauce to any of the curries or soups in this chapter will enhance the authenticity of the dish. You may also want to decrease the other salty ingredients called for in the recipe.

MAKES APPROXIMATELY 2½ CUPS

¼ cup arame (see page 253)
2 cups hot water
2 cloves garlic
2 tablespoons freshly squeezed lemon juice
1 tablespoon rice vinegar
2 teaspoons sea salt
1 teaspoon agave nectar or organic sugar, optional

1. Place the arame in a bowl and cover with the hot water; let soak for 15 minutes. Transfer arame and water to a blender with the remaining ingredients and blend well.
2. Pour the mixture through a strainer and store in a glass container in the refrigerator for up to a week for use in all of your Thai dishes.

Chefs' Tips and Tricks

Looking for that fish-saucy flavor without wanting to make the fish-free sauce? Try using a bit of Bragg's Liquid Aminos in your recipes. It has a unique salty flavor that will do in a pinch.

SRIRACHA

This is a homemade variation of the wildly popular hot sauce that adorns virtually every table in Thai restaurants across America. Sriracha is actually a region in Thailand, though the hot sauce has usurped the title and most think of the sauce when they hear the name. Use the small Thai red hot chile peppers if you can find them in an Asian market. You may want to wear latex gloves as you work with the peppers. Definitely wash your hands immediately if they come in contact with the chiles.

MAKES APPROXIMATELY ¾ CUP

1 cup de-stemmed Thai red chile peppers, red jalapeño peppers, or other hot chile peppers
3 cloves garlic
1 tablespoon agave nectar or organic sugar
2 tablespoons rice vinegar
2 tablespoons mirin, optional
1 teaspoon Fish-Free Sauce, optional
½ teaspoon sea salt, or to taste

Place all of the ingredients in a blender and blend well. Store in a glass container in the refrigerator for up to two weeks.

PART THREE

  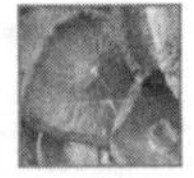

The Cuisine of China

Virtually everything about eating in China is different from eating in the West—from the selection of vegetables, to the pan the food is cooked in, right up to the utensil that puts it in your mouth. Chinese food is steeped in tradition, spirituality, and sophisticated systems of nutrition and health guidelines. We find this rabbit hole of Chinese cuisine to be exciting. And re-creating our favorite dishes in our own kitchen with fresh, local ingredients is downright intoxicating.

As we demystified the skills needed to prepare such classic dishes as Dim Sum Dumplings, Mu Shu Vegetables, and Chow Mein we also created westernized twists like Peking Seitan and Orange-Glazed Tofu. Willing to go even further with our endeavor of delivering authentic Chinese flavor into the hands of the West, we added Pumpkin Pine Nut Soup, Hoisin Eggplant Cutlets, and Green Onion Hotcakes.

For some super simple dishes with unintimidating ingredients lists, try Garlic Lover's Eggplant, Chinese Fried Rice, Sesame Garlic Stir-Fry with Snow Peas, and Mango Custard Pudding. Even the Lotus Root Salad, Seitan and Broccoli, and the Szechuan Tempeh and Veggies are very simple dishes once you grow accustomed to some new and exciting additions to your grocery list.

Most major cities have thriving Chinatowns, and specialty markets abound these days where Asian food aficionados can stock up on an abundance of otherwise obscure ingredients. And there is always the World Wide Web. See our Resource Section (page 245) for tips on procuring the ingredients you need without leaving the comfort of your home. In the words of Lao Tzu, "The journey of a thousand miles must begin with one step."

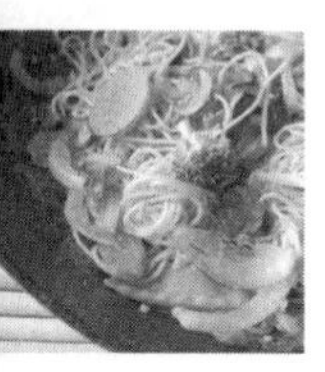

The Asian Pantry: China

Arrowroot: Reputedly cultivated for over 7,000 years, arrowroot is the powdered root of a tropical plant that can be used to replace cornstarch as a thickening agent in recipes. Most Asian recipes you see call for cornstarch. Arrowroot has a more neutral flavor. It works at a lower temperature and with acidic ingredients. In general, 1 tablespoon of arrowroot thickens 1 cup of liquid. You can use 1 tablespoon of arrowroot to replace 2 teaspoons of cornstarch in any given recipe.

Fermented Black Beans: These black soy beans, preserved in salt, impart a strong salty and slightly bitter flavor to dishes. They are frequently used in hoisin sauce and other Chinese dishes of the Canton province. Look for them at your local Asian market or check out our resource guide in Appendix C to order online. Please note that these are different than the black beans typically used in Mexican cooking.

Five-Spice Powder: As the name suggests, this is a blend of five spices that together provide all five flavors—sweet, salty, sour, pungent, and bitter. It consists of ground peppercorns (use Szechuan peppers if possible), star anise, clove, cinnamon, and fennel.

Lotus Root: Popular in Asian cooking, the rhizome of the lotus flower has the appearance of a long potato. When sliced, a wagon-wheel design is revealed. Lotus root makes a crunchy artistic addition to salads and stir-fries.

Seitan: Originating in China and also called "wheat meat," "meat of wheat," and even simply "gluten," seitan is made from wheat gluten. It is high in protein and is commonly used to replace beef or chicken in dishes traditionally made with animal products. Because it's all gluten, individuals with gluten intolerance will want to steer clear of it. Many flavored varieties are available, or you can create your own.

Szechuan Peppers: Also called Szechwan or Sichuan peppers, and widely used in Asian cooking, the Szechuan pepper is not related to the peppercorn or the chile pepper! Chinese pepper, anise pepper, fagara, and flower pepper are additional names for this pepper, whose unique flavor has a hint of lemon and a slightly tingling/ numbing effect that accentuates the spicy heat of chiles, peppercorns, and other spices. A little goes a long way; use sparingly. Popular in the Sichuan province of China, where it originates, as well as in Nepal, Tibet, Japan, and Indonesia, the pepper is available whole, ground, and even in an infused oil. Visit a local Asian market or check out our resource guide in Appendix C to special order.

Tofu: Originating in China, tofu is made from soybeans and is formed into a block. It is another food that crosses cultural boundaries throughout Asia. There are several forms available, including soft, firm, extra-firm, and silken varieties. Please see page 225 for more intriguing information and for tips and tricks on working with tofu.

Wonton Wrappers and Gyoza Skins: These flour-based sheets are perfect for creating quick appetizers or hors d'oeuvres. Both are used to wrap a variety of foods that feature prominently in Dim Sum (see page 96). Be on guard and make sure to check the ingredients: most of the commercially prepared varieties available at the supermarket do contain eggs. You can, however, often find egg-free varieties at an Asian market.

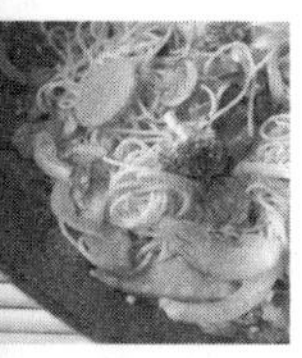

PUMPKIN PINE NUT SOUP

This is a creamy and thick soup that is filling and perfect in autumn, when a wide variety of pumpkins and squash are available. Experiment with the different types of squash such as butternut, buttercup, or acorn. Serve with Green Onion Hotcakes (page 112).

SERVES 6 TO 8

1 tablespoon sesame oil
1 yellow onion, chopped (1½ cups)
2 cloves garlic
1 tablespoon peeled and minced fresh ginger
1 small pumpkin, butternut, or buttercup squash, seeded and cubed (4 cups)
5 cups water or vegetable stock (see page 228)
3 tablespoons soy sauce
1¼ teaspoons five-spice powder
½ teaspoon ground coriander
1 tablespoon agave nectar or sweetener of choice
1 teaspoon sea salt, or to taste
¼ teaspoon ground black pepper
¾ cup pine nuts, cashews, or macadamia nuts, or combination, toasted (see page 225)
1 cup corn, fresh or frozen
1 tablespoon minced fresh cilantro

1. Place the oil in a large pot over medium-high heat. Add the onion, garlic, and ginger and cook for 2 minutes, stirring occasionally. Add the pumpkin and stir well. Lower the heat to medium, add the water, and cook until the pumpkin is soft, approximately 15 minutes.
2. Add the remaining ingredients except the corn and cilantro, and stir well. Using a blender and working in small batches, carefully blend the contents of the pan and transfer to a large tureen or serving bowl. Add the corn and mix well. Garnish with cilantro before serving.

Variations

- If you have more time, instead of sautéing the pumpkin you can roast it on a well-oiled baking sheet in a 400°F oven until a knife can pass easily through any portion of it. Blend with other ingredients as in the recipe above.
- Replace the pine nuts with ¾ cup coconut, soy, rice or almond milk (see page 229).

HOT AND SOUR SOUP

Some like it hot, some like it sour, and some like it hot and sour. Chinese hot and sour soup is considered a regional dish in both Mandarin and Sichuan cuisines. The hot comes from chile pepper and the sour comes from vinegar. Feel free to substitute the rice vinegar with apple cider vinegar. Start with a smaller quantity and adjust to taste, as the rice vinegar has a milder flavor (see Box on page 135).

SERVES 6 TO 8

1 tablespoon sesame oil or toasted sesame oil
2 teaspoons minced garlic
1 tablespoon peeled and minced fresh ginger
1 hot chile pepper, seeded and diced, or cayenne pepper to taste
6 cups water or vegetable stock (see page 228)
1 cup sliced mushrooms (try straw or shiitake)
8 ounces canned bamboo shoots
1 cup chopped tomatoes
1 cup chopped zucchini
1 cup chopped carrots
1 tablespoon agave nectar or organic sugar
¼ cup plus 2 tablespoons rice vinegar
2 tablespoons arrowroot powder dissolved in ½ cup cold water
¼ cup plus 2 tablespoons soy sauce, or to taste
Half (14-ounce) package extra-firm tofu, grated, optional (see page 226)
¼ cup diced green onions

1. Place the oil in a medium pot over medium heat. Add the garlic, ginger, and chile pepper, and stir constantly for 1 minute. Add the water, mushrooms, bamboo shoots, tomatoes, zucchini, and carrots and cook for 10 minutes, stirring occasionally.
2. Add the agave, vinegar, and arrowroot mixture, and gently stir until the soup thickens. Add the soy sauce and tofu, if using, and cook for an additional 5 minutes or until the vegetables are tender.
3. Add the green onions and mix well before serving.

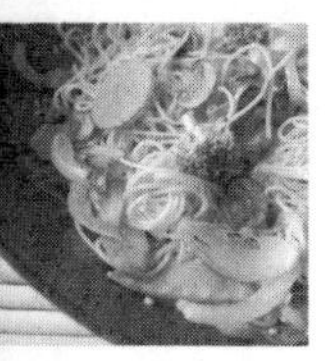

CREAMY CORN SOUP

This is a silky soup that replicates the popular Chinese restaurant dish. Adding the optional grated tofu creates the egglike texture that is included in most versions. We blend the corn with soymilk to create the "creamed corn" effect. Serve as a side with BBQ Tofu with Snow Peas (page 119) and Szechuan Green Beans (page 110).

SERVES 4 TO 6

1 tablespoon toasted sesame oil
1 small yellow onion, chopped small (1¼ cups)
3 cloves garlic, pressed or minced
2 cups vegetable stock (see page 228) or
2 cups water plus 1 tablespoon soy sauce
1 (1-pound) bag frozen corn or 3 cups fresh corn
2 cups soymilk
1 teaspoon sea salt, or to taste
½ teaspoon five-spice powder
¼ teaspoon ground white or black pepper, or to taste
¾ cup grated extra-firm tofu, optional (see page 226)
1 tablespoon mirin, optional
Pinch cayenne
1 tablespoon arrowroot dissolved in ½ cup cold water
(see page 90 for more on arrowroot)
¼ cup diced green onions

1. Place the oil in a medium pot over medium-high heat. Add the onion and garlic and cook for 3 minutes, stirring frequently. Add 1 cup of stock and 2 cups of corn and cook for 3 minutes, stirring occasionally. Transfer the contents to a blender and carefully blend with 1 cup of soymilk.
2. Return the soup base to the pot and add the remaining stock, soymilk, and cup of corn. Add all of the other ingredients except the arrowroot mixture and green onion. Cook over low heat for 10 minutes, stirring occasionally.
3. Add the arrowroot mixture and stir until the soup slightly thickens. Cook for an additional 5 minutes. Garnish with the green onion before serving.

Variations

- Replace the corn with vegetables such as broccoli, cauliflower, or zucchini.
- Replace the soymilk with rice or almond milk (see page 229).

LOTUS ROOT SALAD

The root of the majestic lotus flower, prevalent throughout South and East Asia, is perhaps equally captivating in the culinary world—as far as unique shapes go. When you slice the root, an intricate mosaic pattern is revealed. It is crispy, slightly starchy, and slightly sweet in flavor. Serve on a bed of thinly sliced napa cabbage and grated purple cabbage for a colorful presentation.

SERVES 4 TO 6

1 large fresh lotus root, peeled and thinly sliced (about 2 cups) (see Box below)
1 carrot, peeled into thin ribbons or sliced thinly on the diagonal
¼ cup diced red bell pepper
¼ cup thinly sliced green onion
2 tablespoons peeled and minced fresh ginger
2 tablespoons freshly squeezed lemon or orange juice
1 tablespoon rice vinegar
2 tablespoons water
2 tablespoons sesame oil or 2 tablespoons of water for an oil-free version
¼ teaspoon sea salt, or to taste
⅛ teaspoon ground black pepper
Pinch crushed red pepper flakes
½ teaspoon five-spice powder, optional

1. Place all of the ingredients in a large mixing bowl and gently mix well.
2. Allow it to marinate, tossing occasionally, until ready to serve. The longer the dish has to marinate, the more flavorful and harmonious your dining experience will be.

Chefs' Tips and Tricks

Lotus root contains a lot of fiber, which can be a bit starchy and slightly bitter. Here is a tip for working with this fascinating ingredient. Peel the root, slice, and place it in a bowl of water with a few drops of vinegar to prevent discoloration. We actually enjoy the root in its raw form. However, to remove some of the bitterness, you can steam the root for 5 minutes, or boil it for a few minutes in the water with vinegar.

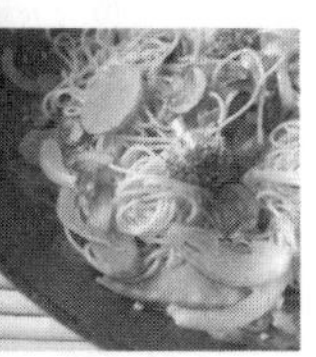

Dim Sum

Consisting of small portions of a variety of dishes, dim sum is a style of cuisine similar in concept to Spanish tapas. It typically involves a wide range of foods including dumplings, buns, and other dishes. Often there is another ritual included in a dim sum meal, namely *chum ya*, or "drinking tea." Dim sum restaurants are very popular in China—there are even 24-hour locations for those with 2 A.M. cravings.

Host your own dim sum party and include the following recipes. Remember to create mini portions—that's half the fun.

Spinach Tofu Dumplings (page 97)

Steamed Wontons (page 99)

Tibetan Dumplings (page 200)

Sweet and Sour Mushrooms (page 103)

Green Onion Hotcakes (page 112)

Hoisin Eggplant Cutlets (page 115)

Small cups of soup such as Creamy Corn (page 94) or Hot and Sour (page 93)

Dim Sum Dipping Sauce (page 101)

Fabulous Fig Dipping Sauce (page 102)

Mango Ginger Sauce (page 61)

SPINACH TOFU DUMPLINGS

Gyoza skins are thicker than wonton skins, round instead of square, and work wonderfully with dumplings. We have also used wonton skins with this recipe with great success! The nutritional yeast–tahini combination gives these treats a cheesy taste. The main time element for this dish is the wrapping and steaming of the dumplings. You can turn this into a 30-minute recipe by making fewer dumplings than the recipe calls for. Using a large bamboo steamer will also save you time because you can steam more dumplings at once. Serve with Dim Sum Dipping Sauce (page 101) or Fabulous Fig Dipping Sauce (page 102).

MAKES 1¾ CUPS FILLING OR ENOUGH FOR ABOUT 20 DUMPLINGS

1½ tablespoons sesame oil
¾ cup diced onion
3 cloves garlic, pressed or minced
1 teaspoon coriander seeds
1 cup grated extra-firm tofu (about half of a 14-ounce block) (see page 226)
1½ cups thinly sliced spinach or kale
¼ teaspoon five-spice powder
2 tablespoons nutritional yeast
2 tablespoons creamy tahini
¼ to ½ teaspoon crushed red pepper flakes
¼ teaspoon sea salt
20 gyoza or wonton skins

1. Place the sesame oil in a small sauté pan over medium-high heat. Add the onion, garlic, and coriander and cook for 5 minutes, stirring occasionally. Add the tofu and cook for 5 minutes, stirring occasionally. Add the spinach and mix well. Add the remaining ingredients. Mix well and cook until the spinach is just cooked, approximately 3 minutes.
2. Place one inch of water in a pot with a bamboo steamer or steamer basket and bring to a boil. Lower the heat to low until the dumplings are ready for steaming.
3. Lay out the gyoza skins on a clean dry surface. Add about 1 tablespoon of filling to the center of each wrapper. Fold in half, creating a semicircle. Seal the edges tightly by pinching the two sides together.

continues

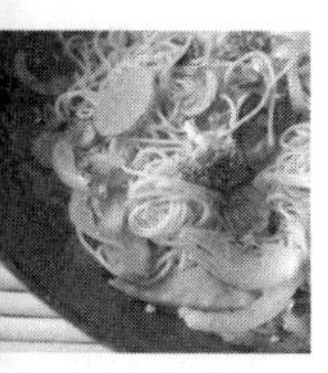

4. Place in the steamer basket and cook with the lid on for 5 to 7 minutes, or until the skins become transparent and shiny. Gently remove with tongs. Garnish with sliced green onion.

Chefs' Tips and Tricks

For an authentic dumpling steamer, try using a bamboo steamer basket. If you are unable to find one at your local Asian market, you can order one online from one of the Web sites in Appendix C.

Variations

- You can also sauté the dumplings rather than steaming them. Use a high-heat oil such as safflower until crisp on both sides. Place them on a paper towel or cloth to absorb excess oil before serving.
- Use the filling for stuffed peppers or mushrooms. For this, remove the stems from the mushrooms and add the filling, or slice a bell pepper in quarters and top with a couple of tablespoons of the filling. Roast on a well-oiled baking sheet in a 375°F oven for 15 minutes before serving.

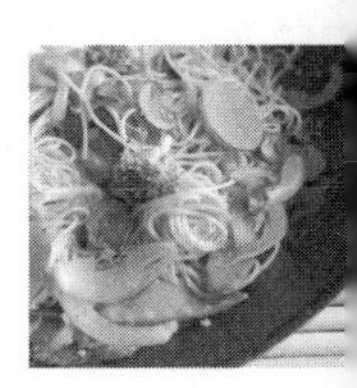

STEAMED WONTONS

Ahhh, the beloved wonton. You can steam them, sauté them, or even boil them, as in the quintessential soup (see Variations on page 100). As with the dumplings, the main time element for this dish is the wrapping and steaming. You can turn this into a 30-minute recipe by making fewer wontons than the recipe calls for. Using a large bamboo steamer will also save you time because you can steam more at once. We love these delicacies on their own with a simple soy sauce topping or served with Dim Sum Dipping Sauce (page 101) or Fabulous Fig Dipping Sauce (page 102).

APPROXIMATELY 1 CUP OF FILLING OR APPROXIMATELY 16 WONTONS

FILLING

1 recipe Marinated Tofu (see below)

1 tablespoon sesame oil

2 teaspoons peeled and minced fresh ginger

2 cloves garlic, pressed or minced

2 teaspoons seeded and diced hot chile pepper, or ¼ to ½ teaspoon crushed red pepper flakes

½ cup diced leek, white and green parts

4 large mushrooms, diced (try shiitake or cremini)

1½ cups thinly sliced bok choy or spinach

2 teaspoons soy sauce

1 teaspoon toasted sesame oil, optional

2 teaspoons rice vinegar

¼ teaspoon sea salt, or to taste

¼ cup sliced green onions

MARINATED TOFU

3 thin tofu cutlets, see step 1 below

2 teaspoons soy sauce

1 teaspoon sesame oil

Few drops liquid smoke

16 wonton skins

1. Preheat an oven or toaster oven to 375°F. Place a block of extra-firm tofu on its side and slice off three ½-inch cutlets from one end. Return the block of tofu to the fridge for use in another recipe. Place the three cutlets on a small baking sheet with the remaining marinade ingredients and flip them for even coating. Bake for 15 minutes. Remove from the oven. Slice each cutlet into thin strips, at least four per cutlet. Dice these strips and set aside.
2. Meanwhile, place the sesame oil in a small sauté pan over medium-high heat. Add the ginger, garlic, and chile pepper and cook for 1 minute, stirring constantly. Add the leek, mushrooms, and bok choy and cook for 5 minutes, stirring frequently. Add all the remaining ingredients, including the tofu (except for the green onions), and mix well. Remove from the heat.

continues

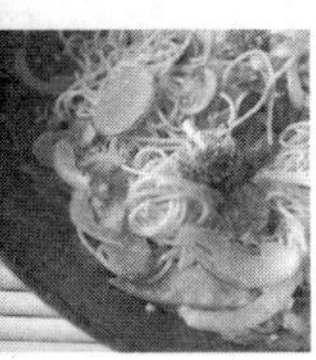

3. Place one inch of water in a pot with a steamer basket and bring to a boil. Lower the heat to low until the wontons are ready for steaming.
4. Lay out the wonton skins on a clean dry surface. Add about 1 tablespoon of filling to the center of each wrapper. Pull the sides up and seal tightly by pressing with your fingers, creating a "purse."
5. Place the wontons in the steamer basket and cook with the lid on for 5 to 7 minutes, or until the skins become transparent and shiny. Gently remove with tongs. Garnish with sliced green onion before serving.

Variations

- If you wish to omit the baking of the tofu, you can dice the tofu according to the instructions in step 1 and add the tofu and marinade ingredients to the sauté pan along with the vegetables.
- Replace the leek with onion or shallot.
- Replace the bok choy with cabbage or spinach.
- Add 1 tablespoon crumbled nuts, such as macadamias or peanuts.
- Replace the tofu with an equal amount of diced seitan.
- You can also sauté the wontons in a high-heat oil such as safflower until crisp on both sides. Drain on a paper towel or cloth before serving.
- For **Won Ton Soup,** instead of steaming the wontons, place them in a pot of boiling water for 5 minutes. In another pot, bring 6 cups of water or vegetable stock to a boil. Lower the heat to low and add 1 cup of thinly sliced spinach, ½-inch peeled and thinly sliced fresh ginger, and ½ cup sliced green onion, and stir well. Add several steamed wontons, several drops of liquid smoke (optional), and 6 tablespoons of soy sauce, or to taste, before serving. For best results, allow the soup ingredients to steep for 20 minutes before adding the wontons.
- For **Rice Noodle Rolls**, another popular dim sum recipe, typically made with a wide rice noodle, we use the rice paper wraps that are used in spring and summer rolls (see page 59). Follow the **Steamed Wontons** recipe. Instead of dicing the tofu, leave it in strips. Follow the rolling instructions for the Thai Summer Rolls on page 59 using approximately ¼ cup of the vegetables and three strips of tofu to the center of each sheet. Place on a serving dish and drizzle each roll with soy sauce or Dim Sum Dipping Sauce (page 101). If you wish for a crispier roll, you can sauté them in a little oil over medium heat for a couple of minutes on each side. Makes four rolls.

DIM SUM DIPPING SAUCE

Salty, spicy, and slightly sweet. Yum!

MAKES ¾ CUP SAUCE

½ cup soy sauce
1 tablespoon plus 1 teaspoon agave nectar or sweetener of choice to taste
1 tablespoon toasted sesame oil
1 teaspoon rice vinegar
1 small clove garlic, minced, optional
1 teaspoon peeled and minced fresh ginger, optional
1 teaspoon seeded and diced hot chile pepper or ¼ teaspoon crushed red pepper flakes, optional

Combine all of the ingredients in a bowl and whisk well.

East Meets West: The Way

The Taoist text *Tao Te Ching* has had a tremendous influence on Chinese thought. The title can be translated as "the way" or "the guiding principle." Written by Chinese sage and philosopher Lao Tzu in the sixth century BC, the book describes guiding principles to live by that create balance. Another book that has had a major influence in China is the *I-Ching*. Check out the recommended reading list in Appendix C for more details.

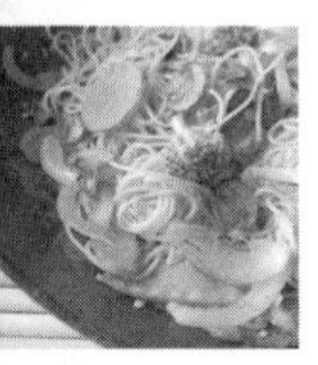

FABULOUS FIG DIPPING SAUCE

A variation of the popular plum sauce, this is a sweet and slightly spicy dipping sauce for all your dim sum needs. It is also wonderful with Samosas (page 7), Thai Summer Rolls (page 59), or Tibetan Dumplings (page 200).

MAKES 2 CUPS

½ cup black mission figs
2 cups water
2 tablespoons sesame oil
½ cup diced yellow onion
1 tablespoon peeled and minced fresh ginger
2 teaspoons seeded and diced chile pepper or ¼ to ½ teaspoon crushed red pepper flakes
1 tablespoon agave nectar or sweetener of choice to taste
1 tablespoon rice vinegar
1 tablespoon soy sauce
½ teaspoon five-spice powder
¼ teaspoon sea salt

1. Place the figs and water in a blender.
2. Place the sesame oil in a small sauté pan over medium-high heat. Add the onion, ginger, and chile pepper and cook for 5 to 7 minutes, stirring frequently. Add to the blender with the remaining ingredients and blend until creamy.

Variations

- For a plum sauce, replace the figs and water with 1 cup of pitted and chopped fresh plums. Adjust the sweetness as necessary. You can also sauté the plums with the onion. Cook until the plums are broken apart, then puree in a blender or food processor before serving.
- Replace the figs with prunes.
- For a ♥ live version, omit the sautéing. Replace the onion with green onion.

SWEET AND SOUR MUSHROOMS

Our vegan rendition of Sweet and Sour offers two sauce variations: one uses apricot preserves, and the other is sweetened with maple syrup. Both get the sour part from rice vinegar. Sweet and sour sauce is quite versatile and can be used as a dipping sauce for recipes from many regions, including Thai Summer Rolls (page 59), Tempura Vegetables (page 142), Samosas (page 7), and Nori Rolls (page 157).

SERVES 4 TO 6

16 large cremini or white button mushrooms, brushed clean, stems removed
1 tablespoon sesame oil
1 lemon, juiced
¼ cup water
1 tablespoon plus 1 teaspoon soy sauce, or to taste
¼ teaspoon five-spice powder, optional
¼ cup sliced green onions

SWEET AND SOUR SAUCE #1

1 cup apricot preserves (about 10-ounces)
2 teaspoons peeled and minced fresh ginger
3 tablespoons rice vinegar
1 tablespoon plus 1 teaspoon soy sauce, or to taste
Pinch crushed red pepper flakes

SWEET AND SOUR SAUCE #2

1 cup water
3 tablespoons maple syrup or organic brown sugar
3 tablespoons rice vinegar
1 tablespoon soy sauce
1 teaspoon tomato paste or ketchup
1 tablespoon arrowroot powder dissolved in ¼ cup cold water

continues

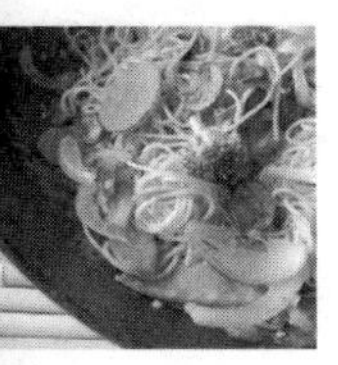

1. Preheat the oven to 375°F. Place the mushrooms, sesame oil, lemon juice, water, soy sauce, and five-spice powder, if using, in a casserole dish and mix well, making sure the mushrooms are evenly coated and gill-side up. Place the dish in the oven and bake until the mushrooms are just tender, approximately 15 minutes.
2. While the mushrooms are cooking, prepare the sweet and sour sauce by combining the ingredients for either version in a bowl and mixing well. As soon as the sauce is completed, add it to the casserole dish with the mushrooms and continue baking them. You can flip the mushrooms at this point.
3. Remove from the oven. Garnish with green onion before serving.

Note: If you wish to make the Sweet and Sour Sauce #1 on its own, simply combine all of the ingredients in a small pot and cook for 5 minutes over low heat, stirring frequently. For version #2, combine all of the ingredients except the arrowroot mixture in a small pan and cook over medium-low heat for 5 minutes, stirring frequently. Add the arrowroot mixture and cook for another few minutes or until the sauce thickens, stirring frequently.

East Meets West: Yin Yang

Most of us are familiar with the yin-yang symbol: it's a circle with two colors, usually black and white, in a wave formation. There is a dot of black in the white side and a dot of white on the black side. This symbol, often used as a symbol of Taoism, represents polar opposites such as hot and cold, contracting and expanding, masculine and feminine. The goal in Taoism is to create harmony between these opposing forces. These principles are also used in traditional Chinese medicine.

CHINESE FRIED RICE

The perfect solution for leftover rice is also one of our nation's favorite comfort foods. You can use 6 cups of cooked rice instead of cooking the basmati rice for this recipe. Grated tofu with a sprinkle of turmeric creates the fried egg effect. The liquid smoke adds—you guessed it—a bit of a smoky flavor that many will find familiar. Serve with Cantonese Lemon Tofu (page 116) or Szechuan Tempeh and Veggies (page 127).

SERVES 6 TO 8

2 cups white basmati rice
3 cups water or vegetables stock (see page 228)
1 teaspoon sea salt
3 tablespoons sesame oil
1 large yellow onion, diced (2 cups)
5 cloves garlic, pressed or minced
½ (14-ounce) package extra-firm tofu, grated (about 1¼ cups) (see page 226)
¼ teaspoon turmeric powder
A few drops of liquid smoke, optional
2 carrots, ¼-inch cubes (1¼ cups)
1¼ cups frozen peas, defrosted
2 tablespoons rice vinegar
¼ cup soy sauce, or to taste

1. Place the basmati rice, water, and salt in a medium pot over medium-high heat. Bring to a boil. Cover and lower the heat to low to simmer. Cook until all of the liquid is absorbed, approximately 10 minutes. Remove from heat and allow the rice to sit for 5 minutes.
2. Place the oil in a large sauté pan or wok over medium-high heat. Add the onion and garlic and cook for 5 minutes, stirring frequently. Add the grated tofu, turmeric, and liquid smoke, if using, and cook for 5 minutes, stirring occasionally.
3. Add the carrots, and cook for 5 minutes, stirring frequently. Add the peas, vinegar, and soy sauce and cook for 2 minutes, stirring frequently.
4. Add the cooked rice and gently mix well. Lower the heat to medium and cook for an additional 10 minutes, stirring occasionally.

Variations

- Replace the carrots and peas with your favorite veggies, such as zucchini, tomatoes, or bell peppers.
- Replace the tofu with 8 ounces of crumbled tempeh or chopped seitan.

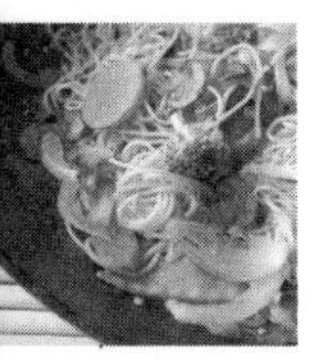

GARLIC LOVER'S EGGPLANT

Chinese eggplants are thinner and longer than their American counterparts and have a thinner skin. You can find them at Asian markets and sometimes in your local supermarket. Both varieties are awesome in this dish. Serve alongside Orange-Glazed Tofu (page 121), Seitan with Black Bean Sauce (page 118), or Kung Pao Tempeh (page 123).

SERVES 4 AS A SIDE DISH

6 cups eggplant, 1-inch cubes
(about 3 Chinese or 2 American eggplants)
2 teaspoons sea salt
2 tablespoons toasted sesame oil
10 cloves garlic, pressed or minced
½ chile pepper, seeded and minced, optional
1 tablespoon soy sauce, or to taste
1 tablespoon rice vinegar
3 tablespoons diced green onion

1. Place the cubed eggplant in a casserole dish and sprinkle with salt. After 10 to 15 minutes, remove the eggplant, place in a colander, and rinse well.
2. When the eggplant is ready, place the oil in a large sauté pan over medium-high heat, add the garlic, and chile pepper, if using, and cook for 2 minutes, stirring frequently. Add the eggplant and cook until tender, approximately 10 minutes, stirring frequently. Add the remaining ingredients, mix well, and enjoy!

Chefs' Tips and Tricks

Sprinkling the eggplant with salt and allowing it to sit for a period of time is called "sweating the eggplant" (not a very appetizing term!). After a few minutes, little water beads start to form, which remove the bitterness. Rinsing the eggplant well washes off most of the salt.

BOK CHOY WITH FIVE-SPICE CASHEWS

Bok choy, a member of the cabbage family, has been grown in China for centuries. If you can't find it in the market, you can substitute Chinese or napa cabbage or any green for that matter. Serve as a side dish with Seitan with Black Bean Sauce (page 118), Cantonese Lemon Tofu (page 116), or Szechuan Tempeh and Veggies (page 127).

SERVES 4 AS A SIDE DISH

1 batch Five-Spice Cashews (see below)
1 large or 2 medium bok choy, or Chinese or napa cabbage, ½-inch chop (12 cups)
1 tablespoon sesame oil
5 cloves garlic, pressed or minced
¼ teaspoon sea salt, or to taste
Pinch crushed red pepper flakes
1 tablespoon rice vinegar

FIVE-SPICE CASHEWS

¾ cup raw cashew pieces
1 teaspoon sesame oil
¼ teaspoon five-spice powder
Pinch sea salt
Pinch cayenne

1. Preheat the oven or toaster oven to 350°F. Place the cashews on a small baking sheet with the remaining Five-Spice Cashews ingredients and mix well. Bake until golden brown, for 3 to 5 minutes. Remove from the heat.
2. Place the chopped bok choy in a colander, rinse, and drain well. Place the oil in a large pot or sauté pan. Add the garlic, salt, and crushed red pepper flakes and cook for 2 minutes, stirring constantly. Add the Five-Spice Cashews and stir well. Add the bok choy and cook until tender, approximately 8 minutes, stirring frequently. Add the vinegar and gently stir well before serving.

Variations

- Replace the bok choy with your favorite greens, such as Chinese or napa cabbage, chard, or collard greens.
- Replace the cashews with pecans, walnuts, or macadamia nuts.
- Replace the rice vinegar with apple cider vinegar.
- If you want to omit the roasting of the cashews, you can add the cashew ingredients along with the garlic at the beginning of the cooking.

MU SHU VEGGIES

This heart-healthy version of a Chinese take-out classic uses mushrooms in place of pork. If you can find any fun Asian mushrooms, such as dried wood ear, this is a great dish to use them in. Otherwise, use whatever mushrooms you can find. This dish is typically served with Hoisin Sauce (see page 115) and with mu shu wrappers (see Box below), but it goes great over rice or quinoa as well.

SERVES 4 TO 6 AS A MAIN DISH

1 tablespoon toasted sesame oil
¼ cup peeled and minced fresh ginger
4 cloves garlic, pressed or minced
¼ teaspoon crushed red pepper flakes, or to taste
3 cups thinly sliced mushrooms (wood ear, shiitake, portobello, cremini, etc.)
1 medium yellow onion, sliced into quarter moons
3 cups assorted thinly sliced vegetables (carrots, celery, fennel bulb, zucchini, red bell pepper)
2 tablespoons soy sauce
2 tablespoons mirin
8 cups shredded napa cabbage, bok choy, or greens of choice
½ cup thinly sliced green onions
1 cup mung bean sprouts

1. Heat a wok or large sauté pan over medium heat. Add the oil, ginger, garlic, and crushed red pepper flakes and stir until the garlic begins to brown. Immediately add the mushrooms and stir for 1 to 2 minutes. Add the onion, stir well, and cover for 2 minutes.
2. Add the vegetables, stir, and cover again for 3 to 4 minutes. Add the soy sauce and mirin and stir well. Add the cabbage, stir well, and cover for 2 more minutes. Uncover and allow it to cook until all of the vegetables are to your desired softness.
3. Turn off the heat, add the green onion and mung sprouts, and stir together. Serve hot.

The Asian Pantry

Authentic mu shu wrappers are thin pancakes made from flour, not unlike Mexican-style tortillas but thinner. If you are unable to find mu shu wrappers at your local Asian market, substitute flour tortillas. Place a small amount of hoisin sauce in the center of each wrapper, fill with a small amount of Mu Shu Veggies, fold up the bottom, and fold the two sides together to enjoy. You can also use cabbage leaves or chard as your mu shu wrapper.

SESAME ASPARAGUS

Have your tongs ready as you prepare this simple and flavorful dish. Use the white sesame seeds if you can find them as they make for a colorful presentation. Serve with Szechuan Tempeh and Veggies (page 127), Seitan and Broccoli (page 125), or Dan Dan Noodles (page 126).

SERVES 2 TO 4

2 teaspoons sesame oil or toasted sesame oil
2 large cloves garlic, minced
1 large bunch asparagus, stem ends trimmed
¾ cup water
1 tablespoon soy sauce, or to taste
2 teaspoons freshly squeezed lemon juice
Pinch crushed red pepper flakes
2 tablespoons white sesame seeds

1. Place the sesame oil in a sauté pan over medium-high heat. Add the garlic and cook for 1 minute, stirring constantly.
2. Add the asparagus and gently stir well with tongs. Add the water and cook until the asparagus is just tender, approximately 5 minutes, depending on the thickness of the asparagus. Most or all of the water should be dissolved by the time it's finished.
3. Add the soy sauce, lemon juice, and crushed red pepper flakes and gently stir well. Top with sesame seeds before serving.

Variations

- Replace the asparagus with broccoli, cauliflower, or zucchini and add more water if necessary.
- Replace the lemon juice with lime juice.
- Replace the garlic with ½-inch piece of fresh ginger, peeled and minced.
- Try toasting the sesame seeds (see page 225).

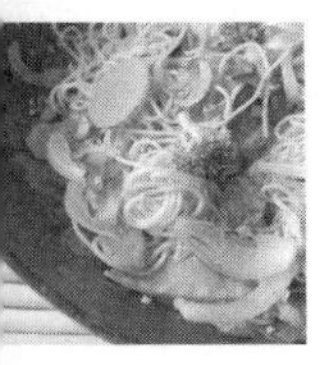

SZECHUAN GREEN BEANS AND RED PEPPER

Szechuan cuisine originates in the Sichuan Province of southwestern China. Almost synonymous with spicy hot, Szechuan dishes abound in hot chile peppers and garlic. If you can find the Szechuan pepper, the dish will be that much more authentic. Serve alongside Cantonese Lemon Tofu (page 116), Kung Pao Tempeh (page 123), or Mu Shu Vegetables (page 108).

SERVES 6 TO 8

½ tablespoon sesame or peanut oil
5 cloves garlic, pressed or minced
1 large red bell pepper, julienned
1 hot red chile pepper, seeded and diced
6 cups string beans, ends trimmed, rinsed well
2 tablespoons rice vinegar
2 tablespoons soy sauce
¼ teaspoon ground anise, optional
¼ teaspoon crushed red pepper flakes, or to taste
¼ teaspoon ground Szechuan pepper or ground black pepper, or to taste
Pinch sea salt, or to taste
½ cup chopped roasted, unsalted peanuts, optional

1. Place the oil in a large sauté pan or wok over medium-high heat. Add the garlic, red bell pepper, and chile pepper and cook for 2 minutes, stirring constantly.
2. Add the green beans and cook until just tender, approximately 7 minutes, stirring frequently with tongs.
3. Add the remaining ingredients except the peanuts, and gently stir well. Garnish with the peanuts before serving.

Variations

- Replace the green beans with a veggie of your choosing, such as broccoli, zucchini, kale, or bok choy.
- Replace the peanuts with cashews, pecans, or macadamia nuts.
- Add hot chile oil to taste.

East Meets West: Chopsticks

Reputably originating in China over 5,000 years ago, chopsticks are a major part of the culinary and cultural traditions throughout Asia, including Japan, Korea, and Vietnam. The use of chopsticks is said to have gained in popularity with the teachings of Confucius (see page 124). Used also in religious ceremonies, chopsticks can help with mindful eating, whereby you eat smaller portions in each mouthful. They come in many sizes and are typically made from bamboo. The best way to learn how to use a chopstick is to ask a trusted companion who has already mastered the art.

GREEN ONION HOTCAKES

The 30-minute sister to Chinese scallion pancakes, these cakes are a cross between a flatbread and a pancake, and they can be whipped up in a jiff. Vary the fillings to create your own unique cakes. Serve them on their own with a dollop of vegan sour cream and chives or as a side with Hot and Sour Soup (page 93) or Sweet and Sour Mushrooms (page 103). You can also make mini pancakes and serve as part of a dim sum meal (see page 96).

MAKES 6 PANCAKES

2 cups spelt flour
½ teaspoon baking soda
¼ teaspoon baking powder
1 teaspoon salt
¼ teaspoon ground black pepper
½ to ¾ cup warm water
¾ cup thinly sliced green onions
2 cloves garlic, pressed or minced, optional
Sesame oil

1. Preheat a griddle or skillet. Place the flour, baking soda, baking powder, salt, and pepper in a mixing bowl and whisk well. Slowly add the water, stirring constantly. You may not need to use the full ¾ cup of water, or you may need slightly more, depending on the environment of your kitchen. You want the dough to be firm and slightly moist.
2. Gently knead the dough for a few minutes. Transfer the dough to a lightly floured surface. Using a rolling pin or your hands, form a 6- by 4-inch rectangle with the dough. Spread the green onions, and garlic if using, in the center of the rectangle. Roll up into a log shape. Slice the log into six pieces. Roll each piece into a ball and flatten to pancake size.
3. Lightly oil the griddle and cook the cakes over medium heat until they are golden brown, flipping occasionally to ensure even cooking. Press down firmly with the spatula to help cook the inside thoroughly.

Variations

- Add ¼ cup of sautéed shiitake mushrooms and/or diced red bell pepper.
- Add 1 teaspoon peeled and minced fresh ginger.
- Add 1 tablespoon sesame seeds along with the flour.

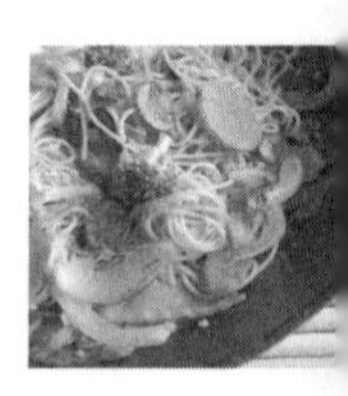

SESAME GARLIC STIR-FRY WITH SNOW PEAS

One of the simplest kinds of stir-fry, this recipe shows how simple it is to create exotic flavor. It pairs magically with Hot and Sour Soup (page 93) and Chinese Fried Rice (page 105).

SERVES 4 TO 6

1 tablespoon sesame seeds
2 teaspoons toasted sesame oil, or to taste
2 cloves garlic, pressed or minced
½ teaspoon sea salt
6 cups snow peas, ends removed
2 teaspoons soy sauce, or to taste
1 teaspoon crushed red pepper flakes or minced fresh chile pepper, optional

1. In a dry sauté pan over medium heat, toast the sesame seeds for about 3 minutes or until they turn light brown and emit a toasty aroma. Transfer to a bowl and set aside.
2. Meanwhile, in a sauté pan over medium heat, add the oil, garlic, and salt and cook for 2 minutes or until the garlic begins to brown, stirring frequently. Add the snow peas and stir-fry for 5 minutes or until the snow peas start to soften but are still bright green.
3. Add the soy sauce and continue to stir-fry for 1 to 2 minutes. Add the toasted sesame seeds and red pepper flakes, if using, and remove from the heat. Serve immediately or allow to cool.

Variations

- Substitute just about any vegetable you like for the snow peas, such as portobello mushrooms, carrots, bok choy, or lotus root. You could also use precooked squash or sweet potatoes.
- Add 2 tablespoons of peeled and minced fresh ginger for even more flavor fun.
- Use black sesame seeds or a combination of white and black seeds.

continues

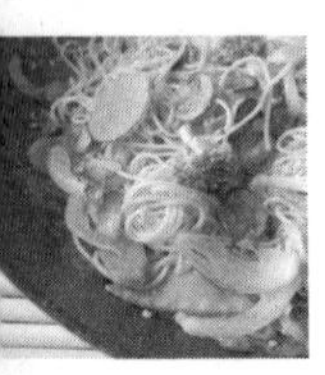

Chefs' Tips and Tricks

Stir-frying is a popular cooking technique in Chinese and other Asian cuisine that involves sautéing ingredients at a very high temperature, often in a wok. There are many tips for a successful stir-fry, including having all of your ingredients prepped beforehand and having them be of a relatively equal size. Also, be sure to add the most dense ingredients first, moving them up the sides of the wok as you add more vegetables to the bottom.

A wok is a large pan with a rounded bottom that is used throughout South and Southeast Asia and may trace its origins back to China. Although they are most well known for high-temperature cooking, woks are also used for braising, deep frying, boiling, steaming (with a steamer basket), and even smoking (with a rack). Use with a long-handled ladle and spatula to prevent burning.

Woks are traditionally cleaned using a bamboo brush rather than submerged in soapy water. This way they stay "seasoned" with that black, well-worn look. For regular cleaning of your wok, simply brush off any food, wipe with a clean towel, and rinse. Then set over a flame on your stovetop to dry off the water. You never want to leave a wok to air dry; this causes rust. If the wok starts to look dull, brush lightly with oil (traditionally peanut or sesame oil) after heating.

HOISIN EGGPLANT CUTLETS

Dishes like this are perfect to have on hand for quick lunches, healthy snacks, or unexpected visitors. Stuff these cutlets in a wrap or serve over a salad or Chinese Fried Rice (page 105). You need to use the regular American eggplant rather than the thinner Asian style eggplant for this recipe.

SERVES 6–8

2 medium eggplants
Kosher salt or sea salt

HOISIN SAUCE

1 cup water
1 tablespoon soy sauce
1 cup black soybeans or 2 ounces fermented black beans (see page 90)
1 tablespoon agave nectar or ¼ cup if using the fermented black beans
2 tablespoons rice vinegar
2 cloves garlic
1 tablespoon toasted sesame oil
½ teaspoon crushed red pepper flakes, or to taste
½ teaspoon five-spice powder, optional
¼ teaspoon ground black pepper

1. Preheat the oven to 350°F. Slice the eggplants into ½-inch thick rounds. Sprinkle them with salt and allow them to sit for a few minutes while you make the sauce.
2. Place all of the hoisin sauce ingredients in a blender and blend until completely smooth. Transfer to a casserole dish or baking tray. Rinse the salt off of the eggplant cutlets and place them in the sauce, flipping them over a couple of times to coat completely.
3. Bake for 15 minutes, flip, and bake for an additional 5 to 10 minutes or until a fork can easily pass through the cutlets. Serve immediately or cool completely before storing in an airtight container in the fridge.

CANTONESE LEMON TOFU

This dish makes use of a lemon marinade to impart a delicate flavor to the tofu, which replaces the fish used in the traditional dish. The turmeric imparts a yellow color to the sauce. If you have more time, go for the variation, which has extra steps but is a more authentic version. Serve alongside quinoa, Chinese Fried Rice (page 105), Sweet and Sour Mushrooms (page 103), or Sesame Asparagus (page 109).

SERVES 4

1½ tablespoons soy sauce
1½ tablespoons water
½ teaspoon five-spice powder
1 (14-ounce) package extra-firm tofu
¼ cup diced green onions

LEMON SAUCE

⅓ cup freshly squeezed lemon juice
1 teaspoon lemon zest
1 tablespoon rice wine vinegar
¼ cup water
2 tablespoons soy sauce
2 teaspoons agave nectar or organic sugar
¼ teaspoon salt, or to taste
¼ teaspoon crushed red pepper flakes
⅛ teaspoon turmeric powder
2 teaspoons arrowroot dissolved in ½ cup cold water

1. Preheat the oven to 375°F. Place the soy sauce, water, and five-spice powder in a casserole dish and stir well. Slice the tofu into quarters widthwise and then cut the quarters in half diagonally to make eight triangles. Place the cutlets in a casserole dish. Flip the cutlets to ensure even coating.
2. Prepare the lemon sauce by heating all of the ingredients except the arrowroot mixture in a saucepan over medium-high heat for 5 minutes, stirring occasionally. Add the arrowroot mixture and cook until the sauce thickens, approximately 3 minutes, whisking constantly.
3. Pour the sauce over the cutlets and bake for 20 minutes. Remove from the oven and top with green onions before serving.

If You Have More Time: Crusted Lemon Tofu Cutlets

1. Marinate the tofu cutlets in a casserole dish with 2 tablespoons of soy sauce and 1 tablespoon of water for 20 minutes. Flip occasionally to ensure even coating.
2. Prepare the lemon sauce by heating all of the ingredients except the arrowroot mixture in a saucepan over medium-high heat for 5 minutes, stirring occasionally. Add the arrowroot mixture and cook until the sauce thickens, approximately 3 minutes, whisking constantly.
3. Blend 3 tablespoons of ground flax seeds with 1 cup of water and place in a bowl. Place 1¼ cups bread crumbs in another bowl.
4. Add a few tablespoons or more of sesame oil to a large sauté pan over medium-high heat. One at a time, dip each tofu cutlet in the flax mixture, making sure they are well coated. Then dip in the bread crumbs, making sure they are completely covered on both sides. (The flax mixture will hold the bread crumbs to the cutlet, though you need to be careful when you flip them to have as much of the bread crumbs stay attached as possible.)
5. Place the cutlets in the pan and cook for 5 minutes. Gently flip and cook another 5 minutes. Carefully remove from the pan and top with the lemon sauce and green onions before serving.

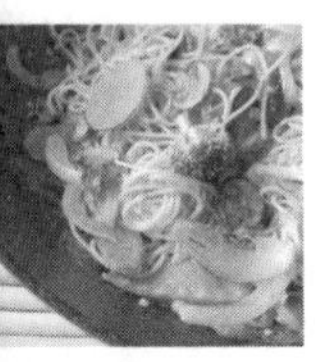

SEITAN WITH BLACK BEAN SAUCE

Although this recipe is typically made with fermented black beans, you can use black soy beans (see page 90) if you are unable to find fermented beans. If you do use the fermented beans, add them to the sauté pan when you add the ginger, and adjust the soy sauce and salt to taste. Seitan is a remarkably versatile product that can mimic the flavor and texture of many animal products (see page 227). You can use the chicken or beef style of seitan for this dish. Serve as a main course with Sesame Asparagus (page 109), Garlic Lover's Eggplant (page 106), or Sweet and Sour Mushrooms (page 103).

SERVES 4 TO 6

- 2 tablespoons toasted sesame oil
- 1 yellow onion, sliced (1½ cups)
- 1 tablespoon minced garlic
- 1 tablespoon peeled and minced fresh ginger
- 1 teaspoon five-spice powder
- 1 teaspoon ground cumin
- 1 green bell pepper, seeded and sliced
- 8 ounces chicken-style seitan (see Box below)
- ½ cup cooked black soybeans or 4 ounces fermented black beans
- ¾ cup water
- 2 tablespoons soy sauce, or to taste
- 1 tablespoon plus 1 teaspoon rice vinegar
- 1 teaspoon agave nectar or organic sugar
- ¼ teaspoon sea salt, or to taste
- ¼ teaspoon crushed red pepper flakes

1. Place the oil in a large sauté pan over medium-high heat. Add the onion, garlic, and ginger and cook for 3 minutes, stirring frequently. Add the five-spice powder, cumin, green bell pepper, and seitan and cook for 5 minutes, stirring frequently.
2. Place the black beans in a mixing bowl and mash with a fork until a paste is formed. It's okay if there are some larger pieces of bean in the mixture. Add to the pan along with the remaining ingredients, lower the heat to low, and cook for 10 minutes before serving.

Chefs' Tips and Tricks

If you are unable to purchase chicken-style seitan, have no fear. Place ¼ cup nutritional yeast, 1 tablespoon garlic powder or 1 teaspoon minced fresh garlic, 1 tablespoon dehydrated onions or 2 teaspoons onion powder, 1 tablespoon soy sauce, 2 teaspoons paprika, ½ teaspoon celery seed, and 1 cup of water in a mixing bowl and whisk well. Add an 8-ounce package of seitan and mix well. Allow it to sit for at least 15 minutes, but ideally an hour or longer, before using in the recipes.

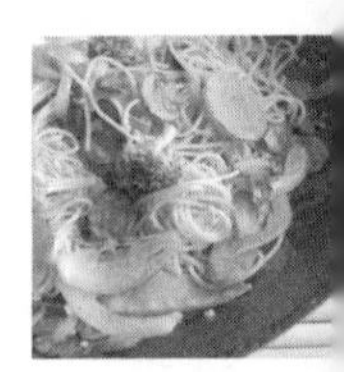

BBQ TOFU WITH SNOW PEAS

Chinese BBQ sauces typically rely on hoisin sauce as their base, instead of the tomato that is used in American-style BBQ sauce. Hoisin sauce in turn is traditionally made with fermented black beans (which are black soybeans). If you are unable to find fermented black beans, tahini makes a tasty replacement. Serve with Vegetable Lo Mein (page 122) or Chinese Fried Rice (page 105).

SERVES 4

2 tablespoons sesame oil
2 tablespoons peeled and minced fresh ginger
3 cloves garlic, pressed or minced
1 teaspoon five-spice powder
1 (14-ounce) package extra-firm tofu
½ pound snow peas, ends trimmed (2 cups)

BBQ SAUCE

3 tablespoons soy sauce
2 tablespoons maple syrup
1 tablespoon sesame oil or toasted sesame oil
1 tablespoon rice vinegar
½ cup water
2 tablespoons fermented black beans (see page 90) or 3 tablespoons tahini
Few drops liquid smoke
Pinch crushed red pepper flakes

1. Place the sesame oil in a large sauté pan over medium-high heat. Add the ginger, garlic, and five-spice powder and cook for 3 minutes, stirring constantly.
2. Slice the tofu in half lengthwise, forming two cutlets. Make three slices lengthwise and three slices widthwise. This yields thirty-two semi-large tofu cubes. (You can make smaller cubes by cutting the block into three cutlets instead of two.) Add to the sauté pan, lower the heat to medium, and cook for 3 minutes, gently stirring occasionally. Add the snow peas and gently stir well.
3. Combine the BBQ sauce ingredients in a small bowl and whisk well. Add to the sauté pan and gently mix. Lower the heat to low and cook for 10 minutes, gently stirring occasionally.

Variations

- Replace the tofu with tempeh or seitan.
- Replace the tofu with 4 cups chopped vegetables of your choosing, such as broccoli, zucchini, mushrooms, or eggplant.

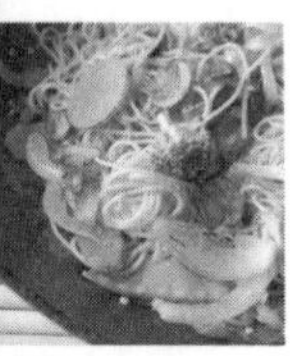

CHOW MEIN

Chow mein means "fried noodles." Generally an egg noodle is used, but many other varieties will work perfectly. Rice and wheat-flour noodles are the most common substitutes. Linguini and fettuccini work if you want a thicker noodle. Rice noodles and bean thread noodles (or vermicelli) are best when you want a thinner noodle. Be sure not to overcook the noodles or they will fall apart when you stir-fry them.

SERVES 4 TO 6

12 ounces noodles (linguini, fettuccini, angel hair, spaghetti, or other pasta)
2 tablespoons toasted sesame oil
6 cloves garlic, pressed or minced
¼ cup peeled and minced fresh ginger
½ teaspoon sea salt
1 yellow onion, chopped
1 cup thinly sliced celery
½ cup sliced snow peas
½ medium red or green bell pepper, thinly sliced
2½ cups sliced mushrooms
1 teaspoon plus 2 tablespoons soy sauce
1 teaspoon plus 1 tablespoon agave nectar
2 tablespoons rice vinegar
1 teaspoon crushed red pepper flakes or fresh minced chile pepper, optional
¼ cup thinly sliced green onions
1 cup mung bean sprouts, optional

1. Prepare the noodles according to the package's instructions.
2. In a large sauté pan, wok, or pot, heat 1 tablespoon of the oil with the garlic, ginger, and salt over medium heat for 2 minutes or until the garlic and ginger start to brown. Add the onion, celery, snow peas, and bell pepper and sauté for 3 minutes, then add the mushrooms. Allow the vegetables to cook until they are just soft.
3. Add 1 teaspoon of the soy sauce, 1 teaspoon of the agave nectar, 1 tablespoon of the rice vinegar, and the crushed red pepper flakes, if using. Continue to cook for 1 to 2 minutes while stirring to ensure even flavoring, then transfer the vegetables to a large mixing bowl.
4. Add the remaining 1 tablespoon of oil to the pan with the noodles and the remaining soy sauce, agave, and rice vinegar. Stir-fry the noodles until they are evenly coated and to your desired taste. Transfer them to the bowl with the vegetables.
5. Top with green onions and mung bean sprouts, if using, and toss the whole mixture well. Serve hot.

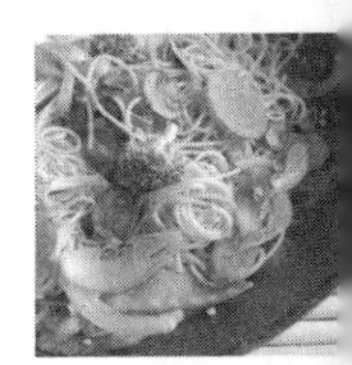

ORANGE-GLAZED TOFU

This is a version of the Hunan-style Orange Chicken, minus the chicken. It's a sweet and savory dish wherein the sauce cooks with the tofu in the same baking dish. There are many different marmalades you can experiment with. Try peach, mango, or apricot. Serve with Green Onion Hotcakes (page 112), Lotus Root Salad (page 95), or Sesame Asparagus (page 109).

MAKES 8 SMALL CUTLETS

1 (14-ounce) package extra-firm tofu
2 tablespoons soy sauce, or to taste
1 tablespoon peeled and minced fresh ginger
½ teaspoon five-spice powder
1 orange, zested and juiced
1 (10-ounce) jar orange marmalade, preferably no sugar added
1 tablespoon arrowroot dissolved in ½ cup cold water
Pinch crushed red pepper flakes
¼ cup thinly sliced green onions

1. Preheat the oven to 350°F. Slice the tofu into quarters widthwise, cut the quarters in half to make eight cutlets, and place them in a casserole dish. Add the soy sauce and flip the cutlets to make sure they are evenly coated. Add the remaining ingredients except the green onion and stir well.
2. Bake for 20 minutes, remove from the oven, and top with the green onions before serving.

Variations

- Replace the tofu with seitan or grilled tempeh (see page 127).
- Replace the tofu with portobello mushrooms or 4 cups of your favorite assorted chopped vegetables, such as carrots, sweet potatoes, beets, parsnips, bell peppers, and/or zucchini. Cook until the thickest vegetable is just soft.
- To tone down the sweetness, you may omit the orange juice.

East Meets West: Tai Chi and Qi Gung

Tai chi and qi gung are Chinese martial art forms that uplift both body and soul. They are types of moving mediations that bring health benefits, promote mental clarity, and reduce stress. There are classes available at gyms, hospitals, and even senior homes. (Mark's Grandma Mollie practiced tai chi at her senior home.) Whereas tai chi has been practiced since the twelfth century, qi gong is a more recent development. *Qi* or *chi* represents life force; *gong* is "working with"; thus it is a practice that enhances life force. Check out the recommended reading section in Appendix C for more on tai chi and qi gong.

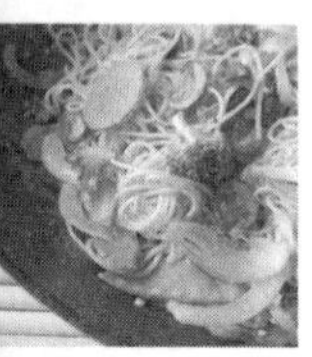

VEGETABLE LO MEIN

Whereas *chow mein* means "fried noodles," *lo mein* literally means "tossed noodles." Egg noodles are the traditional choice, but rice and wheat-flour noodles are commonly substituted. Linguini and fettuccini are great if you want a thicker noodle. Rice noodles and bean thread noodles (or vermicelli) work best when you desire a thinner noodle. As with Chow Mein (page 120), be sure not to overcook the noodles or they will fall apart when you stir-fry them with the vegetables.

SERVES 6

8 ounces noodles (linguini, spaghetti, angel hair, vermicelli, or rice noodles)
1 tablespoon toasted sesame oil
¼ cup peeled and minced fresh ginger
6 cloves garlic, pressed or minced
1 teaspoon crushed red pepper flakes, or to taste
1 medium yellow onion, sliced into quarter moons
4 cups assorted chopped vegetables (carrots, mushrooms, red bell peppers, green beans)
3 tablespoons mirin
3 tablespoons soy sauce, or to taste
2 cups shredded cabbage
½ cup water, if necessary
¼ cup thinly sliced green onions
Mung bean sprouts, optional

1. Cook the noodles according to the instructions on the package. Set aside.
2. Heat the oil in a large sauté pan or wok over medium heat. Add the ginger, garlic, and crushed red pepper flakes and stir frequently for 1 to 2 minutes, until the garlic starts to brown. Add the onion and stir again for 2 minutes, until they begin to turn translucent.
3. Add the chopped vegetables and stir well. Add the mirin and soy sauce, stir well, and cover for 4 to 5 minutes or until the vegetables are just soft. Add the cabbage and mix well to coat with the juices. You may have to add some water during stir-frying to keep the veggies from sticking to the pan.
4. Add the cooked noodles and stir well, adding water if necessary to keep the noodles from sticking to the pan. When the noodles are evenly coated, remove from the heat, sprinkle with green onions and mung bean sprouts, if using, and serve hot.

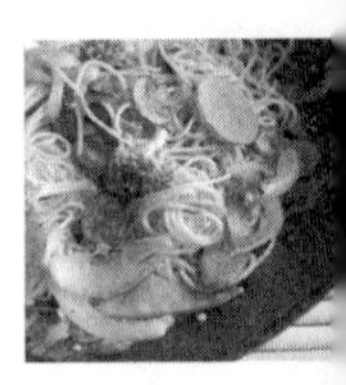

KUNG PAO TEMPEH

Originating in the Sichuan province, this dish packs a spicy punch. It's best if you can find the dried red chiles, otherwise, any hot chile pepper will do. The flavors of this dish wonderfully complement Szechuan Green Beans (page 130), Sesame Asparagus (page 109), or Bok Choy with Five-Spice Cashews (page 107).

SERVES 4 TO 6

MARINATED TEMPEH

2 (8-ounce) packages tempeh, cut into ½-inch cubes
2 tablespoons sesame oil
2 tablespoons soy sauce
2 tablespoons peeled and minced fresh ginger
3 large cloves garlic, pressed or minced
½ cup water

SAUTÉ

1 tablespoon sesame oil or toasted sesame oil
½ cup roasted, unsalted peanuts or cashews
4 or more dried red chiles, or 1 tablespoon seeded and diced chile pepper, or to taste
1 large red bell pepper, thinly sliced
1 large head bok choy, chopped (6 cups)
2 tablespoons soy sauce
1 tablespoon rice vinegar
1½ tablespoons agave nectar
2 tablespoons freshly squeezed lemon juice
1½ tablespoons arrowroot dissolved in 1 cup cold water
Ground Szechuan peppers to taste or a few drops Szechuan oil, optional
¼ cup thinly sliced green onions

1. Preheat the oven to 400°F. Place the marinade ingredients in a casserole dish and mix well. Add the cubed tempeh, flipping to coat all sides. Place in the oven and bake for 15 minutes, stirring occasionally.

continues

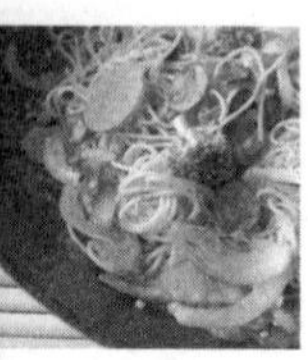

2. Meanwhile, place the sesame oil in a large sauté pan or wok over low heat. Add the peanuts, chiles, and red bell pepper, and cook for 5 minutes, stirring frequently. When the tempeh is done cooking, add the contents of the casserole dish to the sauté pan and gently mix well.
3. Increase the heat to medium-high, add the bok choy, and gently stir well. Add the remaining ingredients except the green onion and cook until sauce thickens, approximately 3 minutes, stirring frequently and adding a small amount of water if necessary to prevent sticking. Top with green onion and additional peanuts if you wish before serving.

Variations

- Replace the tempeh with tofu or seitan.
- You can also replace the tempeh with 6 cups assorted chopped mixed vegetables such as onions, broccoli, carrots, sweet potatoes, or cauliflower.

East Meets West: Confucius says

Confucius was a Chinese philosopher and thinker born in 551 BC. His teachings were highly influential and provided a framework for Chinese political thought for 2,000 years. He shared many wise sayings, such as the Golden Rule: "Do unto others as you would have them do unto you."

SEITAN AND BROCCOLI

This is our version of the ubiquitous cow-based broccoli dish. Look for a marinated brand of seitan for the best flavor (or see page 227 to flavor seitan appropriately). Serve over basmati rice with a side of Szechuan Green Beans (page 110) or Sesame Garlic Stir-Fry Snow Peas (page 113).

SERVES 4 TO 6

2 tablespoons sesame oil
1 yellow onion, sliced (1½ cups)
3 cloves garlic, pressed or minced
½ teaspoon five-spice powder
3 cups small broccoli flowerets
1½ cups water
1 red bell pepper, sliced
1 (8-ounce) package seitan
¼ cup soy sauce
½ to ¾ teaspoon crushed red pepper flakes
1 tablespoon mirin, optional
2 tablespoons arrowroot powder dissolved in
½ cup cold water

1. Place the oil in a large sauté pan over medium-high heat. Add the onion, garlic, and five-spice powder and cook for 3 minutes, stirring frequently.
2. Add the broccoli, ½ cup water, bell pepper, and seitan, and cook for 5 minutes, stirring frequently. Add the soy sauce, remaining cup of water, red pepper flakes, and mirin, if using, and cook for 8 minutes, stirring frequently.
3. Add the arrowroot mixture and stir constantly until sauce thickens. Be careful not to overcook. Serve hot.

Variations

- Add ½ cup roasted cashews at the end of cooking.
- Use chicken-style seitan (page 118).
- Replace the seitan with tofu or tempeh.

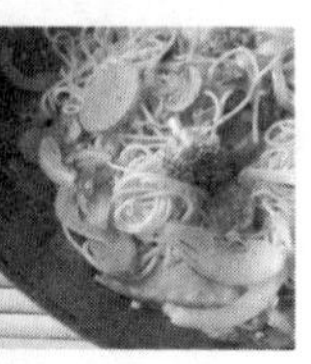

DAN DAN NOODLES WITH TEMPEH

There are many ways to prepare this spicy hot dish from the Sichuan province. Our version uses tempeh because that's how we roll. Serve with Lotus Root Salad (page 95), Sesame Asparagus (page 109), or Garlic Lover's Eggplant (page 106).

SERVES 4 TO 6

14 ounces fettuccini or linguini brown rice pasta or noodle of your choosing
2 tablespoons sesame oil
3 cloves garlic, pressed or minced
2 tablespoons peeled and minced fresh ginger
1 tablespoon hot chile, seeded and diced, or to taste
8 ounces tempeh, chopped small
Few drops liquid smoke or 1 teaspoon smoked paprika (see Box below), optional
Szechuan oil or other hot chile oil, to taste, optional
Ground Szechuan pepper, to taste, optional

DAN DAN SAUCE

¼ cup water
¼ cup sesame oil
¼ cup soy sauce
3 tablespoons rice vinegar
1½ tablespoons agave nectar or sweetener of choice
1¼ teaspoon sea salt, or to taste
1 teaspoon crushed red pepper flakes

1. Cook the pasta according to the instructions on the package. Place in a colander, rinse and drain well, and place in a large bowl.
2. Meanwhile, place the sesame oil in a large sauté pan over medium heat. Add the garlic, ginger, and chile pepper and cook for 2 minutes, stirring frequently. Add the tempeh, and liquid smoke if using, and cook for 10 minutes, stirring frequently and adding water as necessary to prevent sticking. Remove from the heat.
3. Combine the sauce ingredients in a bowl and whisk well. Pour half of the sauce onto the pasta and mix well. Pour the remaining half onto the tempeh and stir well. To serve, place the noodles on each plate, top with hot chile oil, if using, and the Szechuan pepper, if using, and then top with the tempeh.

Variation

- Replace the tempeh with tofu or seitan.

Chefs' Tips and Tricks

Try adding 1 teaspoon of smoked paprika (Pimento de la Vera), if you can find it, instead of the liquid smoke in this recipe and others that call for liquid smoke. It can be ordered at the Spanish Table, www.spanishtable.com/.

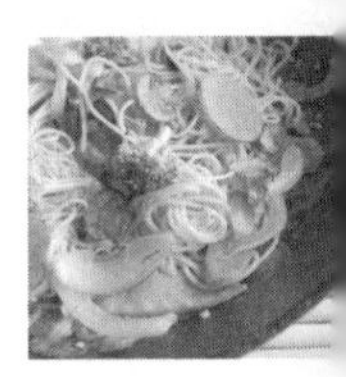

SZECHUAN TEMPEH AND VEGGIES

As we mentioned earlier, Szechuan is generally hot hot hot. Feel free to adjust the spiciness to your liking. This dish creates a Szechuan sauce in which the tempeh and veggies are simmered. Serve with Chinese Fried Rice (page 105) and a bowl of Creamy Corn Soup (page 94).

SERVES 4

1 tablespoon sesame oil
4 to 5 cloves garlic, pressed or minced
1 tablespoon seeded and diced hot chile, or more to taste
1 tablespoon peeled and minced fresh ginger
8 ounces tempeh
1¼ cups water
2 tablespoons mirin or cooking sherry
1 tablespoon plus 2 teaspoons soy sauce, or to taste
1 tablespoon agave nectar, organic brown sugar, or sweetener of choice
2 teaspoons arrowroot powder dissolved in ¼ cup cold water
¼ teaspoon sea salt or to taste
¼ teaspoon ground Szechuan pepper or a few drops of Szechuan oil, or to taste
¼ teaspoon ground black pepper
Cayenne pepper or crushed red pepper flakes to taste
2 cups assorted chopped mixed vegetables (try onions, carrots, broccoli, bell peppers, mushrooms, bok choy, or your favorite green veggie)
¼ cup thinly sliced green onions

continues

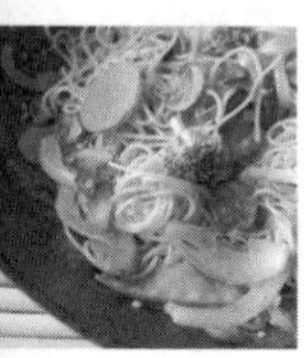

1. Place the oil in a large sauté pan over medium-high heat. Add the garlic, chile, and ginger and cook for 1 minute, stirring constantly. Cut the tempeh into ½-inch cubes and add to the pan. Cook for 3 minutes, stirring frequently and adding a small amount of water if necessary to prevent sticking.
2. Lower the heat to medium-low, add the remaining water, mirin, soy sauce, and agave, and cook for 2 minutes, stirring frequently. Add the arrowroot mixture and stir until the sauce thickens. Add the salt, pepper, and cayenne and stir well.
3. Add the chopped veggies and cook for 10 to 15 minutes, stirring occasionally. Garnish with green onion before serving.

Variations

- Replace the tempeh with tofu or seitan.
- Replace the tempeh with an additional 2 to 3 cups of chopped mixed vegetables.

Chefs' Tips and Tricks

If you want a thicker sauce, dissolve an additional teaspoon of arrowroot in 2 tablespoons of cold water and stir into the pan.

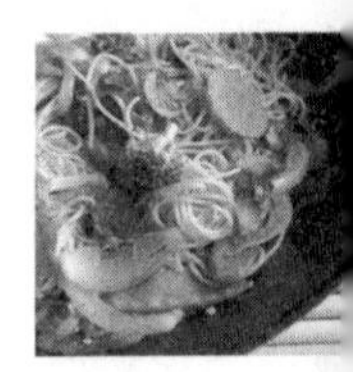

PEKING SEITAN, A.K.A. DAFFY'S RELIEF

We will spare you the details of what goes into creating Peking Duck. For our version, we are using seitan, hence the relief of our favorite duck. Use a convection oven if you have access to one to achieve a crispier, more authentic texture. Serve with Chinese Fried Rice (page 105), Bok Choy with Five-Spice Cashews (page 107), or Garlic Lover's Eggplant (page 106).

SERVES 6

2 tablespoons sesame oil
2 tablespoons peeled and minced fresh ginger
1 cup diced yellow onion
2 (8-ounce) packages seitan, chopped
2 tablespoons maple syrup, agave nectar, or sweetener of choice
2 tablespoons mirin or cooking sherry
1 tablespoon rice vinegar
¼ cup soy sauce
½ teaspoon sea salt, or to taste
¼ teaspoon crushed red pepper flakes, or to taste
1½ tablespoons arrowroot powder dissolved in 1 cup cold water
½ cup thinly sliced green onions

1. Preheat the oven to 425°F. Add the sesame oil to a large sauté pan or wok over high heat. Add the ginger and onion, and cook for 3 minutes, stirring frequently. Add the seitan and cook for 5 minutes, stirring frequently and adding a small amount of water if necessary to prevent sticking.
2. Add the remaining ingredients except the green onion and mix well. Transfer to a casserole dish and bake for 15 minutes. Top with green onion before serving.

Variation

- Replace the seitan with 14 ounces of extra-firm tofu, cubed. Sauté for an additional 15 minutes with the remaining ingredients instead of baking in the casserole dish.

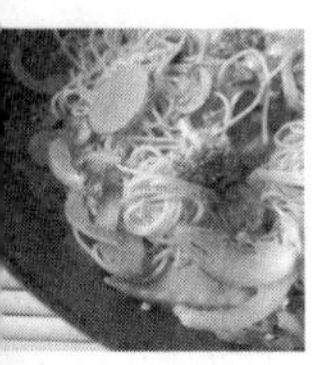

MANGO CUSTARD PUDDING

This custard is simple, fast, and alluring. Though it needs extra time to cool and set, the reward for your patience is generous. You can also use soymilk or soy creamer to make this dish, but you may wish to add ½ teaspoon of coconut extract for the missing flavor. You can check your mango measurement by adding it alone to the blender and whizzing it up to see if it meets the required amount. If you find that your mangoes are a little tart, omit the lemon juice.

SERVES 6

3 medium mangoes, skins and core removed (2¼ cups pureed)
1 teaspoon freshly squeezed lemon juice
1 teaspoon vanilla
¼ cup agave nectar or organic sugar
¾ cup coconut milk
¼ cup arrowroot powder

1. Blend the mango and check to see that you have the proper measurement. Add the lemon juice, vanilla, and agave nectar in a blender on high speed for 20 seconds or until thoroughly blended. Add the coconut milk and arrowroot and blend again for 10 seconds.
2. Transfer the mixture to a pot and place over medium heat. Bring to a boil, stirring frequently with a whisk. When the mixture boils and starts to thicken, whisk constantly for about 5 minutes or until it begins pulling away from the sides of the pot.
3. Transfer to a bowl and chill in the refrigerator for 20 to 30 minutes or until completely cold. Chilling in the freezer will speed up the process.

LIME MINT LYCHEE SORBET

Sublime and simply lovely, this sorbet is a rewarding end to any day. Thanks to our good friend Ali for this killer recipe. You're making Martha proud Ali-cat. For optimal results, an ice cream maker is needed for this recipe. Or, if you're a go-getter like Ali, you can whip up a granita by simply sticking this concoction in the freezer and stirring it up with a fork every 15 to 20 minutes for a few hours! This may seem like a lot of effort but the fanfare is well worth it.

SERVES 4 TO 6

2 (14-ounce) cans lychees in syrup
½ cup less one tablespoon organic sugar
8 fresh mint leaves
¾ cup freshly squeezed lime juice
1 tablespoon freshly squeezed lemon juice

1. Drain the lychee syrup into a small pot and stir in the sugar. Bring the mixture to a gentle boil over medium heat, stirring occasionally, until reduced by half (about 1¼ cups). Remove from the heat, tear the mint leaves and stir them into the hot syrup.
2. Puree the lychees in a blender or food processor on high speed for 20 seconds. Add the syrup mixture and lime and lemon juices, and pulse until well combined.

Variations

- For Lemon Lychee Sorbet (our nephew's favorite variation!), omit the mint, replace the lime juice with 1 cup of lemon juice, and replace the tablespoon of lemon juice with lime juice.
- For a Lychee Colada, follow the Lemon Lychee Sorbet recipe and add ¾ cup of coconut milk along with the other ingredients in step 2.
- Try an unexpectedly lovely Tart Apple Lychee Sorbet by omitting the mint and lime juice and slicing two Granny Smith (or other tart firm apples). Add the apple slices to the syrup mixture in step 1 while the mixture is boiling. Blend the apples, syrup, and lychee together in step 2 along with the lemon juice.

Chefs' Tips and Tricks

Sugar and fat are what make ice cream so smooth and creamy rather than icy. With sorbets, you lose the creamy effect due to the significant reduction in fat. The sugar is essentially what prohibits sorbets from becoming sweet ice cubes. You can also get a little extra help from alcohol and salt, which lower the freezing point and prevent ice crystals from forming. For the following recipe you could try adding ½ cup of Japanese sake and a couple pinches of salt. Otherwise, you could try adding ½ teaspoon of guar gum as a binding, gelling agent.

Photo courtesy Jennifer Murray and Mark Reinfeld.

PART FOUR

The Cuisine of Japan

The land of majestic Mount Fuji, sculpture gardens and temples, and snow monkeys in misty mountain hot springs has made an immense contribution to the culinary scene (especially considering its relatively small size). There has been a proliferation of Japanese sushi restaurants in the West over the past 20 years. Tempura, teriyaki, and miso soup are becoming household words. Some of the modern chef's favorite ingredients—such as shiitake mushrooms, sea vegetables, and miso paste—originated in the Land of the Rising Sun.

It is a delight to provide you with some of our favorite recipes from Japan. We share light salads such as Wakame and Cucumber, Daikon Carrot Salad, and Oshitashi (Spinach Sesame).

Step out of the box with unique dishes like Sesame Tofu with Wasabi Cream Sauce or Roasted Eggplant with Black Sesame Sauce. We also share popular sauce recipes like Teriyaki and Ponzu, which can serve a multitude of flavorful uses. Create your own fan base by hosting a dinner party with Tempura Vegetables and Nori Rolls. Be sure to finish off your meal with light innovative desserts such as Peach Kanten or Mochi Treats. And the chocolate lovers among us will be delighted by the Green Tea Chocolate Bon Bons with Crystallized Ginger.

The Asian Pantry: Japan

Azuki Beans: A very popular legume in Japan, azuki beans (also known as adzuki beans) are used for both sweet and savory dishes throughout East Asia. The most common variety is red, though there are other colors as well.

Edamame: Unripe baby soybeans, still in the pod, edamame are commonly served as an appetizer at Japanese restaurants. As the beans age they become available for use in tofu, miso, oil, and other soy products.

Gomasio: Made from hulled sesame seeds and salt, gomasio is a popular dry condiment in Japanese cuisine. Please see page 174 for our Gomasio recipe.

Green Tea: Japan is well known for its antioxidant-rich green teas. The popular twig tea, *kukicha*, is actually made from the twigs, stems, and stalks of the tea plant. Used widely in macrobiotics (see Box on page 152), it has the lowest caffeine level of any tea, with a nutty, slightly sweet flavor. *Genmaicha* is green tea combined with roasted brown rice. *Bancha* is the most prevalent form of common Japanese green tea. *Matcha* is a powder made from finely ground green tea and forms the basis of the Japanese tea ceremony.

Mirin: A sweet rice wine that is a distinctive ingredient in many traditional Japanese dishes, such as teriyaki sauce, mirin has a strong flavor; a little bit goes a long way. If you do not have any mirin on hand, you can substitute a sweetener such as agave, organic sugar, or even apple juice to compensate for the sweetness mirin provides. You only need to use half the amount: 1 tablespoon mirin = 1½ teaspoons sweetener.

Miso: High in protein, vitamins, and minerals, miso is a cultured soy product with an ancient history of use in Japan. It comes in many varieties including red, white, barley, and even chickpea. Each variety has its own unique flavor, ranging from mild to strong, sweet to salty, and many flavors in between. Become a master of miso by experimenting with as many types as you can. Generally the lighter varieties are recommended in the warmer months, and darker varieties in the colder months. Look for the unpasteurized brands.

Mochi: Mochi is gelatinous or sticky rice pounded into a paste, formed into shapes, and served as a snack. Traditionally eaten during the Japanese New Year, mochi treats are popular year round in Japan, as well as in Hawaii and Taiwan. Mochi flour is available at Asian markets or in the Asian food section in the supermarket. You can also try the pre-made mochi blocks that are sold in natural food stores and come in a variety of flavors. See page 171 for our Mochi Treats recipe.

Mushrooms: To many, Japan is the capital of the fungi kingdom. Some of the most revered mushrooms in the culinary world originate in Japan. Many of them have a long history of medicinal use as well. Be adventurous and try them all to find your favorites. Each has its own unique taste and fascinating shape. Be sure to sample shiitake, maitake, shimeji, matsutake, enoki, and hirataki (oyster mushrooms).

Noodles: Udon and soba noodles are two of the more popular Japanese noodles. Udon are thick, made from wheat flour, and usually served hot with a broth. Soba is a thinner noodle made from buckwheat flour and is used in both hot and cold dishes.

Nori Sheets: Nori sheets are made from a red algae and are paper thin. They are used as a wrapper for Nori Rolls (page 157) or Nori Rice Balls (page 145).

Pickled Ginger: With a strong pungent flavor, pickled ginger is young fresh ginger that has been pickled with brine. See our recipe on page 173 for an amazing homemade version.

Rice Vinegar: Relatively mild and sweet as far as vinegars go, rice vinegar is made from cultured rice. There are different varieties on the market. We recommend using brown rice vinegar. Please note that rice vinegar is not the same as rice wine (mirin).

Sea Vegetables: With many varieties to choose from, sea vegetables, or vegetables of the sea (seaweeds), are a rich source of minerals and impart a salty flavor of the sea to dishes. Varieties to explore include wakame, kombu, nori, kelp, dulse, alaria, laver, Irish moss, sea lettuce, and hijiki. See the glossary for more in-depth descriptions of the popular varieties.

Sushi Rice: A short-grain white rice, sushi rice has a sticky texture when cooked and is widely used in nori rolls. Please see page 157 for instructions on preparing sushi rice.

Umeboshi Plum: Despite the name, umeboshi is a Japanese fruit that more closely resembles an apricot than a plum. This extremely salty and sour pickled condiment is used in macrobiotic cooking and commonly included as a filling in rice balls (see page 145). There is also an umeboshi vinegar, which has a salty, fruity, and sour flavor. Strictly speaking, this vinegar is not actually a vinegar! It's the brine from the umeboshi plum pickling process.

Wasabi: This Japanese horseradish is in the cabbage family of vegetables. The root is used as a condiment in Japanese cuisine. It produces a spiciness that is similar to hot mustard, as opposed to the spicy hot of a chile pepper. As anyone who has tasted it knows, it is a fantastic way to clear the nasal passages. Use sparingly—it sneaks up on you!

MISO SIMPLE SOUP

This soup is the epitome of a quick and easy dish. It's wonderful on chilly days or when you are looking for a light and refreshing meal. Experiment with the many different types of miso (see page 134) for a wide range of flavor profiles.

SERVES 4

6 cups water or dashi (see Box below)
6 tablespoons miso paste, or to taste
2 tablespoons soy sauce, or to taste
½ (14-ounce) block extra-firm tofu, cut into ¼-inch cubes (see page 226)
4 green onions, diced
Small handful arame, soaked in 1 cup warm water for 15 minutes and drained, or 1 nori sheet, cut into small pieces (scissors work best for this)

1. Heat the water in a pot until it just reaches the boiling point.
2. Remove from the heat, whisk in the miso paste and add soy sauce to taste.
3. Pour into serving bowls and add the tofu cubes, green onion, and arame.

Variations

- Add 1 cup thinly sliced spinach, kale, or bok choy.
- Add 1 chopped tomato.
- Some people like to add chopped avocado, minced fresh cilantro, or parsley.
- Spice it up with 1 teaspoon peeled and grated fresh ginger, 1 pressed or minced clove of garlic, or ½ teaspoon crushed red pepper flakes.

Chefs' Tips and Tricks

Have you ever wondered why the miso soup you make at home doesn't taste like it does in restaurants? It's because of dashi. Dashi, a broth made from seaweed and fish, is used as stock in authentic Japanese soups. For **Vegan Dashi** follow this simple recipe: Place two 10-inch strips of kombu in 2 quarts of water along with six dried shiitake mushrooms and, optionally, 2 tablespoons of soy sauce in a pot over medium heat, cover and bring to a boil. Uncover and simmer for 10 minutes, and strain. For added flavor, allow all of the ingredients to soak for an hour to overnight in the refrigerator before boiling. Use Vegan Dashi in place of water in Japanese soups and dishes.

EDAMAME SEA VEGETABLE SOUP

This is a colorful soup that makes use of one of Japan's favorite snack foods—the soybean. Serve as a side along with Arame Garlic Rice (page 153), Teriyaki Tofu (page 159), or Tempura Vegetables (page 142).

SERVES 6 TO 8

¼ cup dried wakame or arame
2 tablespoons toasted sesame oil
1 small yellow onion, diced (1¼ cups)
1 tablespoon peeled and minced fresh ginger
2 large shiitake mushrooms, sliced (1 cup)
½ cup diced red bell pepper
1 large carrot, thinly sliced (1 cup)
1 cup shelled edamame
4 cups water or dashi (see page 136)
¼ cup soy sauce
1 teaspoon sea salt, or to taste
¼ teaspoon crushed red pepper flakes, or to taste
2 tablespoons barley or other miso paste, optional but recommended

1. Place the wakame in a small bowl with 2 cups of warm water.
2. Place the sesame oil in a large pot over medium-high heat. Add the onion, ginger, and shiitake mushrooms and cook for 5 minutes, stirring frequently. Add the red bell pepper and carrots and stir well. Lower the heat to medium, add the edamame and water, and cook for 10 minutes, stirring occasionally.
3. Add the wakame along with the soaking water to the pot with the remaining ingredients. Stir well before serving.

Variations

- Replace the edamame with a bean of your choosing, such as black beans, azuki beans, or navy beans.
- Add 3 cloves of garlic, pressed or minced.

ORANGE GINGER DRESSING

Enter the nirvanic plane by pouring this dressing over a bed of organic mixed greens. This dressing is also utterly delightful as a dipping sauce for Nori Rolls (page 157) or Tempura Vegetables (page 142). The sesame oil adds a distinct, nutty flavor. You can substitute a more mildly flavored oil if you prefer.

MAKES 1¾ CUPS

1 cup sesame oil
¼ cup peeled and minced fresh ginger (see Box below)
3 tablespoons rice vinegar
2 tablespoons water
2 tablespoons freshly squeezed orange juice
1 clove garlic
1 teaspoon Dijon or stone-ground mustard
1 tablespoon plus 1 teaspoon soy sauce
1 tablespoon agave nectar, organic sugar, or sweetener of choice, to taste

1. Combine all of the ingredients in a blender and blend until creamy.
2. Store in a glass container in the refrigerator for up to a week.

Variations

- Substitute safflower oil for the sesame oil.
- Add 1 teaspoon toasted sesame oil.
- Add 2 tablespoons minced fresh herbs like cilantro, parsley, or basil.

Chefs' Tips and Tricks

To mince ginger, we peel it, then cut paper-thin slices. Next, we cut thin julienne strips of the thin slices. Finally, we mince the thin strips. This prevents any long strings of ginger from winding up in your food—something your guests will appreciate!

Thai Summer Rolls • page 59

Edamame Sea Vegetable Soup • page 137

Cucumber Salad with Peanuts and Chile • page 54

Cardamom Cookies • 36, Mango Custard Pudding • 130,
Vanilla Cardamom Rose Lassi • 38

Broccoli and Red Bell Pepper Soba • 164

Lotus Root Salad • 95

Funky Thai Salsa • 58

Kung Pao Tempeh • 123

Curried Potatoes • 11

Vegetable Lo Mein • 122

Red Curry • 70

Tempura Vegetables • 142

Spinach Sesame Salad (Oshitashi) • 150

Black Rice Pudding • 81

Indonesian Seitan Satay • 195

Photo courtesy Jennifer Murray and Mark Reinfeld.

Sesame Tofu with Wasabi Cream Sauce • 160

WAKAME AND CUCUMBER SALAD

This salad is popular at sushi restaurants worldwide. The wakame in this dish imparts the flavor of the sea to the cooling cucumber. Feel free to experiment with different seaweeds, such as arame, hijiki, and even shredded nori. Serve as a side dish with Nori Rolls (page 157), Tempura Vegetables (page 142), and Miso Simple Soup (page 136.)

SERVES 4 TO 6

¼ cup wakame or arame
1 cup warm water
2 tablespoons sesame seeds
1 medium cucumber, peeled, seeded, and sliced thin (approximately 2 cups)
¼ cup diced green onions
2 teaspoons toasted sesame oil
1 tablespoon mirin
¼ teaspoon sea salt, or to taste
1½ teaspoons soy sauce, or to taste
1 tablespoon freshly squeezed lime juice
Pinch crushed red pepper flakes

1. Place the wakame in a small bowl with the warm water and allow it to sit for 15 minutes.
2. Meanwhile, place the sesame seeds in a small sauté pan over medium-high heat and toast for 1 to 2 minutes, or until the seeds begin to pop, stirring occasionally. Remove from the heat.
3. Place the cucumber in a mixing bowl with the green onion, sesame oil, mirin, salt, soy sauce, lime juice, and crushed red pepper flakes, and mix well. Strain and press the water out of the wakame, add it along with 2 tablespoons of the soaking water to the bowl, and gently mix well. Top with the sesame seeds before serving.

DAIKON CARROT SALAD

Daikon is a Japanese word meaning "large root." With origins in Central Asia, daikon is a relatively mild radish when in season. If you can find black sesame seeds, they make for a stunning presentation, but any sesame seed will do. Allow the dish to sit for 20 minutes or longer before serving for optimal flavor. This salad makes a refreshing side dish for many a Japanese meal, including Teriyaki Tofu (page 159), Udon Bowl (page 165), or Nori Rolls (page 157). We even found that it wonderfully complements the Wok-Tossed Cabbage Salad (page 6).

SERVES 4 TO 6

1 large daikon radish, peeled and grated medium (about 2 cups)
3 carrots, peeled and grated (about 2 cups)
1 tablespoon peeled and minced fresh ginger
2 tablespoons freshly squeezed lemon juice
1 tablespoon toasted sesame oil
2 teaspoons soy sauce
2 teaspoons umeboshi vinegar
2 teaspoons mirin, optional
¼ teaspoon sea salt, or to taste
2 tablespoons black sesame seeds

1. Combine the daikon and carrots in a large bowl and mix well.
2. Combine the remaining ingredients except the sesame seeds in a small bowl and whisk well.
3. Pour over the daikon and carrots and gently mix well. Top with sesame seeds before serving.

Variations

- Try toasting the sesame seeds (see page 225).
- Replace the umeboshi vinegar with rice vinegar or your favorite.
- Replace some of the grated carrots with grated beets.
- Add 1 clove garlic, pressed or minced.

East Meets West: The Japanese Tea Ceremony

Also known as "The Way of Tea," the Japanese tea ceremony is a highly ritualized way to prepare and serve the green tea *matcha* (see page 134). It can be a form of meditation wherein mindfulness is brought into everyday actions. The tea gatherings may include sweets and a light meal along with a light tea. They can also be longer affairs, lasting up to 4 hours, with a full meal, dessert, and a stronger tea. The recommended reading section in Appendix C lists a book that can further introduce you to this exquisite ceremony.

BURDOCK ROOT WITH GINGER SESAME SAUCE (GOBO SALAD)

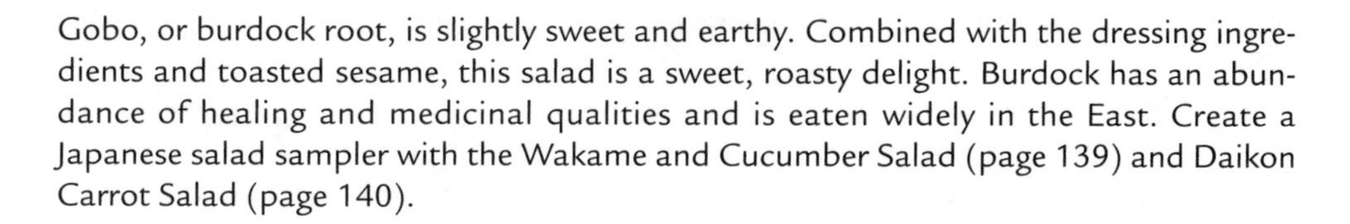

Gobo, or burdock root, is slightly sweet and earthy. Combined with the dressing ingredients and toasted sesame, this salad is a sweet, roasty delight. Burdock has an abundance of healing and medicinal qualities and is eaten widely in the East. Create a Japanese salad sampler with the Wakame and Cucumber Salad (page 139) and Daikon Carrot Salad (page 140).

MAKES 4 SIDE SALADS

2 cups burdock root, peeled, cut into matchsticks (about 2 thin 10-inch pieces of burdock)
½ cup water
1 tablespoon soy sauce
1 tablespoon mirin
1 tablespoon rice vinegar
1½ teaspoons peeled and grated fresh ginger
1 teaspoon sesame seeds
1 cup shredded carrots
2 tablespoons thinly sliced green onion
1 teaspoon toasted sesame oil, optional

1. Place the burdock root in a sauté pan or small pot with the water, soy sauce, mirin, and vinegar. The burdock should be almost submerged in the liquid. Otherwise, add more water until most of the root is covered. Cover and cook for 5 minutes over medium heat.
2. Remove the cover, lower the heat to low, and add the ginger. Cook for another 5 minutes or until the burdock is soft but still a little crunchy.
3. Meanwhile, toast the sesame seeds in a separate, dry sauté pan for 2 or 3 minutes until they are light brown and fragrant. Add them to the burdock or if you are plating the salad yourself, you may wish to sprinkle the sesame seeds on last, after the salad is divided, to keep them from falling off in the dressing.
4. Add the carrots, green onion, and toasted sesame oil, if using. Stir and serve immediately or refrigerate to store.

TEMPURA VEGETABLES

Though deep-frying and healthy living do not go hand in hand, we think you may enjoy this recipe every now and again. And choosing the best-quality ingredients makes a big difference.

Cut the vegetables as flat as possible; this makes them easier to fry in shallow oil. You may wish to lightly pre-steam harder vegetables such as potatoes, squash, or carrots. Please keep in mind that the smaller variety of vegetables you use, the quicker the preparation time will be. Serve with soy sauce, Sweet and Sour Sauce (page 103), Ponzu Sauce (page 148), Mango Ginger Sauce (page 61), or one of the following dipping sauces.

SERVES 4

4 cups mixed vegetables
(onions, zucchini, broccoli, carrots, mushrooms, etc.)

2 cups safflower or sunflower oil or
other oil for frying (16 fluid ounces)

2½ cups flour (try whole wheat or white spelt flour
or for gluten-free tempura use brown rice flour)

½ teaspoon sea salt

2 cups sparkling water

1. Cut the vegetables and set aside near the stove. Pour the oil into a large, deep sauté pan, pot, or wok. Heat the oil over medium heat for a few minutes while you prepare the batter.
2. In a large mixing bowl, stir the flour and salt. Add the sparkling water and stir again to combine. Test if the oil is hot enough by dripping a little bit of the batter into it. If it sizzles and the batter remains at the top, you can begin.
3. Dip the vegetables in the batter, shaking off the excess if necessary, and use tongs to place them into the oil one by one. Fill the pan with as many as can fit without sticking together.
4. Fry on each side for 2 to 3 minutes, or until golden brown. Remove with the tongs, allowing each piece a few seconds to drip off excess oil. Transfer to a baking tray lined with paper towels. Serve immediately.

MISO CASHEW SPREAD

This is an incredibly simple spread to whip up. Use it in your Nori Rolls (page 157), or as a dip for raw veggies like cucumber slices, celery, and carrot sticks. Try it also on rice cakes with sliced avocado and tomato. Experiment with different types of miso paste (see page 134) to experience how it changes the flavor of the dish.

MAKES APPROXIMATELY 2 CUPS

1½ cups cashews, raw (see Box below) or roasted unsalted
¾ cup water
2 tablespoons miso paste
1 tablespoon soy sauce, or to taste
1 tablespoon freshly squeezed lemon juice
1 clove garlic
2 teaspoons mirin, optional

1. Place all of the ingredients in a food processor or strong blender and process until smooth.
2. If you are using a blender, you may need to add more water to get the smooth consistency. Adjust the soy sauce levels accordingly.

Variation

- For a **Miso Tahini Spread**, replace the cashews with 1 cup of tahini paste. Instead of using the food processor, you can combine all of the ingredients in a bowl and whisk well.

The Asian Pantry

Did you know that cashews labeled "raw" are actually not raw? Well, they are raw compared to cashews that are sold as "roasted," but the process of removing the cashew from its shell actually heats the nut to temperatures as high as 200°F.

EDAMAME DIP

The boiling of the edamame gives you plenty of time to cut up some cucumbers, carrots, or fennel for dipping. Health food stores also have different kinds of rice chips, pita chips, rice cakes, and other suitable dippables. Though a food processor is recommended to prepare this dish, you may also use a strong blender.

MAKES ABOUT 3 CUPS

1 (10-ounce) bag frozen shelled edamame
1 tablespoon wasabi powder, or to taste
2 teaspoons peeled and finely grated fresh ginger
1 tablespoon rice vinegar
1 tablespoon mirin, optional
1 tablespoon soy sauce
2 teaspoons barley or other miso paste

1. Boil the edamame according to the instructions on the package. Make sure they are good and soft! Meanwhile, add the remaining ingredients to the bowl of a food processor fitted with the S-blade.
2. Strain the cooked edamame and add it to the bowl. Process on high speed for 30 to 40 seconds or until a hummus-like paste forms. You may need to stop and scrape down the sides once or twice to make sure everything is fully incorporated.
3. Serve immediately or allow it to cool.

NORI RICE BALLS

Not to be confused with nori rolls, this simple snack is called *onigiri* in Japan. It's the ultimate convenience food and is great for traveling. Once you get the hang of rolling the balls, you will become a speed roller. You can fill the balls with any filling you like. A traditional favorite is the umeboshi plum, but feel free to get creative with your fillings. See the variations for some suggestions. If you wish, you can serve the balls with a dipping sauce such as Ponzu Sauce (page 148), Teriyaki Sauce (page 159), or Mango Ginger Sauce (page 61).

MAKES 8 TO 10 BALLS

1¼ cups sushi rice
2 cups water or dashi (see page 136)
1 teaspoon sea salt
1 tablespoon rice vinegar
4 sheets of nori
2 tablespoons umeboshi plum paste (or see Variations on page 146)
Bowl of cold water

1. Place the sushi rice, water, salt, and vinegar in a small pot over medium heat. Bring to a boil. Cover, lower the heat to simmer, and cook until all of the liquid is absorbed, for 10 to 15 minutes.
2. While the rice is cooking, place the nori sheets on a clean cutting board and slice into 2-inch strips. (You may also use culinary scissors to do this.) Set aside.
3. When the rice is cool enough to handle but still relatively hot, you are ready to roll. Creating the balls is a bit of an acquired skill, so be patient with yourself. You will discover your own rolling technique. Wash your hands well and keep them wet through the process. Use a ¼ cup measuring cup to scoop the rice, make a small hole in the rice, and place the plum paste in the center. Use a spoon to remove the rice from the cup, then form it into a ball using your hands. Be sure to cover the plum as much as possible with rice.
4. Once you have your ball, place it in the center of one strip of nori and fold the nori over the ball. Place another strip of nori over the uncovered portion of the ball and fold the nori around the ball. This should completely cover the ball with nori. Now dip your hands in the cold water and coat the ball well. Repeat this process with all of the rice.

continues

Variations

- If you can only find whole umeboshi plums, cut them into ½ teaspoon servings.
- Let your imagination run wild! Instead of using umeboshi, try small pieces of grilled or roasted vegetables, tofu, or tempeh. You can also use pickled ginger and a spread of wasabi paste or umeboshi paste.
- Try coating the rice ball with toasted sesame seeds before covering with nori.
- Replace the sushi rice with Azuki Rice (page 156), adding an extra ¾ cup water to the cooking liquid for a stickier rice.

ARAME LOTUS ROOT SAUTÉ

Here is another dish incorporating the majestic lotus root (see page 90). The flavor of the sea is imparted with the arame, and you can experiment with different Japanese mushrooms to further explore this dish's possibilities. Enjoy with Teriyaki Tofu (page 159), Braised Tempeh with Green Beans (page 168), or Tempura Vegetables (page 142) and then knock 'em dead with the Lime Mint Lychee Sorbet (page 131).

SERVES 4 TO 6

¼ cup dried arame
3 tablespoons arame soaking water
2 tablespoons toasted sesame oil
¼ cup diced shallots
2 tablespoons peeled and minced fresh ginger
2 cloves garlic, pressed or minced
¼ pound maitake or shiitake mushrooms (2 cups chopped)
¾ pound lotus root, peeled and thinly sliced (about 1 cup)
1 tablespoon mirin, optional
1 tablespoon plus 1 teaspoon soy sauce
2 tablespoons freshly squeezed lime juice
¼ teaspoon crushed red pepper flakes, or to taste
½ teaspoon sea salt, or to taste
Sesame seeds for garnish

1. Place the arame in a small bowl with 1 cup of warm water and allow it to soak until soft, approximately 15 minutes. Drain well, reserving 3 tablespoons of the soaking water.
2. Meanwhile, add the sesame oil to a sauté pan over medium-high heat. Add the shallots, ginger, garlic, and mushrooms and cook for 5 minutes, stirring frequently.
3. Add the lotus root and cook for 10 minutes, stirring frequently and adding small amounts of water if necessary to prevent sticking. Remove from the heat and place in a mixing bowl with the remaining ingredients, including the arame and soaking water, but not including the sesame seeds. Garnish with the sesame seeds before serving.

Variations

- Experiment with different mushrooms such as oyster, enoki, or shimeji.
- Add 1 seeded and diced hot red chile pepper or ¼ cup diced red bell pepper for color.
- Replace arame soak water with Fish-Free Sauce (page 85) and adjust salt accordingly.

GRILLED SHIITAKE MUSHROOMS WITH PONZU SAUCE

Ponzu sauce is a thin, tangy sauce. An authentic version often makes use of a citrus called yuzu. If your local market is out of yuzu, you can use lemon, lime, or a combination of both. Instead of grilling the mushrooms you can broil or sauté them. Serve the sauce as a dipping sauce for Nori Rolls (page 157), Nori Rice Balls (page 145), or Tempura Vegetables (page 142) as well.

SERVES 4 TO 6

16 large shiitake mushrooms or
4 large portobello mushrooms, quartered
2 tablespoons sesame oil
1 tablespoon soy sauce
3 tablespoons Ponzu Sauce (recipe follows)

PONZU SAUCE

MAKES 1 CUP

2 tablespoons arame, chopped
¼ cup warm water
¼ cup soy sauce
2 tablespoons mirin
3 tablespoons rice vinegar
1 teaspoon peeled and minced fresh ginger
2 tablespoons freshly squeezed lime juice
2 tablespoons freshly squeezed lemon juice
Pinch crushed red pepper flakes

1. Preheat a grill. Place the mushrooms, sesame oil, and 1 tablespoon soy sauce in a shallow dish. Mix well to evenly coat the mushrooms.
2. Meanwhile, make the Ponzu Sauce: soak the arame in the water for 15 minutes. Place the remaining sauce ingredients in a small bowl and whisk well. Remove 3 tablespoons of this mixture and add it to the mushrooms. Place the remaining sauce in a small pot over low heat.
3. Add the arame along with the soaking water into the pot with the sauce ingredients and cook for 5 minutes, stirring occasionally. Transfer the sauce to a bowl for dipping (you can strain out the arame if you wish).
4. Grill the mushrooms until char marks appear, flipping a few times to ensure even cooking. Serve them on a platter with the Ponzu Sauce for dipping.

Variations

- You can grill, broil, or sauté other vegetables such as zucchini, bell peppers, carrots, or eggplant.
- Try marinating and roasting tofu or tempeh (see page 227) using the Ponzu Sauce for the marinade and dipping sauce.

SPINACH SESAME SALAD (OSHITASHI)

This cold salad is not only a super simple dish to prepare, it also makes for a beautiful presentation. It is wonderful as a side dish when served with Sesame Tofu with Wasabi Cream Sauce (page 160), Nori Rolls (page 157), or Tamari Ginger Tofu (page 162).

SERVES 4

¾ pound fresh baby leaf spinach, rinsed and drained well (6 cups tightly packed)
1 tablespoon plus 1 teaspoon soy sauce
1 tablespoon mirin
1½ teaspoons toasted sesame oil
Gomasio (page 174) or sesame seeds

1. Place the spinach in a small pot or sauté pan with a little water over medium-high heat. Cook until the spinach is just soft and turns a darker green, approximately 3 minutes, using tongs to gently stir. Be sure not to overcook.
2. Place the spinach in a colander and rinse with cold water. Drain well and place in a bowl with the remaining ingredients except the Gomasio and gently mix well.
3. Form the spinach into four individual portions of your desired shape. Try forming squares, circles, rectangles, or oval "towers." Sprinkle with the Gomasio before serving.

Variation

- For **Versatile Sautéed Greens**, sauté 3 cloves of garlic, pressed or minced, in 1 tablespoon of sesame oil. Add the spinach or replace with your favorite green vegetable such as kale, chard, collard greens, bok choy, or napa cabbage. Cook until the greens are just soft. Add 1 tablespoon freshly squeezed lemon juice, a pinch of crushed red pepper flakes, and salt and pepper to taste. If desired, top with some vegan butter.

East Meets West: Bento Box

Perhaps the ultimate lunch box, bento boxes are takeaway containers with compartments so that small portions of several dishes can be enjoyed without having them all wind up in one big pile. Traditionally the boxes are made from black lacquer. Many Japanese restaurants serve meals bento-box style. A vegan bento box might include Nori Rolls (page 157) or Nori Rice Balls (page 145), Wakame and Cucumber Salad (page 139), Daikon Carrot Salad (page 140), Tempura Vegetables (page 142), and a Mochi Treat (page 171).

ROASTED EGGPLANT WITH BLACK SESAME SAUCE

Black sauces are cool! This one is made with black sesame seeds, which when combined with the eggplant give this dish a "baba ganoush of the Far East" effect. Use Japanese eggplant, which are thinner and smaller than American eggplant, if you can find them. If you do use the regular variety, slice the eggplant into thick cutlets.

Serve as a side with Ramen Noodle Stir-Fry (page 167), Tamari Ginger Tofu (page 162), or Teriyaki Tofu (page 159).

SERVES 6 TO 8

4 small Japanese eggplants, sliced in half
1 tablespoon sea salt
Freshly ground black pepper
2 tablespoons diced red bell pepper, optional
Black and white sesame seeds

BLACK SESAME SAUCE

¼ cup black sesame seeds
½ cup water
1 tablespoon freshly squeezed lemon juice
1 tablespoon plus 1 teaspoon soy sauce
⅓ cup sesame oil
1 tablespoon agave nectar or sweetener of choice to taste
1 tablespoon mirin
½ teaspoon crushed red pepper flakes
1 teaspoon toasted sesame oil
¼ teaspoon sea salt, or to taste

continues

1. Preheat the oven to 425°F. Place the eggplant halves in a casserole dish, sprinkle with salt, and allow them to sit for 5 minutes. Rinse well, lightly oil the casserole dish, and return the eggplant to the dish. Top with freshly ground pepper and a sprinkle of sea salt. Place in the oven and bake until a knife can easily pass through the eggplant, approximately 20 minutes.
2. Meanwhile, place the Black Sesame Sauce ingredients in a blender and blend well. Pour into a small sauté pan and keep warm over low heat until the eggplant is done cooking.
3. When the eggplant is done cooking, spread some sauce on each cutlet, top with diced red bell pepper, if using, and sprinkle with black and white sesame seeds before serving.

Variations

- Try serving the Black Sesame Sauce with roasted acorn squash. For a stunning presentation, you can stuff the squash with cooked black forbidden rice. Garnish with roasted red bell peppers and minced fresh cilantro.
- The sauce pairs nicely with any grilled or roasted vegetables.
- If you have more time, allow the eggplant to "sweat" for up to 20 minutes (see page 63).

East Meets West: Macrobiotics

Macrobiotics is a lifestyle approach that emphasizes balance in diet. It is essentially a whole-grain diet that includes cooked vegetables and legumes. Some principles include eating locally and seasonally and avoiding refined products. Many individuals have experienced great improvements in their health by following a macrobiotic diet. A sample meal might include miso soup, a grain dish, a bean dish, some cooked squash or other vegetables, a small amount of sea vegetables, and some toasted nuts or seeds. There is an emphasis on cooked foods and eating heavier foods in the winter and lighter foods in the summer. Check out the *Hip Chick's Guide to Macrobiotics* by Jessica Porter to learn more about macrobiotics.

ARAME GARLIC RICE

We could easily call this dish "garlic lover's rice." If you haven't had whole cloves of garlic cooked along with the rice, it's something that is not to be missed. This is another quick and simple side dish that can accompany any entree. Try it with Sesame Tofu with Wasabi Cream Sauce (page 160), Teriyaki Tofu (page 159), or Kung Pao Tempeh (page 123).

SERVES 6

½ cup arame soaked in 1½ cups hot water
2 cups white basmati rice
3 cups water or vegetable stock (see page 228)
1 teaspoon salt, or to taste
8 to 10 garlic cloves
2 tablespoons mirin, optional

1. Place the arame and hot water in a small bowl and allow it to sit for 10 minutes.
2. Drain well and place in a medium pot with the remaining ingredients over medium-high heat.
3. Bring to a boil, cover, lower the heat to low, and simmer until all of the liquid is absorbed, approximately 10 minutes. Allow it to sit for 5 minutes before gently mixing well.

Variations

- Try replacing the arame with hijiki and soak for an additional 10 minutes before using.
- Add 1 cup of chopped onion or veggies such as celery, shallots, bell peppers, or mushrooms.
- If you have more time, replace the basmati rice with brown rice or another grain and cook according to the instructions on page 230.

Chefs' Tips and Tricks

The scientific way to get garlic out of its skin is to place a clove on a clean cutting board and gracefully thump it with the bottom of a bottle or jar or the flat side of a knife. The clove will then easily peel out of the skin.

SPICY SHIMEJI MUSHROOMS

An extremely popular mushroom in Japan, shimeji is a generic term for about twenty varieties of mushrooms. They come in clusters that are quite artistic. Experiment with different varieties to experience the subtle and not so subtle flavor profiles. You can also substitute the more common shiitake or cremini mushroom. Serve as a side dish with any of our Japanese entrées or use as a filling in Nori Rolls (page 157) or Nori Rice Balls (page 145).

MAKES 2 TO 4 SMALL SERVINGS

1 tablespoon toasted sesame oil
2 cloves garlic, pressed or minced
1 hot chile pepper, seeded and diced
½ pound shimeji mushrooms, whole (about 3 cups)
½ cup diced red bell pepper
2 tablespoons thinly sliced green onion
1 tablespoon freshly squeezed lemon juice
1 tablespoon soy sauce, or to taste
2 teaspoons mirin
Ground cayenne pepper or crushed red pepper flakes to taste
White sesame seeds

1. Place the sesame oil in a small sauté pan over medium-high heat. Add the garlic and chile pepper and cook for 2 minutes, stirring frequently. Add the mushrooms and red bell pepper and cook until the mushrooms are soft, approximately 7 minutes.
2. Add the remaining ingredients except the sesame seeds and mix well. Garnish with the sesame seeds and enjoy!

Variation

- Add 2 tablespoons vegan butter and gently mix well before serving.

TOASTED SESAME–ROASTED VEGETABLES

Here's a simple marinade for all of your roasting needs. Change up the different vegetables and have yourself a good ol' time. The vegetables are the perfect side dish for Teriyaki Tofu (page 159), Arame Garlic Rice (page 153), and Coconut Mashed Parsnips (page 186).

SERVES 4

2 medium tomatoes, cut in half
2 zucchini, sliced
2 heads baby bok choy, cut in half

MARINADE

½ cup water
2 tablespoons toasted sesame oil
2 tablespoons soy sauce
1 tablespoon rice vinegar
2 teaspoons seeded and diced hot chile pepper

1. Preheat the oven to 400°F. Place the marinade ingredients in a large casserole dish. Add the tomatoes and zucchini and cook for 15 minutes. Add the bok choy and cook for 10 minutes longer. Use tongs to flip the bok choy periodically to keep it moist.
2. To serve, place the vegetables on a plate and drizzle with the marinade.

AZUKI RICE

Adding cooked beans is a simple way to bump up the flavor and nutritional profile of a rice dish. Feel free to substitute your bean of choice for the azuki, which is very popular in Japanese cuisine. Cross cultural boundaries and serve with Red Curry (page 70), Sesame Garlic Stir-Fry (page 113), or Madras Curry (page 25).

SERVES 8 TO 10

2 cups white basmati rice
3½ cups water or vegetable stock (page 228)
1 tablespoon rice vinegar
1¼ teaspoons sea salt, or to taste
1 (15-ounce) can cooked azuki beans, drained and rinsed, or 1¾ cups home-cooked beans (see page 230)
½ cup thinly sliced green onions
3 tablespoons sesame seeds

1. Place the rice, water, rice vinegar, and salt in a medium pot over high heat. Bring to a boil. Cover, reduce the heat to simmer, and cook until all of the liquid is absorbed, approximately 10 minutes. Remove from the heat and allow to sit for 5 to 10 minutes.
2. Meanwhile, place the azuki beans in a small pot with a little water. Simmer over low heat, stirring occasionally, until the rice is ready. Add more water if necessary to prevent sticking.
3. Combine the rice, beans, green onions, and sesame seeds in a large bowl and gently mix well. To serve in a creative shape, pack the mixture tightly in a ramekin dish or in a 1-cup measuring cup. Flip onto individual plates.

Variations

- If you have more time, replace basmati rice with brown rice or another grain and cook according to the instructions on page 230.
- Try toasting the sesame seeds.

NORI ROLLS

Sushi rolls can be as fun to dream up as they are to serve. With such a nice presentation, you can hardly go wrong. Everyone is always wowed by these simple yet delicate edible treasures. Though it will take time to build proficiency in rolling, the technique is dependable. Keep it tight, don't overstuff them, and work with cooled sticky rice. You don't even need a bamboo mat, although some people swear by them, in order to get the roll as tight as can be. We use a little extra water to cook the rice to get that desired sticky consistency. The authentic Japanese kitchen steams the rice instead of boiling it. Easier than you think, the technique involves covering a steamer basket with cheesecloth before steaming the rice as you would any vegetable. An electric rice steamer also works well. Our other secret to good rice is preparing it early in the morning (perhaps as you get ready for work). Then just leave it sitting on the stove or countertop, covered, until ready to roll. This way the rice will be thoroughly cooled but not hard from being refrigerated.

For filling the rolls we recommend that you start simple, with two or three ingredients. Choose from avocado, cucumber, green onions, shredded carrots, red or yellow bell peppers, seaweed, daikon, sprouts, or micro greens. Sometimes we even enjoy some chopped macadamia nuts in our rolls.

Take a step up with slightly more involved fillings like steamed asparagus, sautéed or grilled mushrooms, roasted tofu or tempeh (see page 227), Kim Chi (page 214), or Gomasio (see page 174).

Flavor up the scene with some umeboshi paste, Miso Cashew Spread (page 143), Wasabi Cream Sauce (page 160), or Cilantro Pesto (page 181). Spread 1 to 2 tablespoons over the rice (perhaps only 1 or 2 teaspoons of the umeboshi paste) before adding your fillings.

MAKES 4 NORI ROLLS

SUSHI RICE

2 cups sushi rice (or brown rice)
4¼ cups water or vegetable stock (see page 228)
1 tablespoon rice vinegar, optional
2 tablespoons mirin, optional

continues

1. Bring the rice and water to a boil, cover, and simmer for 10 to 15 minutes or until the rice is soft and most of the water is absorbed. A little excess water is okay and will make the rice stickier as it cools.
2. If using, add the rice vinegar and mirin to the cooked rice and stir together.
3. Allow it to cool either on the countertop, or, if pressed for time, in the refrigerator. You can still roll with warm rice but you will have to work faster as the heat softens the nori, which will tear while rolling if you wait too long.

Rolling Instructions

4 nori sheets
¼ cup pickled ginger, or to taste
Wasabi to taste
Soy sauce to taste

1. Fill a small bowl with water. Lay out all four nori sheets on a clean countertop with the long side running parallel to the counter's edge (this gives you longer rolls).
2. Scoop ¾–1 cup of the rice mixture onto each sheet. Use your hands, a spoon, or a rice paddle to spread the rice over each sheet, leaving only a 1-inch strip along the top edge. Dipping your hands in the water will prevent the rice from sticking to you.
3. Clean your hands off and add your preferred filling, lining everything up about 1½ inches from the near edge of the sheet. You can let some of the veggies stick out the ends for an artistic presentation.
4. Grab the near edge and roll it up using a good amount of pressure to keep the roll as tight as possible. Work quickly so that it doesn't have time to wobble around. Dip your fingers in the water, wet the exposed 1-inch strip of nori, and keep rolling until that edge is on the bottom. Press firmly, and leave it with the seam side down while you move on to the other rolls.
5. When all four are rolled, start with the first roll and transfer it to a cutting board. Cut a diagonal line through the middle with a serrated knife, then cut straight lines halfway through each half. Set on plates and garnish with pickled ginger, wasabi, and soy sauce.

Chefs' Tips and Tricks

If the nori does tear, keep rolling, and then wrap it in another nori sheet. You may want to dab some water across the second sheet to get it to stick to the first one.

TERIYAKI TOFU

Teriyaki is comprised of two Japanese words—*teri,* meaning "luster," and *yaki*, meaning "grill" or "broil." The word is used liberally these days, especially in the West, and anything cooked in teriyaki sauce merits use of the name. Make a double batch of the sauce and save it for noodles or as a dipping sauce for Nori Rolls (page 157) or Tempura Vegetables (page 142).

SERVES 4

1 (14-ounce) package extra-firm tofu
½ cup thinly sliced green onions

TERIYAKI SAUCE

MAKES 1 CUP

½ cup soy sauce
½ cup mirin
2 teaspoons peeled and minced fresh ginger
2 cloves garlic, pressed or minced
2 teaspoons maple syrup or organic brown sugar
1 tablespoon toasted sesame oil
Pinch crushed red pepper flakes
2 teaspoons arrowroot powder dissolved in 1 tablespoon cold water

1. Preheat the oven to 375°F. Slice the tofu diagonally across the top to form two triangles. Cut each of these triangles into quarters, forming eight thin cutlets. Place them in a casserole dish.
2. Prepare the Teriyaki Sauce by combining all of the ingredients except the arrowroot mixture in a small sauté pan over medium heat and whisking well. Add the arrowroot mixture and cook until the sauce begins to thicken, approximately 3 minutes, stirring frequently. Pour the sauce over the tofu cutlets and bake in the oven for 15 to 20 minutes, flipping the cutlets halfway through.
3. Remove from the oven and top with green onions before serving.

Variation

- Replace the tofu with tempeh, seitan, portobello mushrooms, or your favorite veggies.

SESAME TOFU WITH WASABI CREAM SAUCE

This innovative dish is a variation of one that we have come to enjoy at a local eatery here on Kaua'i. You need to move pretty quickly to fit this into the 30-minute time frame, but we assure you, it can be done. Serve with a side of quinoa or rice. The cutlets can also be matched with another sauce, such as Teriyaki (page 159) or Korean BBQ (page 218).

MARINATED TOFU

1 (14-ounce) package extra-firm tofu
2 tablespoons soy sauce
1 tablespoon toasted sesame oil
1 tablespoon rice vinegar
2 tablespoons water

TAHINI SPREAD

3 tablespoons creamy tahini
1 tablespoon freshly squeezed lemon juice
3 tablespoons water
1 teaspoon soy sauce

SESAME COATING

½ cup sesame seeds (black, white, or a combination)
Pinch crushed red pepper flakes
⅛ teaspoon sea salt
⅛ teaspoon ground black pepper

WASABI CREAM SAUCE

2 cups soymilk
2 tablespoons wasabi powder
2 teaspoons mirin
2 teaspoons agave nectar, organic sugar, or sweetener of choice, or to taste
1½ tablespoons arrowroot powder dissolved in ½ cup cold water
2 teaspoons freshly squeezed lemon juice
½ teaspoon soy sauce, or to taste
½ teaspoon sea salt, or to taste
⅛ teaspoon ground black pepper

1. Preheat the oven to 350°F. Slice the tofu in half to form two blocks. Slice each block into four small cutlets. (Alternatively, you can slice the tofu on the diagonal to form two triangles and slice these triangles into four small triangle-shaped cutlets.) Add the remaining marinade ingredients to a small casserole dish, stir well, and add the tofu. Flip the tofu to ensure even coating. Place in the oven and bake for 10 minutes.
2. While the tofu is cooking, prepare the tahini spread by combining all of the ingredients in a small bowl and whisking well.
3. Prepare the sesame coating by combining all of the ingredients in a small bowl and mixing well. When the tofu is done cooking, spread a thin layer of the tahini spread on the top of each cutlet, coat well with the sesame seed mixture, and return to the oven for an additional 10 minutes. There is no need to drain off the marinade.
4. Place the soymilk in a saucepan over medium-low heat. Add the wasabi powder and whisk well. Add the mirin and agave and whisk well. When the sauce is hot (be careful not to boil) add the arrowroot mixture. Whisk well until the sauce thickens, about 4 minutes. Add the lemon, soy sauce, salt, and pepper and whisk well.
5. Place the cutlets on a plate or platter and drizzle with the sauce before serving.

Variations

- Try replacing the tofu with tempeh or veggies such as portobello mushrooms or eggplant.
- You can alter the coating in many ways. Replace the sesame seeds with an equal amount of your favorite nut or seed. Process in a food processor until coarsely ground. Add minced herbs, spices, or toasted coconut to form many innovative crusts.

TAMARI GINGER TOFU WITH GREEN ONION

This tofu dish is the height of simplicity, which is a good thing for the 30-minute kitchen. Use this recipe as a starting point for your exploration into the world of tofu. Tamari has a deeper and richer flavor than other types of soy sauce. (See the Box on page 163 to learn all you ever wanted to know about soy sauces.) Prepare a batch of the cutlets to have on hand for use in salads, wraps, or even as a snack with a dipping sauce such as Peanut Sauce (page 64), Ponzu Sauce (page 148), or Cilantro Pesto (page 181).

SERVES 3 TO 4

1 (14-ounce) package extra-firm tofu
2 tablespoons tamari or other soy sauce (see Box on page 163)
1 tablespoon rice vinegar, optional
¼ cup water
2 tablespoons peeled and minced fresh ginger
1 tablespoon sesame oil or toasted sesame oil
1 tablespoon freshly squeezed lemon or lime juice
2 teaspoons agave nectar or maple syrup
¼ cup plus 2 tablespoons thinly sliced green onions

1. Preheat the oven to 375°F. Slice the tofu in half to form two blocks. Slice each block into four small cutlets. (Alternatively, slice the tofu on the diagonal to form two triangles and slice these triangles into four small triangle-shaped cutlets.)
2. Place the remaining ingredients except 2 tablespoons of the green onions in a casserole dish and whisk well. Add the tofu cutlets and flip to coat both sides. If you have more time, allow the cutlets to marinate for 20 minutes or longer, flipping occasionally. If you are pressed for time, you can place the casserole dish in the oven immediately or after 5 or 10 minutes.
3. Bake for 20 minutes. You can flip the cutlets midway through if you wish. To serve, place them on a serving plate and top with a bit of marinade and green onions.

Variations

- Replace the sesame oil with olive or coconut oil.
- Add a dash of the Mediterranean by replacing the rice vinegar with balsamic vinegar.
- Add 1 tablespoon of Dijon or stone-ground mustard.
- Experiment with different soy sauces.

The Asian Pantry: Soy Sauce

Originating in China thousands of years ago, soy sauce is used throughout Asia and beyond.

Soy Sauce: Made by fermenting soy beans with a culture, many products sold as soy sauce contain preservatives, sugar, and other unwelcome ingredients. Check the label.

Shoyu: Since the 1600s the Japanese have produced a soy sauce called *shoyu.* Reputed to be of very high quality, shoyu is brewed with wheat as well as soybeans and has more of an alcohol flavor than tamari.

Tamari: A by-product of the miso making process, tamari can have some wheat in it but is also frequently marketed as a wheat-free variety of soy sauce. It is thicker, darker, and more strongly flavored than other soy sauces.

Nama Shoyu: Literally translates as "raw soy sauce"; this unpasteurized version is also made with wheat.

BROCCOLI AND RED BELL PEPPER SOBA

This colorful and simple dish uses soba noodles, another popular pasta in Japan. Serve cold or hot with a Japanese feast of Miso Simple Soup (page 136), Arame Lotus Root Sauté (page 147), and Peach Kanten (page 170).

SERVES 4

2 (8.8 ounces each) packages soba noodles
¾ cup water
4 cups small broccoli flowerets
1½ cups thinly sliced carrots
¼ cup toasted sesame oil
1 large red bell pepper, thinly sliced (2 cups)
2 cloves garlic, pressed or minced
¼ cup soy sauce
1 tablespoon mirin, optional
1 tablespoon freshly squeezed lime juice
½ teaspoon crushed red pepper flakes, or to taste
¼ cup chopped fresh cilantro
½ cup thinly sliced green onions
Sesame seeds

1. Cook the soba noodles according to the package's instructions. Transfer the soba to a colander and rinse with cold water to stop the cooking process. Drain well. Place in a large mixing bowl.
2. Meanwhile, place the water in a large sauté pan over medium-high heat. Add the broccoli and carrots and cook until all of the liquid is absorbed, stirring frequently, approximately 5 minutes. Lower the heat to medium, add 2 tablespoons of sesame oil, and stir well. Add the red bell pepper and garlic, and cook until all of the veggies are just tender, approximately 5 minutes.
3. Place 2 tablespoons of sesame oil, ¼ cup water, the soy sauce, the mirin, if using, lime juice, and crushed red pepper flakes in a small bowl and whisk well. Add half of this mixture to the soba noodles and toss well. Add the remaining half to the sauté pan with the vegetables and stir well.
4. To serve, place a portion of the soba noodles in a serving bowl. Top with some vegetables and garnish with the green onions, cilantro, and sesame seeds.

Variations

- Try replacing the broccoli with an equal quantity of cauliflower.
- Replace the carrots and red bell pepper with mushrooms, zucchini, yellow bell pepper, or summer squash.

PAN-SEARED SHIITAKE UDON BOWL

The pan-seared mushrooms add a delightful touch to this hardy noodle bowl. You may add whichever vegetables strike your fancy to the broth. Enjoy this dish as soon as it is prepared. The noodles will break apart if left in the water for long periods of time.

SERVES 4 TO 6

1 recipe Marinated Shiitake Mushrooms (recipe follows)
2 tablespoons toasted sesame oil
2 cloves garlic, pressed or minced
1 tablespoon peeled and minced fresh ginger
6 cups water or dashi (see page 136)
1 large carrot, sliced (1½ cups)
1 large tomato, chopped (1¼ cups)
6 ounces udon noodles
1½ cups chopped spinach or kale, tightly packed
1 tablespoon mirin
2 tablespoons soy sauce, or to taste
½ teaspoon sea salt, or to taste
¼ teaspoon ground black pepper, or to taste
¼ cup thinly sliced green onions

MARINATED SHIITAKE MUSHROOMS

8 medium-large shiitake mushrooms
2 tablespoons water
1 tablespoon soy sauce
1 tablespoon mirin
1 teaspoon toasted sesame oil

continues

1. Make the Marinated Shiitake Mushrooms: Place the mushrooms and all marinade ingredients in a shallow casserole dish and allow them to marinate for 15 minutes or longer. Toss occasionally to coat all of the mushrooms.
2. Meanwhile, place 1 tablespoon of the sesame oil in a large pot over medium-high heat. Add the garlic and ginger and cook for 1 minute, stirring constantly. Add the water, carrot, and tomato, and cook for 5 minutes, stirring occasionally.
3. Place 1 tablespoon of the sesame oil in a small sauté pan over high heat. Transfer the mushrooms to the pan, reserving the marinade. Cook the mushrooms, flipping occasionally, until they are cooked through and slightly browning, approximately 5 minutes. Place them and the marinade into the pot and mix well.
4. Add the udon noodles to the pot, mix well, and cook for 5 minutes, stirring occasionally. Add the remaining ingredients except the green onions and cook for 5 minutes, stirring frequently. Garnish with the green onions before serving. You can use as much or as little of the broth as desired.

Variations

- Add roasted tofu or tempeh cubes (see page 227).
- Change up the vegetables by replacing them with bok choy, shallots, zucchini, or cabbage.
- If you wish, you may grill the mushrooms instead of pan-searing them.

RAMEN NOODLE STIR-FRY

Ramen noodle packages are the favorite quick and easy meal of college students everywhere. Just add hot water and stir. It doesn't get much more simple than that! In our recipe we use authentic ramen noodles, fresh vegetables, and seasonings to take our stir-fry up to the next level. If all you can find is the instant Ramen soup packages, use only the noodles and leave out the flavoring packets when you follow this recipe. Substitute rice noodles if you are unable to find ramen. Serve with Miso Simple Soup (page 136) and Green Tea Chocolate Bon Bons (page 172).

SERVES 4 TO 6

4 ounces ramen noodles
3 tablespoons toasted sesame oil
1 yellow onion, sliced (1½ cups)
3 cloves garlic, pressed or minced
1½ tablespoons peeled and minced fresh ginger
5 large shiitake mushrooms, thinly sliced (about 1 cup)
8 ounces seitan, sliced
1 small daikon radish, thinly sliced (about 1 cup)
1 carrot, sliced
2 cups snow peas or sugar snap peas
1 red bell pepper, sliced
2 tablespoons mirin
3 tablespoons soy sauce
1 hot chile pepper, seeded and diced, or ¾ teaspoon crushed red pepper flakes
¼ cup sliced green onions
Black and white sesame seeds

1. Bring water to boil in a small pot. Add the ramen noodles and cook until just soft, approximately 5 minutes. Place in a colander, rinse with cold water, and drain well.
2. Meanwhile, place the sesame oil in a large sauté pan or wok over medium-high heat. Add the onion, garlic, ginger, and mushrooms, and cook for 3 minutes, stirring frequently. Add the seitan, daikon, and carrot and cook for 5 minutes, stirring frequently.
3. Add the ramen noodles, snow peas, and red bell pepper and cook for 5 minutes, stirring frequently. Add the remaining ingredients except the green onions and sesame seeds and stir well. Garnish with the green onions and sesame seeds before serving.

Variations

- Replace the seitan with cubed and roasted tofu or tempeh (see page 227).
- Replace the daikon with burdock root, parsnip, or carrots.
- Replace the seitan with 3 cups of assorted chopped vegetables such as zucchini, broccoli, and cabbage.

BRAISED TEMPEH WITH GREEN BEANS IN SESAME SAUCE

Get your tongs out for this hardy and satisfying way to enjoy tempeh. If you have a large enough sauté pan, you can prepare your main course and side dish in the same pan. Depending upon the consistency of the tahini used, you may need to adjust the water quantity. Serve with Arame Garlic Rice (page 153), and a mixed organic green salad with Orange Ginger Dressing (page 138).

SERVES 2 TO 4

2 tablespoons plus 2 cups water
2 tablespoons soy sauce
3 tablespoons freshly squeezed lemon juice
2 tablespoons toasted sesame oil
1 tablespoon mirin
8 ounces tempeh, sliced into quarters
1 pound green beans, ends trimmed off
¼ cup plus 3 tablespoons tahini
½ teaspoon sea salt, or to taste
¼ cup thinly sliced green onions
Sesame seeds

1. Place 2 tablespoons of the water, 1 tablespoon of soy sauce, 1 tablespoon of lemon juice, 1 tablespoon of the sesame oil, and the mirin in a shallow dish and whisk well. Add the tempeh and allow it to marinate for 5 minutes, flipping occasionally.
2. Place the remaining tablespoon of sesame oil in a large sauté pan over medium-high heat. Add the tempeh and the marinade, and cook for 5 minutes, gently flipping occasionally. Add the green beans and 1 cup of water, and cook until almost all of the water is dissolved and the green beans are a vibrant green, approximately 7 minutes, gently stirring frequently. Lower the heat to medium.
3. Place the remaining 1 cup of water, 1 tablespoon of soy sauce, 2 tablespoons of lemon juice, and the tahini in a small bowl and whisk well. Add to the pan and cook for 5 minutes, gently stirring the green beans and flipping the tempeh occasionally (be careful not to break up the tempeh). Add a little more water if necessary and adjust the salt to taste. Garnish with the green onions and sesame seeds before serving.

Variations

- Replace the tempeh with tofu, seitan, or portobello mushrooms.
- Replace the green beans with a vegetable of your choosing such as broccoli, zucchini, or carrots.
- If you don't have a large sauté pan, you can steam the green beans separately and add them before serving.

Chefs' Tips and Tricks

Braising is a cooking technique in which you sauté food at a high temperature to brown the outside, then simmer in liquid to cook through. The simmering can take place in a pan in the oven or on the stovetop.

PEACH KANTEN

Welcome to the Jell-O of the East! The sea vegetable agar works like gelatin and is popular throughout Asia. Called *kanten* in Japan, this dish varies in sweetness, depending on the juice and the types of fruit used. With chill time, it takes more than 30 minutes. Be sure to clear space before you begin. You can speed up the time by placing this dish in the freezer.

SERVES 10 TO 12

4 cups peach nectar, apple juice, or fruit juice of choice
3 tablespoons agar flakes (see Box below)
2 tablespoons agave nectar, maple syrup, or organic sugar, or to taste, optional
4 peaches, chopped small (approximately 3½ cups)

1. Bring the juice to a boil in a pot, and then lower the heat to low.
2. Add the agar flakes and cook until they are dissolved, approximately 10 minutes, whisking frequently. Add the agave, if using, and whisk well.
3. Meanwhile, place the chopped peaches in a 9 x 13-inch casserole dish. When the agar flakes have dissolved, pour the juice mixture into the casserole dish and place it in the refrigerator until firm, approximately 45 minutes. Cut into squares or fanciful shapes and eat as you would Jell-O.

Chefs' Tips and Tricks

Agar is a sea vegetable that can be found in stores in flaked or powdered form. It imparts a firming, gelatinous texture to dishes. When making kanten, the more acidic the juice, the more agar is needed for the juice to thicken. In general, 1 teaspoon of powdered agar is required to thicken 2 cups of neutral liquid. Six times the amount of flakes are necessary when using an acidic juice (2 tablespoons in this case). Agar is sometimes found in bar form as well. The bar will need to be broken into pieces, boiled with 3 cups of liquid, and simmered for about 15 minutes. Definitely purchase the powder or flakes if you have the option.

MOCHI TREATS

Mochi is a chewy Japanese rice cake made from sticky rice. It is traditionally served as part of the New Year celebration and enjoyed year round in various forms. This dish is called *daifuku* in Japanese. The mochi is stuffed with a sweet bean paste, called *anko,* made from azuki beans and is extremely popular in Japan.

MAKES 10 MOCHI TREATS

ANKO FILLING

¾ cup cooked azuki beans, drained, rinsed very well, and drained again
¼ cup agave nectar, organic sugar, or your favorite sweetener, to taste

Approximately ¼ cup anko filling
1¼ cups water
¼ cup plus 2 tablespoons organic sugar
¼ teaspoon sea salt
1½ cups mochi flour (mochiko)
Mochi flour for dusting

1. Prepare the anko filling by combining the ingredients in a food processor and processing until smooth. Set aside in a small bowl. There will be leftover paste, which you can store in the refrigerator for up to 3 days.
2. Prepare the mochi cake by placing the water, sugar, and salt in a pot over medium heat. Cook for a few minutes, stirring occasionally. Slowly add the mochi flour and stir constantly until all of the liquid is absorbed. Keep stirring for a few minutes more, kneading the dough. A wooden spoon works great for this. (Avoid using a whisk as you will be confronted with the arduous task of removing the sticky dough from the center of the whisk—we are speaking from experience!)
3. Transfer the dough to a clean cutting board dusted with mochi flour. Allow it to cool for 3 to 5 minutes. Place a small amount of mochi flour on a plate. Roll the dough out on the cutting board into a log approximately 2 inches in diameter. Slice the log into ten uniform pieces. Flatten each of the pieces into a small circle, add 1 teaspoon of the anko filling, fold in the sides, and roll into a ball. Dust with mochi flour before serving.

Variations

- For an American version, replace the anko paste with chocolate chips! Add a few chips to each mochi treat. Dust with cocoa powder.
- Replace the anko paste with small pieces of dried fruit, such as dates, apricots, or papaya.

GREEN TEA CHOCOLATE BON BONS WITH CRYSTALLIZED GINGER

These treats are the vegan bomb. Matcha is powdered green tea; it imparts a somewhat smoky flavor to the chocolate. The green tea is packed with antioxidants and gives an extra boost to the chocolate reverie.

MAKES 20 SMALL BON BONS

2 cups vegan chocolate chips
2 teaspoons matcha powder
2 tablespoons water
3 tablespoons agave nectar, maple syrup, or sweetener of choice, or to taste
½ cup tahini
¼ cup chopped crystallized ginger
Sesame seeds (optional)

1. Melt the chocolate chips by heating them in a double boiler over medium heat until the consistency is smooth, lump-free, and creamy, stirring only once or twice. (If you don't have a double boiler, you can place a glass or steel bowl on top of a pot with 1 to 2 inches of boiling water in it.)
2. Place the matcha powder and water in a small bowl and stir well until all of the powder is absorbed. When the chocolate is melted, transfer it to a large bowl with the remaining ingredients, including the matcha and water, and stir well.
3. Using a small scoop or a rounded tablespoon, form small balls or mini cookie shapes. Place on a parchment paper-lined or lightly-oiled baking sheet and top with sesame seeds, if using. Refrigerate until firm (approximately 15 minutes) or until you can't restrain yourself, whichever comes first.

Variations

- Replace the matcha powder and water with 2 bags of green tea steeped in 3 tablespoons of hot water for 15 minutes. Squeeze the tea bags to get maximum flavor.
- Replace the tahini with almond or peanut butter.
- Replace the crystallized ginger with ¼ cup toasted coconut flakes.
- Add ½ teaspoon ground cinnamon and ¼ teaspoon ground cardamom.

Note: This dish will come out sweeter if you use the more common semisweet chocolate chips, which contain cane sugar. Sunspire sells a variety that we prefer, which is grain-sweetened, but either one will work.

PICKLED GINGER

Most Japanese restaurants serve pickled ginger that is alarmingly pink. As you'll notice when you make this mouth-watering version, a pink color is the result of the salt-coated ginger interacting with the vinegar. But the color is slight, not neon, and the end result is far more akin to the natural color of ginger than most packaged varieties. Adding a few drops of beet juice can also give you the color if you so desire. Using a mandoline will yield the thinnest slices of ginger.

MAKES 2 CUPS

1 pound fresh young ginger, very thinly sliced
2 teaspoons sea salt
2 cups rice vinegar
1 cup agave nectar

1. In a medium bowl, combine the sliced ginger with the sea salt and let it sit on the counter for 1 hour.
2. Boil the vinegar and agave nectar together over medium heat. Stir in the ginger mixture and turn off the flame. Transfer to a sterilized jar and allow the mixture to cool. Refrigerate for at least one week for optimal flavor.

The Asian Pantry: Young Ginger

The glory of young ginger cannot be fully expressed. With a thin skin and a tender flavor, it is the ginger of choice when available. The organic variety of young ginger does not need to be peeled.

GOMASIO

The ubiquitous Japanese condiment is made from two ingredients—sesame seeds and salt. Use as a topping on salads, stir-fries, inside nori rolls or other wraps, and any time you wish to add a little salty pizzazz to a dish.

MAKES 1 CUP

1 cup sesame seeds
2 tablespoons sea salt

1. Toast the sesame seeds in a large dry sauté pan over medium-high heat until golden and fragrant, approximately 3 minutes, stirring frequently.
2. Add to a bowl with the salt and mix well. Place in a strong blender or spice grinder and pulse for a few seconds. Store in a shaker bottle for all your culinary needs.

Variations

- Vary the amount of salt, adding less or more depending upon your preference.
- Add the salt to the sauté pan with the sesame seeds.
- Some like it hot—add 2 teaspoons wasabi powder or to taste.
- Create a designer gomasio by adding dulse flakes or grated nori.

PART FIVE

 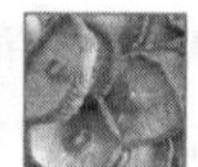 

Asian Fusion

From the heights of the Mighty Himalaya in Tibet to the plains of Uzbekistan, this section is devoted to the cuisine of a wide range of Asian countries. We share recipes from Korea, Indonesia, Vietnam, the Philippines, Tibet, Afghanistan, and Nepal. We also had a longing to include recipes from Central Asian countries such as Turkmenistan, Uzbekistan, and Iran.

In addition to our translations of traditional dishes, we include recipes that are inspired by the ingredients of Asia without being identified with any particular country–Asian Fusion.

Among these Asian-inspired creations are Lemon Rice, Asian Slaw, Coconut Mashed Parsnips, an Asian smoothie, and even Cilantro Pesto. Our selection of Korean recipes includes Pine Nut Porridge, Kim Chi, and a simple roasted barley tea. From Vietnam we share a recipe for the popular Pho Bo Noodle Soup and our version of Vietnamese Happy Pancakes. From Tibet we have the beloved momo (dumpling). Treasures from Indonesia include Gado Gado and Indonesian Coconut Tempeh.

We believe you will have as much fun making these somewhat esoteric dishes as we had developing them. We are trendsetting for the vegan scene in Uzbekistan, Turkmenistan, and Iran, creating vegan versions of popular traditional dishes. Check out the Uzbeki Chickpea Salad, Tajikistani Pilau Rice, and the Iranian Lima Bean and Dill recipes and spread the word!

The Asian Pantry

Asian Fruit: Though we stick to the more common Asian fruits in our recipes, such as pears, papayas, bananas, mangoes, and dates, the continent is most known for its more exotic gems. Try experimenting with starfruit, rambutans, persimmon, jack fruit, or yuzu when you see some available in your local market. Though rare and short-lived, most of these do come around when they are in season and can be substituted for the more common fruits listed in our recipes here. (And it never hurts to ask your grocer if you are interested in something specific.)

Cilantro/Coriander: *Cilantro* is the word used mostly in North and South America; the rest of the world's population refers to both the leaves and seeds of the plant as *coriander.* Frequently seen in Asian cooking, coriander leaves are usually added at the end of the cooking process to preserve their delicate flavor. The seeds, which are used in both sweet and savory foods, are sold whole or ground and impart a slight citrus flavor. A versatile herb, coriander is also referred to as Chinese parsley.

Cumin: Cumin ranks second behind black pepper as the most popular spice in the world. Cultivated and used throughout Asia, each region having its own word for it, cumin brings a deep warm flavor to dishes. Cumin resembles fennel and caraway seeds and is also sold ground.

Mung Beans: Popular throughout Asia, the mung bean is a versatile small green legume. It is used whole and split in dhals in India and Pakistan, as bean thread noodles in China, sprouted in Thailand, made into spring roll wrappers in Vietnam, and ground into pancakes in Korea. It also features prominently in the Philippines.

Peanuts: Generally eschewed in modern health circles, the humble peanut is used frequently in Asian cuisine—though we must mention that the peanuts commonly available to us in the West are a lot different than what is used in Asia. It is a common sight at Asian farmers' markets to see fresh and boiled peanuts. See the Box on page 64 for more exciting peanut information.

Pistachios: This tasty nut features prominently in Central Asian countries such as Iran. Pistachios are generally sold as a snack, salted and roasted in the shell. Many natural food stores carry them raw in bulk as well as roasted unsalted.

Saffron: The hand-picked stigma or the saffron crocus flower is the most precious and expensive spice in the world. Saffron imparts a bright orange-yellow color and an exotic flavor and aroma to dishes. It is found in many cuisines from around the world, including Central Asia, China, and India.

Tempeh: Originating in Indonesia, tempeh is a soybean product with more protein and fiber than tofu. It is made with whole soybeans that are cultured and formed into cakes. Tempeh needs to be thoroughly cooked before eating. There are many different flavors and varieties on the market. You can also make your own tempeh! Check out www.tempeh.info for all you need to know.

Turmeric: A relative of ginger, turmeric is smaller, bright orange-yellow, and more bitter than its well-known cousin, as well as far more extensively used. In addition to the dried powder commonly found in spice collections, turmeric is used in cosmetics, as a food additive and bug repellant, and as a dye. Turmeric is currently being widely studied for its significant healing properties.

ASIAN DREAM BOAT SMOOTHIE

We drink a whole lot of smoothies over here in Hawaii. So it is nice to switch them up by incorporating fresh, exotic, and taste-bud captivating flavors. Give this one a whirl and experience the Orient for breakfast with the widely used flavors of lime, ginger, and mango as well as the chiefly Indian spice cardamom and the popular Thai coconut milk.

MAKES 24 OUNCES

2 medium mangoes
2 medium bananas
½ cup coconut milk, optional
2 kaffir lime leaves or 1 tablespoon of freshly squeezed lime juice
1 teaspoon peeled and minced fresh ginger
½ teaspoon ground cardamom, optional

Place all of the ingredients in a blender, whirl together, and imbibe wholeheartedly.

Variations

- For a chilled smoothie you can either add 1 cup of ice, or refrigerate or freeze the fruit before preparing. Remember that bananas must be peeled before freezing. And fruits like mangoes, pineapple, or papaya should be peeled, seeded, and cubed. Store all fruits in airtight containers in the freezer.
- Replace the mango with 2 medium papayas or ½ of a pineapple.
- Add a handful of kale, chard, or spinach for a Green Asian Dream Smoothie.
- Replace the coconut milk with coconut water, apple juice, or your favorite fruit juice.

CILANTRO PESTO

Although pesto may have you thinking of gondolas and Michelangelo, this recipe has an Asian twist. It uses cilantro and sesame oil instead of the basil and olive oil you'd find in Italian pesto. Serve as a dipping sauce for crudités, a spread for wraps, part of the filling in Thai Summer Rolls (page 59), or spread on Hoisin Eggplant Cutlets (page 115).

MAKES ¾ CUP

2 bunches cilantro, coarsely chopped (2 cups)
1 hot chile pepper, seeded
2 large cloves garlic
2 tablespoons freshly squeezed lemon or lime juice
1 tablespoon peeled and minced fresh ginger
½ cup chopped cashews, toasted (see page 225)
3 tablespoons sesame oil
1 tablespoon toasted sesame oil
1 tablespoon soy sauce, or to taste

Place all of the ingredients in a food processor or strong blender and process until smooth. For a thinner consistency, add more oil. Adjust soy sauce to taste.

Variation

- For a ♥ live version, replace the cashews with macadamia nuts and omit the toasted sesame oil, or replace it with cold-pressed olive oil.

CABBAGE ROLLS WITH FIVE-SPICE PÂTÉ

Five-spice powder blends well with pepitas—Spanish for pumpkin seeds. These raw food rolls are wonderful on their own or served with sauces such as Mango Ginger Sauce (page 61) or Dim Sum Dipping Sauce (page 101). The pâté can be enjoyed on its own as a side for salads, or used as a spread on Green Onion Hotcakes (page 112). If you have more time, soaking the pumpkin seeds for up to two hours will produce a softer, more luxurious texture and flavor.

SERVES 6 TO 8

1 recipe Pepita Pâté (recipe follows)
6 to 8 thin slices avocado
6 to 8 thin slices tomato
6 to 8 thin slices cucumber
6 to 8 Chinese cabbage leaves

PEPITA PÂTÉ

1¼ cups pumpkin seeds
2 tablespoons freshly squeezed lime juice
2 tablespoons thinly sliced green onion
1 tablespoon peeled and minced fresh ginger
2 tablespoons minced fresh cilantro
2 teaspoons seeded and diced hot chile pepper
3 tablespoons sesame oil
¼ cup water
¾ teaspoon five-spice powder
½ teaspoon sea salt, or to taste
¼ teaspoon ground black pepper
2 tablespoons nutritional yeast
2 teaspoons nama shoyu

1. Place the pumpkin seeds in a large bowl with a few cups of water. Allow them to sit for 15 minutes, place in a colander, rinse, and drain well. If you have more time, soak the pumpkin seeds longer, up to 2 hours.
2. Meanwhile, prep the avocado, tomato, and cucumber. Rinse and pat dry the cabbage leaves.
3. When the pumpkin seeds have finished soaking, place them in a food processor with the remaining pâté ingredients and process until smooth.
4. Place a small amount of pâté in the center of each cabbage leaf. Add the avocado, tomato, and cucumber (or your desired fixings), wrap, and roll your way to lunch!

Variations

- Replace the cabbage with chard, collards, or lettuce. You can also use nori sheets. See page 158 for nori rolling instructions.
- Get creative with your fillings. Add grated carrots, daikon radish, or beet. Add sprouts of your choosing.
- Replace the pumpkin seeds with sunflower seeds.
- Create an Indian flare to the pâté by replacing the five-spice powder with 1½ teaspoons curry powder and 1 teaspoon cumin powder.

KALE AND SNOW PEAS

Kale salad is big around our house, decorated with all manner of seasonal goodies. Snow peas, ginger, and sesame oil bring a taste of China to the table. Massaging oil into the leaves helps break down the toughness, making it easier to love. Another option is to quickly toss the kale in boiling water for a few seconds. This is a good choice if you are serving the salad right away, though it won't be raw anymore.

SERVES 2 TO 4

1 lemon, juiced (about 2 tablespoons)
1 bunch curly kale, stems removed, torn in small pieces (about 8 cups)
1 tablespoon sesame or olive oil
1 cup snow peas
1 teaspoon peeled and grated fresh ginger
2 tablespoons soy sauce or Bragg's Liquid Aminos
1 to 2 teaspoons maple syrup or agave nectar
2 tablespoons minced sweet onion

1. Squeeze the lemon over the kale and add the oil. Rub the lemon juice and oil into the leaves of the kale for 1 to 2 minutes, until thoroughly coated. Set aside.
2. If you'd like the snow peas to be softer, blanch them by covering them with boiling water for about 20 seconds. You don't want them to get too soft, just take the rough edge off. Slice them into strips (it is okay if the peas come out) and add them to the kale.
3. Add the remaining ingredients and stir well. Serve immediately or refrigerate for up to 3 days.

Variations

- For some extra protein, color, and crunch, add 2 tablespoons of white sesame seeds along with the ingredients in step 3.
- If you are a fan of raw garlic, press or mince 2 cloves and add them along with the ingredients in step 3.
- The sweet crispiness of jicama is a great seasonal substitute for the snow peas.

ASIAN SLAW

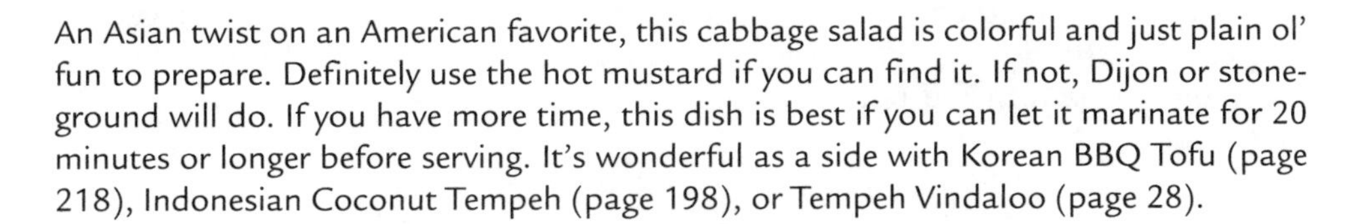

An Asian twist on an American favorite, this cabbage salad is colorful and just plain ol' fun to prepare. Definitely use the hot mustard if you can find it. If not, Dijon or stone-ground will do. If you have more time, this dish is best if you can let it marinate for 20 minutes or longer before serving. It's wonderful as a side with Korean BBQ Tofu (page 218), Indonesian Coconut Tempeh (page 198), or Tempeh Vindaloo (page 28).

SERVES 6

6 cups thinly sliced Chinese or napa cabbage
1½ cups thinly sliced purple cabbage
1 cup snow peas or sugar snap peas, thinly sliced
1 cup grated carrots
1 cup grated daikon
½ cup thinly sliced green onions
2 tablespoons minced fresh cilantro
1½ tablespoons peeled and minced fresh ginger
3 tablespoons sesame oil
1 tablespoon prepared hot mustard
1 tablespoon freshly squeezed lime juice
1 tablespoon rice vinegar
1 tablespoon plus 1 teaspoon soy sauce, or to taste
2 teaspoons seeded and diced hot chile pepper
2 teaspoons toasted sesame oil
1 kaffir lime leaf, optional, or ½ teaspoon lime zest
¾ teaspoon five-spice powder, optional

1. Place the Chinese cabbage, purple cabbage, snow peas, carrots, daikon, green onions, cilantro, and ginger in a large bowl and mix well.
2. Place the sesame oil, hot mustard, lime juice, rice vinegar, soy sauce, chile pepper, toasted sesame oil, kaffir lime leaf, if using, and five-spice powder, if using, in a blender and blend well. Add to the bowl and toss well.

COCONUT MASHED PARSNIPS

Creamy and somewhat sweet, steamed parsnips are combined with coconut milk and a hint of chile pepper to create this Asian Fusion dish. Parsnips are a starchy vegetable that has deep flavor. For a gourmet presentation serve with Toasted Sesame Roasted Vegetables (page 155) and Teriyaki Tofu (page 159).

SERVES 4

2 large parsnips, chopped small (4 cups)
1 tablespoon sesame oil
¼ cup diced shallots
2 cloves garlic, pressed or minced
2 teaspoons seeded and diced chile peppers
1 cup coconut milk
¾ teaspoon sea salt, or to taste

1. Place 1 inch of water in a pot and position a steamer basket inside. Add the parsnips and steam over medium heat until the parsnips are just soft, approximately 10 minutes.
2. Meanwhile, place the sesame oil in a small sauté pan over medium heat. Add the shallots, garlic, and chile pepper and cook for 3 minutes, stirring frequently. Lower the heat to low and add the coconut milk and salt and mix well. Cook for 5 minutes.
3. When the parsnips are done cooking, add them to the sauté pan with the coconut milk and salt and gently mash well with a fork, the bottom of a strong whisk, or a potato masher.

Variations

- Replace the parsnips with potatoes, yams, or squash.
- For **Wasabi Mashed Parsnips**, add 1 to 1½ teaspoons wasabi powder to the coconut milk.

LEMON RICE

Most Asian cultures serve rice at nearly every meal, with every region having its specialty pilafs. We find that seasoned grain dishes are a simple way to dress up dinner. With just a little more effort, the whole meal is elevated. Change around the spices and add diced vegetables that suit your meal. Although you might think the lemon is what makes the rice yellow, the color really comes from the turmeric.

SERVES 4 TO 6

2 cups white basmati rice or jasmine rice
3½ cups water or vegetable stock (see page 228)
1 tablespoon brown mustard seeds
1 tablespoon sesame or toasted sesame oil
¼ teaspoon turmeric powder
10 curry leaves (see Note on page 6)
½ medium red onion, chopped small
1 teaspoon sea salt, or to taste
2 tablespoons minced fresh parsley
2 tablespoons freshly squeezed lemon juice, or to taste

1. Place the rice and water in a pot over high heat and bring to a rapid boil. Cover and simmer over low heat for 15 minutes or until most of the water is absorbed and the rice is soft.
2. Meanwhile, in a dry sauté pan over medium heat, toast the mustard seeds for 2 minutes or until they are popping a lot with a toasty aroma. Add the oil, turmeric, and curry leaves and sauté for 1 to 2 more minutes. Add the red onion and salt and sauté until the onion is soft.
3. When the rice is done, toss it in a bowl with the onion mixture until the rice is evenly coated. Add the parsley and lemon juice to taste. Serve immediately.

ASIAN CHOCOLATE PARFAIT

As we approached the end of our recipe development, we realized we were a little underrepresented in the chocolate department. In response, we include this Asian Fusion chocolate sensation. Agar flakes are used to thicken the coconut layer, but if you are unable to find this ingredient you can use the sweetened coconut milk as a sauce. If you want to take it to the next level, top each parfait with some Mango Custard Pudding (page 130). To fit this dish into a 30-minute time frame, we place the parfaits in the freezer to chill. Make sure you have space available!

MAKES 6 PARFAITS

LE CHOCOLATE LAYER

1½ cups chocolate chips (see Note on page 172)
1¼ cups soft silken tofu
1 tablespoon maple syrup, agave nectar, or sweetener of choice, to taste
1 teaspoon vanilla extract, preferably alcohol-free
¼ teaspoon ground cinnamon
⅛ teaspoon ground cardamom
Pinch ground anise or allspice

LE COCONUT LAYER

1 (14-ounce) can coconut milk
3 tablespoons agave nectar, or sweetener of choice, to taste
1 tablespoon agar flakes

ACCOUTREMENTS

Fresh berries
Mint leaves

1. Melt the chocolate chips by heating them in a double boiler over medium heat until the chips are glossy and the consistency is smooth, lump-free, and creamy, stirring only once or twice. (If you don't have a double boiler, you can place a glass or steel bowl on top of a pot with 2 inches of boiling water in it.) Place the remaining Chocolate Layer ingredients in the food processor.
2. Meanwhile, place the coconut milk and agave in a small sauté pan over medium-high heat and bring to a low boil. Add the agar flakes, lower the heat to low and simmer until the agar completely dissolves, approximately 7 minutes, whisking frequently. Remove from the heat. Stir periodically while you prepare the chocolate layer.
3. Add the melted chocolate chips to the food processor and process until smooth. Pour into 6 parfait glasses.
4. Pour the coconut mixture on top of the chocolate layer and place them in the freezer until firm, approximately 12 minutes. Garnish with fresh berries and mint leaves before serving.

Note: This dish will come out sweeter if you use the more common semi-sweet chocolate chips, which use cane sugar. We prefer a variety made by Sunspire that is grain-sweetened, but either one will work.

Variations

- For a soy-free version, replace the tofu with ripe avocado and adjust the sweetener to taste.
- If you have more time, you can place the parfaits in the refrigerator to chill.

VIETNAMESE HAPPY PANCAKES

Traditionally served with fresh mint and basil, these savory pancakes are fun and so simple to whip up once you get the hang of it. The more creative you get with the topping, the happier these pancakes make you! Pancake + topping = delightful dinner. So use what you love, what you have on hand, or whatever entices you at the market in place of the prescribed ingredients; the instructions will be much the same. You can cook the toppings or leave them raw, use fruit and sweet sauces, or even just eat the pancakes plain! They're also delightful with the traditional Nuoc Cham dipping sauce (see page 192).

MAKES 4 SMALL OR 2 LARGE PANCAKES

PANCAKE

¾ cup brown rice flour
½ teaspoon sea salt
¼ teaspoon turmeric powder
1 cup water
¼ cup thinly sliced green onions
1 tablespoon oil for coating the pan

TOPPING

1 teaspoon sesame oil
1 clove garlic, pressed or minced
½ medium yellow onion, sliced into thin quarter moons
¼ teaspoon sea salt
2 cups thinly sliced mushrooms
2 cups thinly sliced napa cabbage
Handful mung bean sprouts

1. For the pancake batter, whisk together the flour, salt, and turmeric. Add the water and mix well. Fold in the green onions and set the mixture aside for 15 minutes, during which time it will thicken slightly.
2. Meanwhile, prepare the topping by heating the oil in a sauté pan over medium heat. Add the garlic, onion, and salt and sauté for 1 to 2 minutes to soften the onion. Add the mushrooms and continue to sauté until the mushrooms are soft and juicy, about 5 minutes. Add the cabbage, stir, and cook for 1 more minute before removing from the heat. Mix in the mung sprouts and set aside, near your stove.
3. Heat a skillet or griddle until it is piping hot and brush on a very light coating of oil. (You can test it to see if it's ready by sprinkling it with a little water. If the water sizzles, you're ready to go.) Stir up the batter again and pour ⅓ cup onto the skillet in a very thin layer (if you use a griddle you can cook all four at once). Layer the toppings on top, and allow the pancake about 5 minutes to cook. It is ready when it is crispy and the edges turn brown (you can also use a spatula to peek underneath). Serve them open-faced like they are in the pan.

Variations

- Other savory topping options include thinly sliced collard greens or kale. Arugula, mustard greens, and shredded carrots also work well. If you have some squash or sweet potato already cooked in your fridge, slice it up and use it here.
- Try adding other minced fresh herbs into the pancake batter, such as parsley, chives, tarragon, oregano, or thyme.
- Be efficient and resourceful by using some leftovers as the topping.
- You can also try sweet happiness using strawberries, sliced bananas, apples, pears, or mangoes. Omit the green onion and turmeric and reduce the salt to a pinch. Top with a sprinkle of powdered sugar or maple syrup. Go even further with some chocolate or caramel sauce. There are even some really nice vegan whipped creams out there these days.

NUOC CHAM

The quintessential Vietnamese dipping sauce. Use it to dip everything from crudités to Tempura Vegetables (page 142) to Thai Summer Rolls (page 59) and beyond.

MAKES ¾ CUP

¼ cup soy sauce, tamari, or Bragg's Liquid Aminos
2 tablespoons rice vinegar
2 tablespoons water
¼ cup freshly squeezed lime juice
½ teaspoon crushed red pepper flakes
1 clove garlic, pressed or minced

Combine all of the ingredients in a small bowl and serve immediately or store in an airtight container in the refrigerator for up to a week.

VIETNAMESE SEITAN AND NOODLE DISH (PHO BO)

A popular dish in Vietnam, pho bo involves noodles, a brothy soup with vegetables, and typically an animal product. Star anise, a beautiful spice (shaped like a star), adds a subtle flavor to the broth. Serve with Vietnamese Happy Pancakes (page 190).

SERVES 6 TO 8

14 ounces rice noodles
2 tablespoons sesame oil
1 tablespoon coriander seeds
1 cup diced yellow onions
8 ounces seitan, chopped
½ cup diced shallots, or another ½ cup diced onion
2 tablespoons peeled and minced fresh ginger
3 cloves garlic, peeled and minced, optional
1 hot chile pepper, seeded and diced
5 large mushrooms, sliced (try shiitake, oyster, or cremini)
6 cups water or vegetable stock (see page 228)
4 whole star anise
2 cups sliced greens (try kale, spinach, collards, or mustard greens)
2 tablespoons soy sauce, or to taste
2 tablespoons minced fresh cilantro
1 teaspoon sea salt
A few drops liquid smoke
Mung bean sprouts
Cilantro leaves

1. Cook the pasta according to the package's instructions. Place in a colander, rinse well with cold water, and drain well.
2. Meanwhile, place the sesame oil in a large pot over medium-high heat. Add the coriander seeds, onion, and seitan and mix well. Add the shallots, ginger, garlic, chile pepper, and mushrooms and cook for 5 minutes, stirring frequently.
3. Add the water and star anise and cook for 10 minutes, stirring occasionally. Add the greens and the remaining ingredients except the mung bean sprouts and cilantro leaves, and cook for 5 minutes, stirring occasionally.
4. Remove the star anise and show your guests how cool they look. To serve, place the noodles in each dish. Top with the vegetables and broth. Garnish with the mung sprouts and cilantro leaves.

INDONESIAN COCONUT RICE (NASI UDUK)

This dish packs a punch of flavor and boasts a winning combination of rice, coconut milk, lemongrass, and hot chiles. Serve as a side with Indonesian Seitan Satay (page 195), Tofu Tikka Masala (page 33), or Loving Jungle Princess (page 72).

SERVES 6 TO 8

4 lemongrass stalks, bottoms and outer stalks removed
2 cups white basmati rice
1 (14-ounce) can coconut milk
1¾ cups water
1¾ teaspoons sea salt, or to taste
1 tablespoon sesame oil
3 cloves garlic, pressed or minced
2 tablespoons peeled and minced fresh ginger
1 cup thinly sliced green onions
1 teaspoon ground cloves
¼ teaspoon crushed red pepper flakes, or to taste
½ cup shredded unsweetened coconut
or coconut flakes, toasted (see page 225)

1. Crush the lemongrass by lightly pounding it with a wooden spoon or other heavy object. Place them in a large pot with rice, coconut milk, water, and salt, and bring to a boil over high heat. Lower the heat to simmer, cover, and cook until all of the liquid is absorbed, approximately 15 minutes. Remove from the heat.
2. Meanwhile, place the sesame oil in a large sauté pan over medium heat. Add the garlic, ginger, and green onions and cook for 3 minutes, stirring frequently. Add the remaining ingredients except the toasted coconut and cook for 2 minutes, stirring frequently.
3. When the rice is done cooking, combine all of the ingredients except the toasted coconut in a large mixing bowl and gently mix well. Remove the lemongrass stalks and garnish with toasted coconut before serving.

Variations

- Add 2 cups diced vegetables, such as red bell peppers, mushrooms, or celery, to the sauté pan along with the green onions.
- Replace the basmati rice with brown rice, or even with quinoa. Use 2 cups of quinoa and 4 cups of total liquid for this recipe.

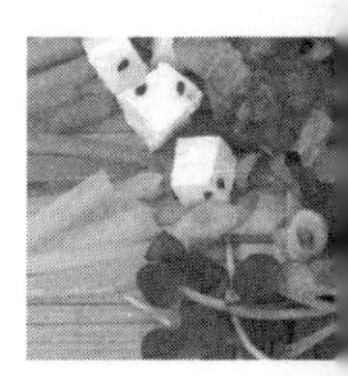

INDONESIAN SEITAN SATAY

Originating in Indonesia and making its way across Southeast Asia, satay is a popular dish across all borders. Typically served on skewers with a spicy dipping sauce, our version replaces the meat with marinated seitan. Turmeric is traditionally used to impart a yellow color to the dish. Serve as part of an appetizer sampler with Samosas (page 7), Thai Summer Rolls (page 59), and Steamed Wontons (page 99).

MAKES 4 APPETIZER PORTIONS

1 (8-ounce) package seitan
1 tablespoon sesame or peanut oil
1 cup sliced yellow onions
2 cloves garlic, pressed or minced
⅛ teaspoon turmeric powder
2 teaspoons soy sauce
2 teaspoons rice vinegar
1 cup or more Peanut Sauce (page 196)
4 bamboo or other skewers

1. Slice the seitan into approximately sixteen equal pieces.
2. Heat the oil in a sauté pan over medium-high heat. Add the onions and garlic and cook for 2 minutes, stirring frequently. Add the seitan and turmeric and cook for 10 minutes, stirring occasionally. Add the soy sauce and vinegar, stir well, and lower the heat to low.
3. Prepare the peanut sauce by following the instructions on page 197. Pour into a small bowl.
4. Place four pieces of seitan on each skewer and serve with the sauce. You can serve the onions alongside the skewers or place some on top of each skewer.

Variations

- Try grilling the seitan and the onion.
- Replace the seitan with marinated and roasted tempeh or tofu (see page 227).
- Add 1-inch slices of red, green, and yellow bell pepper, as well as mushrooms, and create the kebab of your dreams!

INDONESIAN GADO GADO

Gado gado is a traditional Indonesian dish, typically including a mixture of cooked and raw vegetables served with a peanut sauce dressing. The sauce is quite versatile. We use it for Indonesian Seitan Satay (page 195) and as a dipping sauce for Thai Summer Rolls (page 59). Try it as a sauce for your next stir-fry or soba dish (see page 164).

SERVES 6

8 cups assorted vegetables—try green beans, potato, cabbage, carrots, cauliflower, or your faves

1 cucumber, sliced

1 tomato, large slices

½ cup thinly sliced green onions

PEANUT SAUCE

MAKES 2½ CUPS SAUCE

1 tablespoon sesame or peanut oil

3 tablespoons minced shallots or onion

2 cloves garlic, pressed or minced

2 teaspoons peeled and minced fresh ginger

1 teaspoon seeded and diced jalapeño or other hot pepper

1 cup coconut milk

¾ cup water

1 cup crunchy peanut butter

2 teaspoons Fish-Free Sauce, optional (page 85)

1 tablespoon maple syrup, organic brown sugar, or sweetener of choice

1 tablespoon plus 1 teaspoon soy sauce, or to taste

1½ teaspoons tamarind paste (see Box on page 197) or 1 tablespoon freshly squeezed lime juice

½ teaspoon sea salt, or less if using Fish-Free Sauce

Crushed red pepper flakes to taste

1. Place 1 inch of water in a pot with a steamer basket over medium-high heat. Steam the vegetables until just soft. Arrange them on a plate with the cucumber and tomato slices.
2. To prepare the peanut sauce, place the oil in a pot over medium heat. Add the shallots, garlic, ginger, and jalapeño and cook for 3 minutes, stirring frequently. Lower the heat to low and add the remaining ingredients, stirring occasionally. Pour the sauce into a bowl and serve warm alongside the veggies. Garnish each serving wth the green onions or add them to the peanut sauce.

Variations

- Add grilled or roasted tempeh or tofu to the veggie plate (see page 227).
- Replace the peanut butter with almond butter.

The Asian Pantry

Tamarind is available as a paste, pulp, and—in some markets—fresh pods. Tamarind sauces are also available, but these will contain added ingredients. Check with your local grocer to see if tamarind is available to you or could be ordered. Otherwise check out the Resource Section in Appendix C for Web sites that sell tamarind products. See the food pantry on page 2 for more information.

INDONESIAN COCONUT TEMPEH

This is a decadent dish wherein the tempeh is first marinated and roasted and then stewed in creamy coconut milk and spices. YUM! For best results, toast the dried coconut that is used to garnish the dish. Serve with quinoa and a side of Indonesian Tamarind Vegetables with Lemongrass (page 199). The sauce actually makes enough for another 8 ounces of tempeh. If you wish to use more tempeh, just add an extra tablespoon of soy sauce and ¼ cup more water.

SERVES 2 TO 6

TEMPEH MARINADE

1 pound tempeh
Zest of 1 lemon
3 tablespoons freshly squeezed lemon juice
3 tablespoons soy sauce
¼ cup water

INDONESIAN COCONUT SAUCE

1½ teaspoons ground coriander
1 tablespoon sesame or peanut oil
¾ cup sliced onions
2 garlic cloves, pressed or minced
1 to 2 teaspoons seeded and diced hot chile pepper
1 (14-ounce) can coconut milk
2 bay leaves
2 teaspoons agave nectar, organic sugar, or sweetener to taste
½ teaspoon ground nutmeg
Pinch of ground cinnamon
¼ teaspoon sea salt, or to taste
¼ cup shredded unsweetened coconut, optionally toasted (see page 225)

1. Preheat the oven or toaster oven to 350°F. Slice the tempeh into eight cutlets. Pour the remaining marinade ingredients onto a small baking sheet (the one that fits in the toaster oven works fine) or casserole dish. Add the tempeh and flip to coat evenly. Place in the oven and bake for 10 minutes.
2. Meanwhile, place the coriander in a large sauté pan over medium-high heat. Stir constantly for 1 minute. Add the oil, onions, garlic, and chile pepper and cook for 3 minutes, stirring frequently. Add the coconut milk and the remaining sauce ingredients except the shredded coconut, stir well, and lower the heat to low.
3. When the tempeh is done cooking, add the cutlets to the sauce. Cook over low heat for 10 minutes, stirring occasionally. Remove the bay leaves and top with shredded coconut before serving.

INDONESIAN TAMARIND VEGETABLES WITH LEMONGRASS

This is a light and tangy dish with delicate flavors. It can be adapted to use whatever vegetables are fresh and available. Serve as a side with Lemon Rice (page 187) and Kung Pao Tempeh (page 123).

SERVES 4 TO 6

2 carrots, sliced
1 parsnip, sliced
2 zucchini, thick slices
1 yellow squash, thick slices
¼ cup minced lemongrass (white and yellow portion only)
1 tablespoon tamarind paste or 2 tablespoons freshly squeezed lime juice
¾ cup water
1 tablespoon agave nectar, maple syrup, or sweetener of choice
2 tablespoons sesame oil
2 tablespoons soy sauce
½ teaspoon crushed red pepper flakes
2 tablespoons minced fresh cilantro
½ teaspoon sea salt, or to taste
¼ teaspoon ground black pepper, or to taste
¼ cup thinly sliced green onions

1. Place the carrots and parsnips in a steamer basket and steam for a few minutes. Add the zucchini and squash and steam until the vegetables are just tender, approximately 5 minutes. Transfer to a mixing bowl.
2. Place the remaining ingredients except the green onions in a strong blender and blend well. Pour over the vegetables and gently mix well. Garnish with green onions before serving.

Variations

- Replace the vegetables with 6 to 8 cups of assorted chopped vegetables, such as broccoli, cauliflower, potatoes, yams, kale, or your favorites.
- Add marinated and roasted tofu or tempeh cubes (see page 227).

Chefs' Tips and Tricks

When steaming vegetables, place the hardier vegetables in the steamer first. Add softer vegetables later in the steaming process.

TIBETAN DUMPLINGS (MOMOS)

"Momos" to those in the know, these delightful dumplings are an extremely popular dish in the Tibetan community. They can be steamed, baked, or fried as you wish. For steaming, we recommend using a bamboo steamer. Serve with soy sauce or a dipping sauce such as Dim Sum Dipping Sauce (page 101), Mango Ginger Sauce (page 61), or Sweet and Sour Sauce (page 103). It is a bit of a stretch to finish this recipe within 30 minutes, but give it your best shot and you will come close.

MAKES 6 LARGE MOMOS

FILLING

2 tablespoons sesame oil
½ cup diced yellow onion
1 tablespoon peeled and minced fresh ginger
2 cloves garlic, pressed or minced
½ cup diced mushrooms
½ cup diced cabbage
½ cup grated extra-firm tofu (see page 226)
2 teaspoons soy sauce
¼ to ½ teaspoon crushed red pepper flakes
¼ teaspoon sea salt

DOUGH

1¼ cups whole wheat pastry flour, unbleached white flour, or white spelt flour
¼ teaspoon sea salt
¼ to ½ cup water

1. Place the sesame oil in a small sauté pan over medium-high heat. Add the onion, ginger, garlic, and mushrooms and cook for 5 minutes, stirring frequently. Add the remaining filling ingredients and cook for 5 minutes, stirring frequently. Remove from the heat.
2. Place the flour and salt in a bowl and mix well. Add the water and mix well, forming it into a dough. Knead the dough for a few minutes and place on a clean, lightly floured surface. Dough should be slightly moist and flexible. Roll into a log about 12 inches long.

3. Place a bamboo or lightly oiled steel steamer basket in a large pot with 1 inch of water and bring to a boil. Cut the dough into six pieces. Roll each piece to form a very thin 6-inch diameter circle. Place 1 heaping tablespoon of the filling in the center of the circle. Fold in half to form a semicircle and pinch the edges to seal tightly.
4. Place each dumpling in the steamer basket and steam for 7 minutes. Make sure the dumplings are not touching as they have a tendency to stick together. Serve warm.

Variations

- Sauté the dumplings in a high-heat oil such as safflower until crisp on both sides.
- You can bake the dumplings by placing them on a well-oiled baking sheet and baking for 15 minutes in a 400°F oven.
- For a quicker version, replace the dough with wonton wrappers or gyoza wrappers (see page 91).

East Meets West: Tibet

Controversially a part of China since the 1950s, Tibet sits at 16,000 feet above sea level and is thus the highest inhabited region on Earth. Known for centuries as the crossroads of Asia, Tibet became a household word in the United States in 1997 when two movies were released within months of each other. *Seven Years in Tibet* stars Brad Pitt as an Austrian mountaineer, and *Kundun* (directed by Martin Scorsese) chronicles the life of the Fourteenth Dalai Lama.

The Fourteenth Dalai Lama (known in the West simply as *the* Dalai Lama) has managed to become an extremely highly regarded international ambassador of peace and compassion. Though he is the spiritual leader of the Tibetan Buddhist religion, he promotes harmony among all religions. His name is familiar throughout the West due to his many speaking engagements, television appearances, and the somewhat popular Free Tibet campaign with its flags and bumper stickers.

TIBETAN NOODLE SOUP (THENTHUK)

Thenthuk is a hardy soup in which the "noodles" are actually small pieces of dough. It will definitely keep you warm and happy in the high Himalayas. Create your own designer thenthuk by adding what's fresh in your garden. Serve with a warm cup of Korean Toasted Barley Tea (page 219).

SERVES 4 TO 6

"NOODLES"

¾ cup spelt flour
¼ teaspoon sea salt
3 tablespoons water

SOUP BASE

6 cups water or vegetable stock (see page 228)
1 small onion, chopped
4 cloves garlic, chopped
1 hot chile pepper, seeded and diced, or 3 dried red chiles
1 tomato, chopped
2 cups small cauliflower flowerets
1 cup chopped cabbage
3 tablespoons soy sauce
1 teaspoon sea salt, or to taste
2 cups chopped kale or spinach
2 tablespoons minced fresh cilantro

1. Make the "noodles": place the flour and salt in a bowl and mix well. Add the water and mix well, forming it into a dough.
2. Place the water in a large pot over medium-high heat. Add the remaining soup ingredients except the kale and cilantro and bring to a boil, stirring occasionally. Lower the heat to medium and cook until the cauliflower is just soft.
3. Pinch off small pieces of the dough, flatten with your fingers, and add them to the soup. Cook for 5 minutes, stirring occasionally. Add the kale and cilantro, cook for 2 minutes longer, and mix well before serving.

Variations

- Replace the vegetables with potatoes, broccoli, squash, carrots, zucchini, or mushrooms.
- Try adding roasted tofu or tempeh cubes (see page 227).

NEPALESE DHAL BHAT

Mark feasted daily on local versions of this rural Nepal staple during his trek in the Himalayas. It typically consists of lentils and whatever vegetables happen to be available. It is served with rice and makes a filling and grounding meal. To prepare this dish in 30 minutes, start on the lentils before you begin chopping any vegetables.

SERVES 6

2 tablespoons sesame oil
2 teaspoons cumin seeds
1½ teaspoons coriander seeds
¾ cup red lentils or split mung beans
5 cups water or vegetable stock (see page 228)
1 yellow onion, diced (1¼ cups)
1½ tablespoons peeled and minced fresh ginger
3 to 4 garlic cloves, chopped
1 tablespoon seeded and diced hot chile pepper
1 cup chopped cauliflower flowerets
1 carrot, thinly sliced
1 cup chopped cabbage
1 tomato, chopped
2 teaspoons tamarind paste or 1 tablespoon freshly squeezed lemon or lime juice
2 teaspoons sea salt, or to taste
1 tablespoon soy sauce, or to taste
3 tablespoons minced fresh cilantro

1. Place the sesame oil in a large pot over medium-high heat. Add the cumin seeds and coriander seeds and stir well. Add the lentils and water and stir well.
2. Add the remaining ingredients except the salt, soy sauce, and cilantro, and cook until the lentils are soft, approximately 20 minutes.
3. Add the salt, soy sauce, and cilantro, and mix well before serving.

continues

Variations

- Replace the red lentils with green lentils or mung beans. Add more water, and adjust spices as necessary.
- Replace the vegetables with your favorites, such as zucchini, broccoli, mushrooms, kale, or spinach.

Chefs' Tips and Tricks

One of our favorite dishes is kitchari, which consists of a grain and a legume cooked together in the same pot with a good amount of water over medium heat. To create your own, add 1 cup of lentils or mung beans and 1 cup of rice or quinoa to a pot with 6 or more cups of water or vegetable stock. Add a few cups of chopped vegetables, a few tablespoons of minced herbs, and salt and pepper to taste. Cook until the grain and legume are thoroughly cooked. Add more water if necessary as you go. Depending upon the legume and grain, it may take over 30 minutes to cook. It's so worth it! Kitchari takes moments of your time to prepare, and a healthy and balanced meal is your reward.

AFGHANI EGGPLANT WITH TOMATO (BONJAN SALAD)

It's all the rage in Kabul, and now you can experience this Afghani treasure for yourself. Resembling an Italian ratatouille with its eggplant and tomato combination, bonjan salad includes mint and cinnamon for a tantalizing twist. You can turn this into a 30-minute dish by reducing or eliminating the eggplant "sweat time," though the longer the eggplant sweats, the less bitter it will be. Create a fusion meal and serve warm or cold with Persian Rice (page 210) and Braised Tempeh with Green Beans (page 168).

SERVES 4 TO 6

1 large eggplant
1 tablespoon plus 1 teaspoon sea salt, or to taste
2 tablespoons sesame oil
1 small yellow onion, sliced (1¼ cups)
2 cloves garlic, pressed or minced
1 hot chile pepper, seeded and diced
2 tomatoes, chopped (2 cups)
1 tablespoon tomato paste
¼ teaspoon ground black pepper, or to taste
2 tablespoons minced fresh mint
2 teaspoons ground cinnamon

1. Cut the eggplant into 1-inch cubes (makes about 6 cups) and place in a large casserole dish. Sprinkle with salt, allow it to sit for 15 minutes, and rinse well.
2. Meanwhile, place the sesame oil in a large sauté pan over medium heat. Add the onion, garlic, and chile pepper and cook for 5 minutes, stirring occasionally. Increase the heat to medium-high, add the eggplant, cover, and cook until the eggplant is soft, approximately 15 to 20 minutes, stirring frequently and adding water as necessary to prevent sticking. Add the tomatoes and the remaining ingredients and cook for 5 minutes, stirring frequently.

FILIPINO MONGO (MUNG BEAN STEW)

Mongo is a popular dish in the Philippines that makes use of the humble and highly nutritious mung bean. We are quite sure that you will not find this dish served with tofu pups in Manila, though we feel it makes a great replacement for the animal product typically included. The mung beans take closer to 35 minutes to cook. If you're looking for a 30-minute dish, replace the mung beans with a can of your favorite cooked beans, such as azuki or black. Even though this dish does go over the 30-minute time frame, we wanted to include it because of its popularity in the Philippines and the highly nutritious nature of the mung beans.

SERVES 6

6 cups water or vegetable stock (see page 228)
½ cup mung beans, rinsed well
2 tablespoons coconut or sesame oil
1 yellow onion, sliced (1¼ cups)
3 cloves garlic, pressed or minced
1 hot chile pepper, seeded and diced
6 large shiitake mushrooms, sliced
4 ounces seitan or vegan hot dogs, sliced
1 large tomato, chopped
1½ cups thinly sliced kale or spinach, tightly packed
3 tablespoons soy sauce, or to taste
Pinch crushed red pepper flakes
2 tablespoons Fish-Free Sauce, optional (page 85)
Few drops liquid smoke, optional

1. Place the water and mung beans in a medium pot over high heat. Bring to a boil. Lower the heat to medium and cook until the mung beans are soft, approximately 35 minutes.
2. Meanwhile, place the coconut oil in a sauté pan over medium-high heat. Add the onion, garlic, chile pepper, and shiitake mushrooms and cook for 5 minutes, stirring frequently. Add the seitan and tomatoes and cook for 5 minutes, stirring frequently. Remove from the heat.
3. When the mung beans are done cooking, add the contents of the sauté pan and the remaining ingredients to the pot with the mung beans and mix well before serving.

Variation

- Combine all of the ingredients except the soy sauce, salt, Fish-Free Sauce, if using, and cilantro in a large pot over medium heat and cook until the mung beans are soft. Add the remaining ingredients and mix well before serving.

If You Have More Time

For maximum digestibility, it's recommended to soak the mung beans for a few hours or overnight before using. Drain and rinse well before using in the recipe. If the beans are presoaked before following this recipe, reduce the water called for by 1 cup.

UZBEKISTANI CHICKPEA SALAD

The talk of the town in most villages in Uzbekistan, this is a simple and flavorful dish made with turnips and carrots, which appear often in Uzbeki cuisine. The chickpeas give this dish an almost Mideastern flair. Serve on its own with a mixed green salad, or with Persian Rice (page 210) or Indonesian Coconut Rice (page 194).

SERVES 6

1½ tablespoons sesame oil
1 yellow onion, chopped small (1¼ cups)
2 cloves garlic, pressed or minced
2 carrots, sliced thin (1½ cups)
1 turnip, chopped small (1½ cups)
1 (15-ounce) can chickpeas, rinsed and drained, or 1¾ cups cooked chickpeas (see page 230)
1 tablespoon minced fresh dill, tightly packed
1½ teaspoons ground coriander
¾ teaspoon ground cumin
½ cup vegan sour cream (see Note below)
¼ cup water
1 teaspoon sea salt, or to taste
¼ teaspoon ground black pepper
Pinch cayenne

1. Place the sesame oil in a large sauté pan over medium-high heat. Add the onion, garlic, carrots, and turnip and cook for 5 minutes, stirring frequently.
2. Add the chickpeas and cook for 10 minutes, stirring frequently and adding water as necessary to prevent sticking.
3. Add the remaining ingredients and gently mix well before serving.

Variations

- Replace the garbanzo beans with black beans, fava beans, navy beans, or your favorite.
- Replace the dill with cilantro, parsley, or basil.

Note: For homemade vegan sour cream, add the juice of 1 lemon to 1 cup of vegan mayonnaise (such as Vegenaise) and mix well.

TAJIKISTANI PILAU RICE (PLOV)

Plov, the national dish of Tajikistan, traditionally includes rice, vegetables, and meat. All of the ingredients are cooked in the same pot, and it is served family style, eaten with your hands and washed down with a cup of green tea. For your culinary delight, we replaced the horse meat traditionally used in Tajikistani dishes with seitan. We think you will be quite pleased with the difference. This dish is a meal unto itself served with slices of tomato and cucumber. Note: If you cook all the ingredients together it may go over 30 minutes, counting cooking time. You can prepare it within 30 minutes if you cook the rice separately.

SERVES 6 TO 8

2 tablespoons sesame oil
1 yellow onion, chopped small (1½ cups)
7 garlic cloves, quartered or halved
1 tablespoon fennel seeds
8 ounces seitan, chopped
1¼ cups white basmati rice
3 cups water or vegetable stock (see page 228)
2 teaspoons sea salt, or to taste
2 carrots, cut into thin matchsticks
1 turnip, peeled and chopped into small cubes
¼ cup minced Italian parsley

1. Place the sesame oil in a large pot or wok over medium heat. Add the onion, garlic, fennel seeds, and seitan and cook for 3 minutes, stirring frequently. Add the rice, water, and salt, gently stir well, and cover. Add the carrots and turnip cubes to the pot and gently mix well.
2. Cook until all of the liquid is absorbed and the rice is soft and cooked through, approximately 20 minutes, stirring occasionally. Add more water if necessary to cook the rice completely. Garnish with parsley before serving.

Variations

- If you have more time, replace the basmati rice with 1 cup brown rice and use 3½ cups of water. Cook until the rice is done, approximately 40 minutes.
- Replace the seitan with roasted tofu or tempeh cubes (see page 227).
- Replace the carrots and turnip with vegetables of your choosing, such as broccoli, parsnips, or portobello mushrooms.

PERSIAN RICE

The long-guarded secret of the ayatollahs finally revealed, this dish makes use of some traditional ingredients in Persian cuisine. The vegan yogurt adds creaminess and helps us approximate the flavor of the original dish. Serve with Uzbekistani Chickpea Salad (page 208) or Iranian Lima Bean and Dill (page 212).

SERVES 6

2 cups white basmati rice
3¼ cups water or vegetable stock (see page 228)
1 teaspoon sea salt, or to taste
2 teaspoons coriander seeds
2 to 3 tablespoons soy yogurt or vegan butter
1 tablespoon fresh minced dill or 1 teaspoon dry
2 to 3 tablespoons currants or raisins
¼ to ½ cup shelled pistachio nuts
⅛ teaspoon saffron threads soaked in 3 tablespoons hot water

1. Place the rice, water, sea salt, coriander seeds, and vegan yogurt in a medium pot over medium-high heat. Bring to a boil. Lower the heat to low, cover, and simmer until all the liquid is absorbed, approximately 10 minutes.
2. Allow the pot to sit off the heat for 5 minutes. Add the remaining ingredients, including the saffron and soaking water, and gently fluff with a fork. To make sure you get all of the saffron, you can place some rice in the bowl with the saffron remnants and mix well before returning the rice to the pot.

The Asian Pantry

Although not common throughout Asia, yogurt and other dairy products are widely used in Central Asian cuisine. As we mentioned earlier, for the vegan pantry, there are several varieties of vegan yogurt on the market to choose from.

East Meets West: Persia

Persian literature's influence on Western writing and thought has been profound, though subtly understood. Emerson, Nietzsche, Goethe, and others indicated that much of their depth and passion for expression arose from their study of Persian literature. It is said that the Persian and Arabic languages are capable of expressing a lyrical emotion hard to capture in other tongues. Rumi and Hafiz, two names popular in the West, are among the great Persian writers. Though Rumi adored his native tongue, he believed that "love will find its way through all languages on its own." Apparently he was correct—he was acknowledged as the "most popular poet in America in 2007."

IRANIAN LIMA BEAN AND DILL

As we drift toward the Mediterranean in our Asian adventures, we begin to notice its influence on the cuisine. Here we use olive oil instead of the sesame oil found in the other recipes in this book, as well as Central Asian ingredients like dill and lima beans. Serve along with Persian Rice (page 210) and Asian Slaw (page 185).

1 pound frozen lima beans (approximately 4 cups)
1½ cups water or vegetable stock (see page 228)
1 tablespoon olive oil
1 onion, diced (1½ cups)
3 cloves garlic, pressed or minced
1 tablespoon freshly squeezed lemon juice
2 teaspoons red wine vinegar
2 tablespoons fresh dill, or 2 teaspoons dried dill
¾ teaspoon sea salt, or to taste
¼ teaspoon ground black pepper, or to taste
¾ cup vegan yogurt

1. Bring the lima beans and water to boil in a large pot. Cover and lower the heat to simmer. Cook until the beans are tender, for 12 to 15 minutes.
2. While the lima beans are cooking, add the olive oil to a sauté pan over medium-high heat. Add the onions and garlic and cook until the onions are translucent, approximately 5 minutes, stirring frequently. Transfer to a large bowl.
3. When the lima beans are done cooking, drain well and add them to the bowl with the onions. Add the remaining ingredients and mix well before serving.

Variations

- Replace the lima beans with black beans, azuki beans, or garbanzo beans.
- Replace the dill with minced cilantro, basil, or Italian parsley.

KOREAN PINE NUT PORRIDGE

One of our favorite restaurants in New York, Hangawi, serves Korean vegan cuisine, including the heavenly porridge jat juk. It's quite rich, so only a small portion is necessary. Though it is traditionally served with jujube dates (see Box below), any date will due in a pinch. We find it quite nourishing and soothing to the soul. Enjoy first thing in the morning or as a midnight snack.

SERVES 4

½ cup pine nuts
1½ cups water
⅛ to ¼ teaspoon sea salt
¼ cup brown rice flour
3 tablespoons agave nectar or sweetener of choice
4 dates, finely chopped
Pinch cinnamon

1. Place the pine nuts in a blender with 1 cup water and blend on high speed until smooth. Transfer to a pot over medium heat.
2. Place the flour in a sauté pan over medium-high heat. Cook for 3 minutes, stirring frequently. Slowly add the remaining water and whisk constantly until a smooth paste is formed, with no lumps. Add the pine nut mixture and salt and stir well. Whisk until the porridge is creamy and begins to thicken, approximately 5 minutes.
3. Add the agave and mix well. Pour the porridge into serving bowls and top with the dates and a pinch of cinnamon.

The Asian Pantry: Jujube Dates

Cultivated for more than 4,000 years, jujube dates, also called Chinese dates, are used in traditional medicine in both China and Korea to alleviate stress.

Chefs' Tips and Tricks

If you cannot find rice flour, make your own by adding rice to a strong blender and processing it until finely ground. Try it with different types of rice to experience the variety of flavors possible.

KIM CHI

Though it needs to ferment for a few days, homemade kimchi is well worth the wait. Considered by many to be the national dish of Korea, kim chi is a spicy and tangy, cultured vegetable dish, typically with cabbage as the base (consider it the sauerkraut of the East!). There are countless varieties, each making use of different vegetables, spices, and pickling ingredients. This is a simple version, which takes a short while to prepare. Serve as a side with Lemon Rice (page 187), with all your Asian meals, and as a filling in Nori Rolls (page 157).

MAKES APPROXIMATELY 4 TO 6 CUPS

1 large head green or napa cabbage
2 tablespoons sea salt, or to taste
¼ cup minced fresh garlic
2 inches peeled and minced fresh ginger
1 jalapeño or other hot pepper, seeded and minced
1 tablespoon ground cayenne or other hot chile powder, to taste
1 tablespoon unpasteurized miso paste, optional
1 tablespoon agave nectar, Sucanat, or organic sugar
1 cup diced mixed vegetables, optional
(try green onions, cucumbers, carrots, cauliflower, broccoli, bok choy, or daikon)
1 cup water

1. Rinse the cabbage well and remove the outer leaves and the root. Save the outer leaves for later use. Chop the remaining cabbage into ½-inch strips and place in a 2-quart mason jar (or two 1-quart jars). Add 2 tablespoons of the salt and fill the jar with water. Allow it to sit for 1 to 2 hours.
2. Meanwhile, combine the remaining salt and all of the other ingredients in a large bowl with just enough water to create a creamy paste.
3. Drain and rinse the cabbage well. Add to the bowl with the paste, and mixed vegetables, if using. Mix until everything is well coated.
4. Return this mixture to the mason jar, add water to cover, and top with the outer cabbage leaves. Loosely place the cover on the jar. Allow the jar to sit at room temperature, out of direct sunlight, for 3 to 5 days, depending on the climate. The final product should have a spicy and tangy flavor. After this time it is then ready for the fridge, where it can continue to ferment for at least a month and even longer.

Chefs' Tips and Tricks

As is seen in cultures around the world, pickling foods is the most ancient method of food preservation. It assists in breaking down food, making it more easy to digest. The pickling process also provides beneficial bacteria that can assist in digestive health.

KOREAN MUNG BEAN PANCAKES

Ground split mung beans create the flour for these flavorful hotcakes. If you have more time, you can soak the mung beans for 4 or more hours before blending. If you make mini cakes, they make innovative hors d'oeuvres. Serve on their own with soy sauce or with any of the assorted chutneys (page 40), or with a dipping sauce like Mango Ginger Sauce (page 61), Teriyaki Sauce (page 159), or Dim Sum Dipping Sauce (page 101).

MAKES 8 PANCAKES

1 cup split mung beans
3 tablespoons spelt or brown rice flour
3 tablespoons thinly sliced green onion
1 teaspoon baking powder, sifted
1 teaspoon sea salt, or to taste
½ teaspoon chile powder, optional
2 tablespoons sesame oil
2 cloves garlic, pressed or minced
1 tablespoon peeled and minced fresh ginger
2 teaspoons seeded and diced hot chile pepper
2 mushrooms, diced (about ½ cup—try shiitake, oyster, or cremini)
1 cup water
Oil for sautéing

1. Place the mung beans in a high-powered blender or food processor and blend until the beans are powdered. Place them in a mixing bowl. Add the flour, green onion, baking powder, salt, and chile powder, if using, and mix well.
2. Place the sesame oil in a small sauté pan over medium-high heat. Add the garlic, ginger, chile pepper, and mushrooms and cook for 5 minutes, stirring frequently and adding a small amount of water if necessary to prevent sticking. Transfer to the mixing bowl and mix well. Slowly add the water and mix well, until all of the liquid is absorbed.
3. Place the oil in a large sauté pan or on a griddle over medium-high heat. Scoop out pancake-size portions of the batter and place in the pan as space allows. Cook for 6 to 8 minutes, flipping periodically to ensure even cooking. Use a spatula to flatten the pancakes so that the insides are cooked as well. You are looking for a golden brown crust. Voila!

KOREAN POTATO IN SWEET SOY SAUCE (GAMJA JORIM)

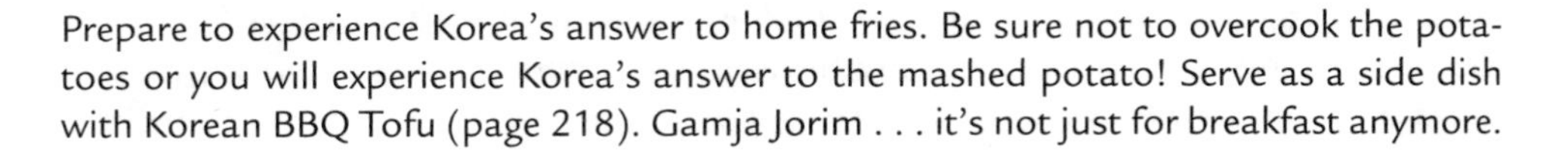

Prepare to experience Korea's answer to home fries. Be sure not to overcook the potatoes or you will experience Korea's answer to the mashed potato! Serve as a side dish with Korean BBQ Tofu (page 218). Gamja Jorim . . . it's not just for breakfast anymore.

SERVES 4 TO 6

2 potatoes, thinly sliced (about 4 cups)
2 tablespoons sesame oil
1 small yellow onion, thinly sliced
2 cloves garlic, pressed or minced
1¼ cups sliced oyster or shiitake mushrooms
1 teaspoon chile powder
1 teaspoon Sriracha (page 86), or 2 teaspoons seeded and diced hot chile pepper
2 tablespoons agave nectar
3 tablespoons soy sauce
½ teaspoon sea salt, or to taste
Sesame seeds

1. Place a steamer basket in a pot filled with approximately 1 inch of water over medium-high heat. Add the potatoes and steam until just soft, approximately 15 minutes. Be careful not to overcook.
2. Meanwhile, place the sesame oil in a large sauté pan over medium-high heat. Add the onions, garlic, mushrooms, and chile powder, and cook until the mushrooms are browned and cooked through, approximately 5 minutes, stirring frequently. Remove the sauté pan from the heat until the potatoes are done cooking.
3. When the potatoes are done, add them to the sauté pan with the remaining ingredients except the sesame seeds, and gently stir well. Garnish with the sesame seeds before serving.

KOREAN BBQ TOFU

A meal at an authentic Korean BBQ restaurant includes the food being grilled right at the table, oftentimes with the grill being built into the table! For this recipe, the longer the tofu sits in the marinade the more flavor it will absorb. Serve with your choice of rice and Asian Slaw (page 185), Spicy Asparagus (page 65), or Kale and Snow Peas (page 184).

SERVES 4

1 recipe BBQ Sauce (recipe follows)
1 (14-ounce) package extra-firm tofu

BBQ SAUCE

¼ cup water
¼ cup diced yellow onion
3 tablespoons soy sauce
2 tablespoons agave nectar, or sweetener of choice to taste
1 tablespoon peeled and minced fresh ginger
2 cloves garlic
1 teaspoon seeded and diced hot chile pepper, or ¼ teaspoon crushed red pepper flakes, or to taste
¼ teaspoon ground black pepper

1. Preheat a grill. Place all of the sauce ingredients in a blender and blend until creamy. Pour into a shallow dish.
2. Slice the tofu into four cutlets and add them to the sauce. Allow them to sit in the sauce for 20 minutes or longer. Transfer the cutlets to the grill and grill until char marks appear on both sides, flipping occasionally. After grilling return the tofu to the sauce. To serve, place the tofu on a plate and drizzle with the sauce.

Variation

- Bake the tofu and BBQ sauce in a 375°F oven for 15 to 20 minutes.

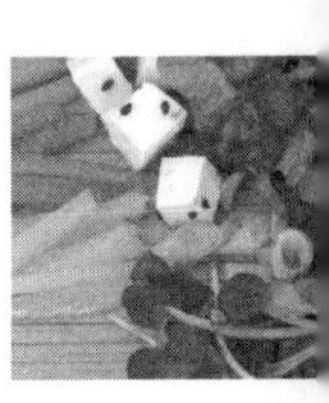

KOREAN TOASTED BARLEY TEA (BORI CHA)

This simple tea has an earthy flavor and a grounding effect.

MAKES TWO 16-OUNCE SERVINGS

¼ cup hulled barley
4 cups water
Agave nectar, optional

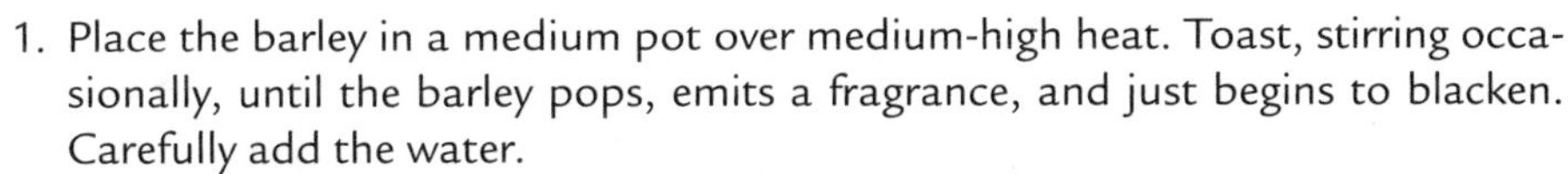

1. Place the barley in a medium pot over medium-high heat. Toast, stirring occasionally, until the barley pops, emits a fragrance, and just begins to blacken. Carefully add the water.
2. Lower the heat to low and simmer for 15 minutes or longer. Delightful as is, or sweeten with agave nectar or your favorite sweetener to taste. You may strain the tea before serving if you wish, and you may reuse the barley again for another batch with a more mellow flavor.

KOREAN BLISS MIX TEA

A highly refreshing fruity beverage that may be enjoyed hot or over ice with a sprig of fresh mint.

MAKES TWO 16-OUNCE SERVINGS

4 cups water
1 inch peeled fresh ginger, sliced thin
4 dates, pitted and sliced
1 cinnamon stick
Pine nuts
2 thin slices persimmon, optional

1. Bring the water to a boil in a small pot. Lower the heat to low, add the ginger, dates, and cinnamon stick, and simmer for 20 minutes or longer.
2. Pour into glasses and top with a few pine nuts and a persimmon slice, if using.

KOREAN PEAR WITH PEPPERCORNS (BAESOOK)

This is a wonderfully refreshing dessert. The peppercorns give a sharp bite that contrasts with the sweet and pungent flavors of the pears and sauce. Simply divine when served warm or cold.

SERVES 6 TO 8

2 cups water
1 tablespoon peeled and minced fresh ginger
1 cinnamon stick
2 tablespoons whole peppercorns
2 large Korean pears, peeled and quartered, or 4 pears, quartered
3 tablespoons agave nectar, or sweetener of choice to taste
2 teaspoons arrowroot dissolved in 2 tablespoons cold water
½ teaspoon ground cardamom
½ teaspoon ground cinnamon
½ cup pine nuts, toasted (see page 225)

1. Place the water, ginger, and cinnamon stick in a large sauté pan over medium heat. Press a few peppercorns into the sides of the pears. Place them on the bottom of the sauté pan and cook for 15 minutes, gently stirring and flipping the pears occasionally. Add the agave nectar and gently stir well.
2. Add the arrowroot and cook until the sauce thickens, approximately 3 minutes, stirring frequently. Garnish each serving with a pinch of cardamom and cinnamon and a sprinkle of pine nuts.

Variations

- Experiment with different varieties of pear such as Bosc, Anjou, or Bartlett.
- Be bold and replace the pears with four apples.
- Garnish each serving with chopped dates and a sprinkle of nutmeg.
- Try adding 1 tablespoon of rose water.

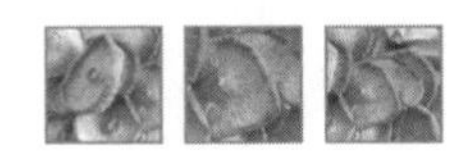

Acknowledgments

Can you thank your parents enough? Not really. So, much love and gratitude to our parents Roberta and Martin Reinfeld and Deborah and Patrick Murray for all of the ways you have supported us throughout our lives. Thank you to all of our friends and family who helped make this book possible. Thanks to our agent, Marilyn Allen of Allen O'Shea Literary Agency. Thank you, Marilyn, for your support and vision.

Many thanks to our Da Capo editors—Renée Sedliar, Collin Tracy, Alex Camlin, and Michelle S. Asakawa.

Tremendous thanks to all of our thorough recipe testers, tasters, and developers: Jessyka Murray, Elizabeth Warfield-Murray, Lisa Parker, Roland Barker, Gabriel Zingaro, Aaron Warfield-Murray, Gia Baiocchi, Roberta Reinfeld, Roger Vossler, Dawn Reinfeld, Bill Townsend, Ryan Hughes, Neil and Erica Greene, Laura Bishop, Jerrod Perry, Kelika Ranke, Natalie and Scott Kuroiwa, Aaron Mauck, and Ali Karasic. We could not have done this without all of you!

Love and gratitude to Sarah Warfield for taking the initiative and persevering with the food photography. Thanks also to Sarah Joy Davis for her invaluable assistance with the food styling and photography.

Thank you to all of the many chefs and culinary creatives out there who have contributed to our knowledge, inspiration, skills, and careers.

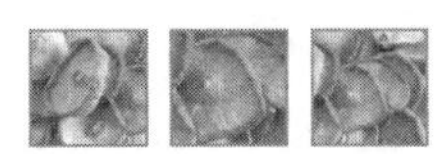

Metric Conversions

- The recipes in this book have not been tested with metric measurements, so some variations might occur.
- Remember that the weight of dry ingredients varies according to the volume or density factor: 1 cup of flour weighs far less than 1 cup of sugar, and 1 tablespoon doesn't necessarily hold 3 teaspoons.

General Formulas for Metric Conversion

Ounces to grams	→	ounces × 28.35 = grams
Grams to ounces	→	grams × 0.035 = ounces
Pounds to grams	→	pounds × 453.5 = grams
Pounds to kilograms	→	pounds × 0.45 = kilograms
Cups to liters	→	cups × 0.24 = liters
Fahrenheit to Celsius	→	(°F − 32) × 5 ÷ 9 = °C
Celsius to Fahrenheit	→	(°C × 9) ÷ 5 + 32 = °F

Linear Measurements

½ inch = 1½ cm
1 inch = 2½ cm
6 inches = 15 cm
8 inches = 20 cm
10 inches = 25 cm
12 inches = 30 cm
20 inches = 50 cm

Volume (Dry) Measurements

¼ teaspoon = 1 milliliter
½ teaspoon = 2 milliliters
¾ teaspoon = 4 milliliters
1 teaspoon = 5 milliliters
1 tablespoon = 15 milliliters
¼ cup = 59 milliliters
⅓ cup = 79 milliliters
½ cup = 118 milliliters
⅔ cup = 158 milliliters
¾ cup = 177 milliliters
1 cup = 225 milliliters
4 cups or 1 quart = 1 liter
½ gallon = 2 liters
1 gallon = 4 liters

Volume (Liquid) Measurements

1 teaspoon = ⅙ fluid ounce = 5 milliliters
1 tablespoon = ½ fluid ounce = 15 milliliters
2 tablespoons = 1 fluid ounce = 30 milliliters
¼ cup = 2 fluid ounces = 60 milliliters
⅓ cup = 2⅔ fluid ounces = 79 milliliters
½ cup = 4 fluid ounces = 118 milliliters
1 cup or ½ pint = 8 fluid ounces = 250 milliliters
2 cups or 1 pint = 16 fluid ounces = 500 milliliters
4 cups or 1 quart = 32 fluid ounces = 1,000 milliliters
1 gallon = 4 liters

Oven Temperature Equivalents, Fahrenheit (F) and Celsius (C)

100°F = 38°C
200°F = 95°C
250°F = 120°C
300°F = 150°C
350°F = 180°C
400°F = 205°C
450°F = 230°C

Weight (Mass) Measurements

1 ounce = 30 grams
2 ounces = 55 grams
3 ounces = 85 grams
4 ounces = ¼ pound = 125 grams
8 ounces = ½ pound = 240 grams
12 ounces = ¾ pound = 375 grams
16 ounces = 1 pound = 454 grams

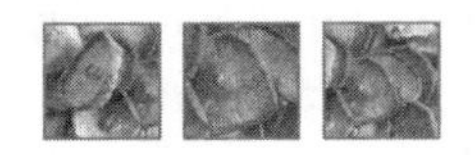

Appendix A: Preparation Basics

In this section we go over some of the basic principles of vegan natural food preparation used in the recipes in the book.

Toasting Spices, Nuts, and Seeds

Toasting brings out a deeper flavor of ingredients. There are two methods we commonly use. One way is to use a dry sauté pan. For this method, place the food in a pan, turn the heat to high, and cook until the item turns golden brown, stirring constantly. This method is good for spices, grains, and small quantities of nuts or seeds. Another method involves preheating an oven to 350°F. Place the food on a dry baking sheet and leave in the oven until golden brown, stirring occasionally and being mindful to avoid burning. This method is best for nuts, seeds, and shredded coconut. Nuts become crunchier after cooling down. If you have more time, you can enhance the flavor even more by roasting at lower temperatures for longer periods of time. Nuts, for instance, roasted at 200°F for 45 minutes have a richer, toastier flavor than roasting at a high temperature for shorter periods of time.

Working with Tofu

Tofu is sold in a number of varieties, including extra-firm, firm, soft, and silken. Each variety lends itself to a particular type of food preparation. The recipes describe which form of tofu is required for the dish.

The silken style may be blended and used to replace dairy products in puddings, frostings, dressings, creamy soups, and sauces.

The soft type may be used cubed in soups or puréed in sauces, spreads, or dips.

The medium, firm, and extra-firm styles may be scrambled, grated in casseroles, or cubed in stir-fries.

The extra-firm style may be grilled or baked as cutlets, or it may be cubed and roasted or cubed and steamed along with vegetables.

Leftover tofu should be rinsed and covered with water in a glass container in the refrigerator. Changing water daily is recommended. Use within 4 days. Firm and extra-firm tofu may be frozen for up to 2 months. Frozen tofu that has been defrosted has a spongy texture that absorbs marinades more than tofu that has not been frozen.

To make tofu cutlets: Slice a 1-pound block of extra-firm tofu into thirds or fourths. If you wish, you can then cut these cutlets in half to yield six or eight cutlets per pound. You can also cut the tofu diagonally to create triangle-shaped cutlets. Cutlets can be marinated and then roasted or grilled.

To make tofu cubes: To make medium-size cubes, slice the tofu as you would for three or four cutlets. Then make four cuts along the length and three cuts along the width of the tofu. You can make the cubes larger or smaller by altering the number of cuts.

To grate tofu: Be sure to use medium, firm, or extra-firm tofu that has been drained well. Slide over the large grate on a standard cheese grater. Be careful with your fingers!

Marinating

Marinade ingredients significantly determine the flavors of a dish. The main rule of thumb is the longer an ingredient sits in the marinade, the more of its flavors it will acquire. Simply placing tofu or a portobello mushroom in different marinades creates dramatically different taste sensations. If possible, allow more time for marinating than the recipe calls for. Up to an hour (or even more) will yield a more flavorful dish.

There is vast room for creative experimentation when it comes to marinades. Some of our favorite marinade ingredients include soy sauce, toasted sesame oil, coconut or olive oil, brown rice vinegar, mirin, mustard, minced garlic or ginger, maple syrup, balsamic vinegar, and a variety of spices and herbs. You can also add sliced or chopped yellow or green onions.

Working with Tempeh

Tempeh needs to be thoroughly cooked before consuming. It is typically available in an 8-ounce package. Several varieties come in a thick square block. Others come as a thinner rectangle. Some cooks recommend steaming the tempeh for 10 minutes before using in dishes to remove any bitterness. Store leftover tempeh in a sealed glass container in the refrigerator for up to 3 days.

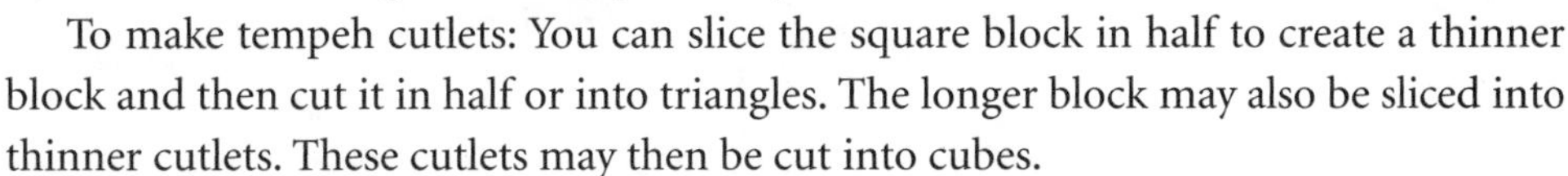

To make tempeh cutlets: You can slice the square block in half to create a thinner block and then cut it in half or into triangles. The longer block may also be sliced into thinner cutlets. These cutlets may then be cut into cubes.

Roasting Tofu and Tempeh

Tofu and tempeh cubes can be marinated, roasted, and then stored for a couple of days in a glass container in the refrigerator to be used in salads, stir-fries, or on their own as a snack.

To roast tofu and tempeh cutlets and cubes, follow these three simple steps:

1. Preheat the oven or toaster oven to 350°F. Cut the tofu or tempeh into cutlets or cubes as mentioned above.
2. Place them in a marinade of your choosing. Allow them to sit for at least 5 minutes and up to overnight. If marinating overnight, store in an airtight container in the refrigerator.
3. Place on a well-oiled baking sheet or casserole dish. Roast until golden brown, approximately 20 minutes, stirring the cubes occasionally to ensure even cooking. If making cutlets, you can flip them after 10 minutes. Try a convection oven or use a broil setting for a crispier crust.

We prefer to use the toaster oven for small quantities of up to 1 pound of tofu or tempeh, which conveniently fits in our toaster oven's baking tray. Be aware that food tends to cook faster in a toaster oven than in a regular oven. Depending on the model, you can typically roast the tofu or tempeh in 15 minutes instead of 20.

Working with Seitan

Originating in ancient China, Seitan is sometimes referred to as "meat of wheat." It is wheat gluten dough that has been cooked in a broth with different types of seasonings.

Seitan can be used as an animal product replacement in virtually any dish. There are several brands available on the market. Experiment with them all to find your favorite. If you are ambitious and wish to make your own, go to www.about.com and enter "making seitan," which gives step by step instructions. Check out page 118 for a quick way to spice-up store-bought seitan and create a "chicken"-style variety. A reminder note: seitan is pure wheat gluten—it's definitely not the dish for the gluten intolerant!

Grilling

We love grilling tempeh and tofu cutlets, as well as many vegetables such as portobello mushrooms, corn, onions, baby bok choy, bell peppers, asparagus, zucchini, coconut meat, pineapple slices, and eggplant. For added flavor, first place the food in a marinade for a few minutes or up to overnight. Baste or brush with oil before and during grilling, and grill until char marks appear and the item is heated thoroughly, flipping periodically. If using a gas grill, avoid placing items over a direct flame.

Another grilling option is to use a stove-top grill. Kitchen supply stores sell cast-iron and nonstick pans that are flat, straddle two burners, and have a griddle on one side and a grooved side for grilling. The flavor is similar to outdoor grilling, and you get the fancy char marks without having to fuss with (or own) a grill.

Broiling

Most ovens come with a broiler setting that allows for quick cooking under direct high heat. We use it to broil tofu or tempeh cubes, or vegetables such as eggplant, zucchini, onion, or any other food that might also be grilled. To broil, place food on a baking tray (either lightly oiled or with a small amount of water) and set the tray on the top rack, a few inches below the heat element. This is a relatively fast cooking process, so be sure to keep your eye on the prize.

Soup Stock

Here are some tips for a simple and satisfying soup stock:

Save your vegetable clippings and scraps used in preparing other recipes. Place them in a large, thick-bottomed stockpot over low heat with water to cover, and simmer until all of the veggies are completely cooked. Experiment with different vegetables and herbs until you determine your favorite combinations.

BASIC NUT OR SEED MILK

Recipe courtesy of *The 30-Minute Vegan*

Use this base recipe to create countless varieties of nut and seed milks. Each combination will provide its own unique flavor. Partake of this milk in all recipes that call for milk or on its own as a refreshing beverage. This recipe also works for rice milk. Just follow the ratios using uncooked brown rice and water. It's a convenient way to save on packaging, it's fresh, and it tastes better than store-bought brands!

If you have more time and for best results, see the chart at the end of the recipe for recommended soaking times.

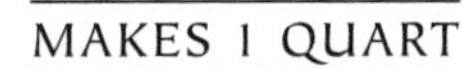

MAKES 1 QUART

1 cup nut or seeds
4 cups water

1. Rinse the nuts or seeds well and drain. Place them in a blender with the water and blend on high speed for 30 seconds or until creamy.
2. Strain the milk through a fine mesh strainer, cheesecloth, or mesh bag. If using a fine mesh strainer, use a spoon or rubber spatula to swirl the nut or seed meal around, which allows the milk to drain faster. If desired, sweeten with agave nectar or maple syrup to taste. Lasts for 3 to 4 days when stored in a glass jar in the refrigerator.

If You Have More Time

Soaking Chart

Rinse nuts or seeds well and place them in a bowl or jar with water in a 1 part nut or seed to 3 or 4 part water ratio. Allow them to sit for the recommended time before draining, rinsing, and using in recipes.

Nut/Seed	Soak Time in hours	Nut/Seed	Soak Time in hours
Almonds	4 to 6	Pecans	4 to 6
Macadamia nuts	1 to 2	Pine nuts	1 to 2
Hazel nuts	4 to 6	Sesame seeds	1 to 4
Cashews	1 to 2	Pumpkin seeds	1 to 4
Brazil nuts	4 to 6	Sunflower seeds	1 to 4
Walnuts	4 to 6		

Try using onions, potatoes, celery, carrots, parsley, parsnips, zucchini, leeks, and garlic. Many people avoid using vegetables that become bitter when simmered, such as bell peppers, radishes, turnips, broccoli, cauliflower, greens, and Brussels sprouts. It is not necessary to add dry herbs or spices to a stock. The stock may be frozen and defrosted for future use. You can also pour the broth into ice cube trays, freeze, and use as needed.

Cooking Grains

Grains are the staple food for many of the world's cultures. A source of fiber, minerals, and B vitamins, these complex-carbohydrate foods provide energy to keep us going. Whole grains contain oil that can become rancid and attract insects if not stored correctly. To store grains, keep them in a tightly sealed container in a cool, dry location. They can be stored in a refrigerator for up to 3 months and in a freezer for up to 6 months. Cooked grains may be kept in the refrigerator for up to 3 days.

Follow these 3 easy steps to cook grains:

1. Rinse the grain thoroughly and drain the excess water.
2. Bring the measured amount of grain and liquid (either vegetable stock or water) to a boil. You can add a dash of sea salt.
3. Cover with a tight-fitting lid, lower the heat to low, and simmer for the recommended time. Do not lift the lid until the grain has finished cooking.

The following chart will give you an approximate cooking time and yield of some of the more popular grains. Cooking times may vary depending on altitude and stove cooking temperatures. The grain is generally finished cooking when it is chewy and all of the liquid is absorbed.

Many grains can be prepared in less than 30 minutes. If you wish to turn a recipe in the book into a 30-minute meal, begin cooking the grain before doing any other recipe preparation, and the grain will typically be finished by the time you are done preparing the other dishes.

Cooking Beans and Legumes

Beans and legumes are a high fiber, low calorie, low fat, low sodium, and cholesterol-free food. They are also relatively high in protein, amino acids, vitamins, and minerals. If you have time to soak and prepare a pot of beans you will save on the packaging of the canned products.

Grain Cooking Chart				
Grain	Liquid/cup of Grain	Approx. Cooking Time (minutes)	Approx. Yield (cups)	Comments
Amaranth	2½	25	2½	Ancient grain of Aztecs; higher in protein and nutrients than most grains.
Barley, pearled	3	45	3½	Good in soups and stews.
Buckwheat	2	15	2½	Hardy, nutty flavor. When toasted it's called kasha. Can be used as a breakfast cereal.
Couscous	1½	15	1½	A North African staple made from ground semolina.
Millet	2½	20	3	A highly nutritious grain that is used in casseroles, stews, and cereals.
Oats				A versatile grain that is popular as a cereal and for baking.
Steel Cut	3	30 to 40	3	
Rolled	3	10	3	
Quick	2	5	2	
Polenta	3	10	3	A type of cornmeal used in Italian cooking
Quinoa	2	20	2½	Ancient grain of the Incans. High in protein and many nutrients. Has a delicate, nutty flavor.
Rice				High nutrient content; a staple in many of the world's cultures.
Brown Basmati	2	35 to 40	2¼	
White Basmati	1½	20	2	Nutty flavor. Used in Indian cooking.

continues

Grain Cooking Chart *continued*

Grain	Liquid/cup of grain	Approx. cooking time (minutes)	Approx. yield (cups)	Comments
Rice *(continued)*				
Brown Long Grain	2	45	3	
Brown Short Grain	2	45	3	
Jasmine	1½	20	2	Fragrant long-grain rice cultivated in Thailand.
Wild	3	60	4	
Teff	3	20	1½	The smallest grain in the world; it's the main ingredient for Ethiopian *injera* flatbread.
Wheat				Primary bread grain.
Bulghur	2	15	2½	Used in Middle Eastern dishes, such as tabouli.
Cracked	2	25	2½	May be used as a cereal.

Before you cook legumes, it is recommended to clean them thoroughly, rinse well, and soak overnight. This improves their digestibility and reduces gas. Digestibility can also be improved by adding some fennel seeds, a handful of brown rice, or a few strips of the sea vegetable kombu to the legumes while cooking. If you do not have time to soak the beans overnight, a quick method is to bring beans and four times the amount of water to a boil, remove from the heat, cover, and allow them to sit for a few hours.

After soaking the legumes or boiling them in this way, discard the soaking water, add the measured amount of vegetable stock or water to a thick-bottomed pot, bring to a boil, cover, lower the heat to simmer, and cook until tender. The times in the following chart are for cooking dry legumes.

Do not add salt to the cooking liquid—it can make the legumes tough. Legumes are done cooking when they are tender but not mushy. They should retain their original shape.

Note: These times are for cooking dry beans. Please reduce cooking time by 25 percent when beans are soaked.

Dried Bean Cooking Chart				
Legume	Liquid/Cup of Legume	Approx. Cooking Time (hours)	Approx. Yield (cups)	Comments
Azuki/Adzuki Beans	3¼	45 min.	3	Tender red bean used in Japanese and macrobiotic cooking.
Anasazi Beans	3	2	2	Means "the Ancient Ones" in Navajo language; sweeter and meatier than most beans
Black Beans (Turtle Beans)	4	1¼	2½	Good in Spanish, South American, and Caribbean dishes.
Black-Eyed Peas	4	1¼	2	A staple of the American South.
Garbanzo Beans (Chickpeas)	4	3 to 4	2	Used in Middle Eastern and Indian dishes.
Great Northern Beans	4	1½	2	Beautiful, large white bean.
Kidney Beans	4	1½	2	Medium-size red beans. Most popular bean in the U.S.; also used in Mexican cooking.
Lentils Green Red	 3 3	 45 min. 25 min.	 2¼ 2¼	Come in green, red, and French varieties. Member of the pea family used in Indian dhal dishes and soups.
Lima Beans, Baby Limas	3 3	1½ 1½	1¼ 1¾	White bean with a distinctive flavor and high in nutrients.
Mung Beans	3	45 min.	2¼	Grown in India and Asia. Used in Indian dhal dishes. May be soaked and sprouted and used fresh in soups and salads.

continues

Legume Cooking Chart *continued*

Legume	Liquid/cup of grain	Approx. cooking time (minutes)	Approx. yield (cups)	Comments
Navy Beans (White Beans)	4	2½	2	A hardy bean used in soups, stews, and cold salads.
Pinto Beans	4	2½	2	Used in Mexican and Southwestern cooking, in soups and as refried beans in burritos.
Split Peas	3	45 min.	2¼	Come in yellow and green varieties. Do not need to be soaked. Used in soups and Indian dhals.

Homemade Coconut Milk

Want to avoid using can upon can of coconut milk? Here is a quick recipe for homemade coconut milk or cream. Open a young coconut by puncturing the coconut with a machete, large knife, or coconut opener. Pour the water through a strainer into a blender. Crack the coconut open using a large heavy knife, scoop out the meat, and put into the blender. Blend until creamy. You can use this liquid to replace the coconut milk in any given recipe.

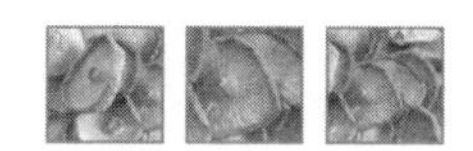

Appendix B: Supplemental Information

Why Vegan?

"In terms of immediacy of action and the feasibility of bringing about [greenhouse gas] reductions in a short period of time, [eating vegetarian meals] clearly is the most attractive opportunity. Give up meat for one day [a week] initially, and decrease it from there."
—Dr. Rajendra Pachauri, chair of the Nobel Prize–winning United Nations Intergovernmental Panel on Climate Change

"Nothing will benefit human health and increase the chances for survival of life on Earth as much as the evolution to a vegetarian diet."
—Albert Einstein

A vegetarian diet is one that does not include meat, fish, or poultry. There are three types of vegetarian diets. A *lacto-ovo vegetarian* diet includes eggs and dairy products. A *lacto-vegetarian* diet includes dairy products, but not eggs. *Vegan* is used to describe a diet and lifestyle that does not include the use or consumption of any animal-based products, including dairy or eggs. This means vegans also avoid wearing leather and silk, and products tested on animals. The phrase *plant-based* is often used instead of the word *vegan.*

The reasons people choose to enjoy vegan foods are many. First and foremost, they taste incredible! People also turn to vegan foods for weight-loss and disease prevention. Numerous studies show that many serious illnesses—such as heart disease, obesity, and diabetes—can be prevented and reversed by enjoying more vegan foods.

Want to be Earth-friendly? In addition to providing an out-of-this-world culinary experience, eating vegan foods also happens to be one of the most effective steps we can take to protect the environment. The UN's Food and Agriculture Organization estimates that meat production accounts for nearly one-fifth of global greenhouse gas emissions—more than the entire world's transportation industry combined. We do more for the environment by switching meals to vegan than by trading in our gas guzzlers for an electric car or jogging to work.

Optimal Health

There is a true revolution occurring in the medical world regarding the benefits of vegan foods. Renowned doctors such as Dr. Caldwell Esselstyn Jr. and Dr. Dean Ornish have successfully reversed instances of heart disease with programs that incorporate vegan foods. Dr. John McDougall, Dr. Neal Barnard, and Dr. Gabriel Cousens have likewise had success reversing certain forms of diabetes.

The evidence continues to mount that overconsumption of the saturated fat and cholesterol in animal products leads to serious health problems, including obesity, heart disease, diabetes, hypertension, gout, kidney stones, and certain forms of cancer.

In addition, animals raised on factory farms are routinely given hormones to accelerate their rate of growth for maximum profit. Antibiotics are used to protect their health as they are housed and transported in less-than-sanitary conditions. These drugs inevitably make their way into the bodies of the humans that consume them.

In a 1995 report, the U.S. Department of Agriculture (USDA) and the U.S. Department of Health and Human Services affirmed that all of the body's nutritional needs can be met through a well-planned plant-based diet.

In 2009 the American Dietetic Association restated its position that "well-planned vegan and other types of vegetarian diets are appropriate for all stages of the life cycle, including during pregnancy, lactation, infancy, childhood, and adolescence." (ADA vol. 109, no. 7, July 2009) It is the association's official opinion (as well as that of the Dietitians of Canada) that "appropriately planned vegetarian diets, including total vegetarian or vegan diets, are healthful, nutritionally adequate, and may provide health benefits in the prevention and treatment of certain diseases."

The ADA goes on to say that

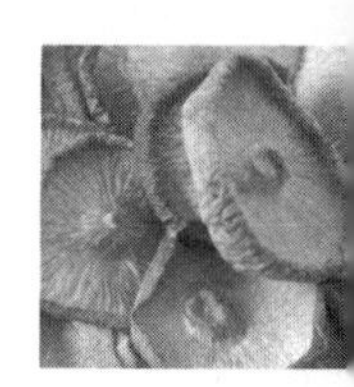

> the results of an evidence-based review showed that a vegetarian diet is associated with a lower risk of death from ischemic heart disease. Vegetarians also appear to have lower low-density lipoprotein cholesterol levels, lower blood pressure, and lower rates of hypertension and type 2 diabetes than non-vegetarians. Furthermore, vegetarians tend to have a lower body mass index and lower overall cancer rates. Features of a vegetarian diet that may reduce risk of chronic disease include lower intakes of saturated fat and cholesterol and higher intakes of fruits, vegetables, whole grains, nuts, soy products, fiber, and phytochemicals. (ADA vol. 109, no. 7, July 2009)

May this forever dispel the myth that a vegan diet is nutritionally lacking in any way. For anyone concerned about this, please rest assured that vegan foods provide all of the protein, calcium, iron, and all other vital nutrients needed for us to thrive.

Preserving the Environment

Why does Dr. Rajendra Pachauri, chair of the United Nations Intergovernmental Panel on Climate Change, go so far as to recommend that we go meatless one day a week as "the most attractive opportunity" to conserve greenhouse gases?

It's because the environmental footprint of a vegan diet is a fraction of that of a meat-based diet. Vegan foods represent the best utilization of the Earth's limited resources. It takes 16 pounds of grain and 2,500 gallons of water to produce 1 pound of beef. It's astonishing to realize this when we see so much in the news about food and water shortages and people going to bed hungry.

We must use the resources of our planet wisely if we are to survive. World scientists agree that global warming poses a serious risk to humanity and life as we know it. The key to reducing global warming is to reduce activities that produce the greenhouse gases that cause the Earth's temperature to rise. According to a 2006 UN report titled "Livestock's Long Shadow," raising livestock for food consumption is responsible for 18 percent of all greenhouse gases emitted. That's a lot of gas! (Food and Agriculture Organization of the United Nations, *Livestock's Long Shadow: Environmental Issues and Options,* 2006.)

Here are some additional topics to consider for those wishing to "go green":

The U.S. livestock population alone consumes enough grain and soybeans each year to feed over 5 times the U.S. human population. Animals are fed more than 80 percent of the corn and 95 percent of the oats that are grown on our soil.

Less than half of the harvested agricultural acreage in the United States goes to feed people.

According to the USDA, 1 acre of land can produce 20,000 pounds of vegetables. This same amount of land can only produce 165 pounds of meat.

It takes 16 pounds of grain to produce 1 pound of meat.

It requires 3½ acres of land per person to support a meat-centered diet, 1½ acres of land to support a lacto-ovo vegetarian diet, and ⅙ of an acre of land to support a plant-based diet.

If Americans were to reduce meat consumption by just 10 percent, it would free up 12 million tons of grain annually.

Half of the water used in the United States goes to irrigate land growing feed and fodder for livestock. It takes approximately 2,500 gallons of water to produce a single pound of meat. Similarly, it takes approximately 4,000 gallons of water to provide a day's worth of food per person for a meat-centered diet, 1,200 gallons for a lacto-ovo vegetarian diet, and 300 gallons for a plant-based diet.

Developing nations use land to raise beef for wealthier nations instead of utilizing that land for sustainable agriculture practices.

Topsoil is the dark, rich soil that supplies the nutrients to the food we grow. It takes 500 years to produce an inch of topsoil. This topsoil is rapidly vanishing due to clear-cutting of forests and cattle-grazing practices.

For each acre of forest land cleared for human purposes, 7 acres of forest is cleared for grazing livestock or growing livestock feed. This includes federal land that is leased for cattle-grazing purposes. This policy greatly accelerates the destruction of our precious forests.

In order to support cattle grazing, South and Central America are destroying their rainforests. These rainforests contain close to half of all the species on Earth and many medicinal plants. Over a thousand species a year are becoming extinct, and most of these are from rainforest and tropical settings. This practice also causes the displacement of indigenous peoples who have been living in these environments for countless generations.

The factory farm industry is one of the largest polluters of our groundwater due to the chemicals, pesticides, and run-off waste that is inherent in its practices.

Over 60 million people die of starvation every year. This means that we are feeding grain to animals while our fellow humans are dying of starvation in mind-staggering numbers.

For those concerned about our environment, it all boils down to the question of sustainability. What is the most sustainable way for us to feed and support the growing human population? When you look at the disproportionate amount of land, water, and resources it takes to support a meat-based diet, it makes a lot of sense for us to introduce more plant-based foods into our way of life. Whether by going completely vegan or simply including more vegan meals each week, every little bit helps.

Much of this environmental information is provided by John Robbins, a pioneer in the promotion of the health and environmental benefits of a plant-based lifestyle. He is the author of the landmark book *Diet for a New America.* His latest work, *Healthy at 100,* is a must-read in-depth exploration of health and longevity. He also founded EarthSave International to educate, inspire, and empower people around the world.

It's Cool to Be Kind

Many people who adopt a vegetarian diet do so out of a commitment toward nonviolence. For them, we are meant to be stewards and caretakers of the earth and its inhabitants and do not wish to support practices that inflict suffering on any creature that has the capacity to feel pain.

The small family farm where husbandry practices engendered a certain respect for the animals that were used for food is becoming a thing of the past. Today, most of the world's meat, dairy, and egg production occurs on massive factory farms that are owned by agribusiness conglomerates. This has brought about practices that view the raising and transportation of farm animals solely in terms of their ability to generate profits.

Animals are routinely given chemicals and antibiotics to keep them alive in these conditions. In order to increase the weight of cows, many are fed sawdust, plastic, tallow, grease, and cement dust seasoned with artificial flavors and aromas. Mother pigs on factory farms are kept in crates that are so small they are unable to turn around. Dairy cows are forced to remain pregnant most of their lives and are injected with hormones to increase milk production.

Male calves born from these cows are often raised to become "veal." This practice consists of confining a newborn calf to a crate that is so small that he is unable to turn around. This is to ensure that the flesh remains tender. They are fed diets that are deliberately iron deficient, a practice that induces anemia and allows the flesh to remain white. After four months or so in these conditions, the calf is slaughtered to produce "veal."

Go Organic

The Organic Trade Association states that "organic farming is based on practices that maintain soil fertility, while assisting nature's balance through diversity and recycling of energy and nutrients. This method also strives to avoid or reduce the use of synthetic

fertilizers and pest controls. Organic foods are processed, packaged, transported and stored to retain maximum nutritional value, without the use of artificial preservatives, coloring or other additives, irradiation or synthetic pesticides."

Some people wonder if it's worth it to buy organic. To that we reply that many of the chemicals in commercial pesticides and fertilizers have not been tested for their long-term effects on humans. Is it worth it to take that chance with your health and the health of your family? Organically grown foods represent a cycle of sustainability that improves topsoil fertility, enhances nutrition, and ensures food security.

Organic farmers employ farming methods that respect the fragile balance of our ecosystem. This results in a fraction of the groundwater pollution and topsoil depletion that's generated by conventional methods. Most people have also found the taste and nutrient quality of organic products to be superior to that of conventionally grown food.

Purchasing local, seasonal, and organically grown food is also an extremely effective way to reduce your environmental impact. Buying local saves the huge amount of energy it takes to transport food—sometimes across oceans and continents.

Another reason to support organic farmers has to do with the health of the farm workers themselves. Farm workers on conventional farms are exposed to high levels of toxic pesticides on a daily basis. Organic farm workers don't have to encounter these risks.

Last, by supporting organic farmers, we are supporting small, family farms. This once-prevalent method of farming is rapidly disappearing. This is due to the small farmer's inability to compete with the heavily subsidized agribusiness farms that use synthetic soil, pesticides, crop dusters, and heavy machinery on lands that encompass thousands of acres.

For more information on organic farming, visit your local farmers' market and talk to the farmers. You can also check out the Web sites for the International Federation of Organic Agriculture Movements, the Organic Consumers Association, and the Organic Trade Association, listed in Appendix C.

Say No to GMO

A GMO (genetically engineered and modified organism) is a plant, animal, or microorganism that has had its genetic code altered—typically by introducing genes from another organism. This process gives the GMO food characteristics that are not present in its original form. Many people feel this practice goes against nature and poses a profound threat to humans, the environment, and our agricultural heritage.

GMO seed manufacturers maintain that this makes the seed more pest resistant, promotes higher yields, or enhances nutrition. The fact is, the long-term effects of these seeds on the consumer and our genetic pool is still unknown. We believe this untested engineering is dangerous to human health in the long term. By definition, eating organic foods eliminates GMO from our food supply.

There are even GMO seeds that are referred to as *assassin seeds.* The plant that grows from these seeds produces seeds that are infertile. This prevents the replication of the genetic bond. This means that farmers must constantly purchase seeds every year from the companies that manufacture them.

Many communities around the world have succeeded in becoming GMO-free. Please join us in this critical movement to move our agriculture away from genetic engineering and toward truly sustainable agriculture. For more information, you may visit the Non-GMO Project at www.nongmoproject.org.

Composting: The Cycle of Life

Composting is the method of breaking down food waste, grass trimmings, and leaves to create nutrient-rich and fertile soil. It's the next step we can take toward creating a more sustainable method of growing our food. Compost contains nitrogen and micronutrients to keep the soil healthy and can be used as a mulch and soil amendment. When the soil is healthy, plant yields are higher and fertilizers and pesticides aren't as necessary.

Composting completes the cycle of life from seed to table and back to the Earth. Many communities sponsor composting programs and can give you all the tools and instructions you need to succeed. Check out www.compostguide.com for a complete guide to composting.

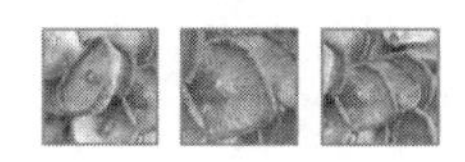

Appendix C: Additional Resources

Further Reading

Want to learn more? Explore this section to deepen your knowledge of the information touched upon in *Taste of the East.*

Vegan Education

Barnard, Neal. *Dr. Neal Barnard's Program for Reversing Diabetes: The Scientifically Proven System for Reversing Diabetes Without Drugs.* New York: Rodale Books, 2006.

Brazier, Brendan. *The Thrive Diet: The Whole Food Way to Lose Weight, Reduce Stress, and Stay Healthy for Life.* New York: Da Capo Press, 2007.

Campbell, T. Colin, and Thomas M. Campbell II. *The China Study: The Most Comprehensive Study of Nutrition Ever Conducted and the Startling Implications for Diet, Weight Loss, and Long-term Health.* Dallas: Benbella Books, 2006.

Esselstyn, Caldwell. *Prevent and Reverse Heart Disease.* New York: Avery Publishing, 2007.

Fuhrman, Joel, M.D. *Eat to Live: The Revolutionary Formula for Fast and Sustained Weight Loss.* Boston: Little, Brown, and Company, 2005.

Jacobson, Michael, Ph.D. *Six Arguments for a Greener Diet: How a Plant-based Diet Could Save Your Health and the Environment.* Washington, D.C.: Center for Science in the Public Interest, 2006.

Lyman, Howard. *Mad Cowboy: Plain Truth from the Cattle Rancher Who Won't Eat Meat.* New York: Scribner, 2001.

Marcus, Erik. *Vegan: The New Ethics of Eating.* Ithaca, NY: McBooks Press, 2001.

Ornish, Dean. *Dr. Dean Ornish's Program for Reversing Heart Disease: The Only System Scientifically Proven to Reverse Heart Disease Without Drugs or Surgery.* New York: Ivy Books, 1995.

Pitchford, P. *Healing with Whole Foods.* Berkeley, CA: North Atlantic Books, 1993.

Reinfeld, Mark, and Jennifer Murray. *The 30-Minute Vegan:* Over 175 Quick, Delicious, and Healthy Recipes for Everyday Cooking. New York: Da Capo Press, 2009.

Reinfeld, Mark, and Bo Rinaldi. *Vegan Fusion World Cuisine.* New York: Beaufort Books, 2007.

Reinfeld, Mark, Bo Rinaldi, and Jennifer Murray. *The Complete Idiot's Guide to Eating Raw.* Indianapolis: Alpha Books, 2008.

Robbins, John. *Diet for a New America.* Tiburon, CA: HJ Kramer, 1987.

———. *Healthy at 100.* New York: Random House, 2006.

Silverstone, Alicia. *The Kind Diet: A Simple Guide to Feeling Great, Losing Weight, and Saving the Planet.* New York: Rodale Books, 2009.

Stuart, Tristram. *The Bloodless Revolution: A Cultural History of Vegetarianism from 1600 to Modern Times.* New York: W. W. Norton, 2007.

Tuttle, Will, Ph.D. *World Peace Diet: Eating for Spiritual Health and Social Harmony.* Brooklyn, NY: Lantern Books, 2005.

East Meets West

Dass, Ram. *The Journey of Awakening : A Meditator's Guidebook.* New York: Bantam, 1990.

Douglas, Bill. *The Complete Idiot's Guide to T'ai Chi and QiGong,* 3rd ed. New York: Alpha Books, 2005.

Hoff, Benjamin. *The Tao of Pooh.* New York: Penguin Books, 1983.

Kabat-Zinn, Jon. *Wherever You Go, There You Are: Mindfulness Meditation in Everyday Life.* New York: Hyperion, 2005.

Lao Tzu. *Tao Te Ching: A New English Version.* Trans. by Stephen Mitchell. New York: Harper Classics, 2006.

McCall, Timothy. *Yoga as Medicine: The Yogic Prescription for Health and Healing by Yoga Journal.* New York: Bantam, 2007.

Nibodhi. *Ayurvedic Cooking for Health and Longevity.* Kerala, India: Mata Amritanandamayi Mission Trust, 2009.

Porter, Jessica. *The Hip Chick's Guide to Macrobiotics: A Philosophy for Achieving a Radiant Mind and a Fabulous Body.* New York: Avery Trade, 2004.

The I Ching or *Book of Changes*, 3rd ed. Trans. by Richard Wilhelm, Cary F. Baynes. Preface by Hellmut Wilhelm. Foreword by C. G. Jung. New Jersey: Princeton University Press, 1967.

Sadler, A. L. *The Japanese Tea Ceremony: Cha-No-Yu.* North Clarendon, VT: Tuttle Publishing, 2008.

Yarema, Thomas, Daniel Rhoda, and Johnny Brannigan. *Eat-Taste-Heal: An Ayurvedic Cookbook for Modern Living.* Kapaa, HI: Five Elements Press, 2006.

Online Resources

Here are some of our favorite Web sites and blogs promoting a vegan and sustainable way of life. We also list some go-to sites for kitchen equipment and to stock up your Asian pantry.

Vegan and Veg-Friendly Web Sites

www.animalconcerns.org
Animal Concerns Community serves as a clearinghouse for information on the Internet related to animal rights and welfare.

www.aspca.org
The American Society for the Prevention of Cruelty to Animals (ASPCA) provides effective means to prevent animal cruelty in the United States.

www.compassionatecooks.com
Compassionate Cooks offers vegetarian cooking classes, cooking videos, and recipes.

www.earthsave.org
Founded by John Robbins, EarthSave is doing what it can to promote a shift to a plant-based diet. It posts news, information, and resources and publishes a magazine.

www.farmusa.org
Farm Animal Reform Movement (FARM) is an organization advocating a plant-based diet and humane treatment of farm animals through grassroots programs.

www.godairyfree.org
Go Dairy Free is a comprehensive Web site with information on how to cook, shop, and dine dairy-free, while still promoting a healthy lifestyle.

www.happycow.net
Happy Cow is a searchable dining guide to vegetarian restaurants, natural health food stores, and information on vegetarian nutrition, raw foods, and vegan recipes.

www.hsus.org
The Humane Society of the U.S. (HSUS) works to create a world where humans relate to animals with compassion.

www.ivu.org
The World Union of Vegetarian/Vegan Societies had been promoting vegetarianism worldwide since 1908.

www.keepkidshealthy.com
A guide for raising vegan children with advice on providing your child with an early start to leading a long and healthy life.

www.pcrm.org
The Physicians Committee for Responsible Medicine (PCRM) is a nonprofit organization that promotes preventive medicine, conducts clinical research, and encourages higher standards for ethics and effectiveness in research.

www.peta.org
People for the Ethical Treatment of Animals (PETA), the largest animal rights organization in the world, is dedicated to establishing and protecting the rights of all animals.

www.tastyandmeatless.com
Tasty and Meatless is a weekly vegetarian television series on Time Warner Cable.

www.thekindlife.com
Alicia Silverstone's Web site in conjunction with her book, *The Kind Diet*, offers a forum, videos, recipes, and the latest from a hip celebrity vegan activist.

www.thevegetariansite.com
An extensive online source for vegan and vegetarian living, including health and nutrition info, animal rights info, news, and complete online shopping.

www.vegan.com
The popular site of Eric Marcus, geared toward the aspiring and long-term vegan, that features articles, interviews, product evaluations, book reviews, and more.

www.vegan.org
Vegan Action is a nonprofit grassroots organization dedicated to educating people about the many benefits of a vegan lifestyle.

www.veganbodybuilding.com
The Web site of vegan body builder Robert Cheeke features articles, videos, products, and a forum for the active vegan.

www.veganfitness.net
Vegan Fitness is a community-driven message board that provides a supportive, educational, and friendly environment for vegans, vegetarians, and those seeking to go vegan.

www.veganfusion.com
This is our own Web site, where you can sign up to receive the free *Vegan Fusion* newsletter with recipes and the latest current vegan events.

www.vegan.meetup.com
Meet up with other vegans in your town!

www.veganpassions.com
Vegan Passions is a free online dating site for meeting single vegans.

www.veganpeace.com
Vegan Peace is striving toward peacefully sharing our Earth and includes information about veganism, animal cruelty, recipes, cookbook reviews, and nutrition.

www.veganpet.com.au
Veganpet provides nutritionally complete and balanced pet food and information on raising vegan pets.

www.vegansociety.com
The Vegan Society promotes ways of living free of animal products for the benefit of people, animals, and the environment.

www.vegcooking.com
Features hundreds of vegetarian and vegan recipes with spotlights on vegetarian and vegan foods, products, menus, and restaurants.

www.vegdining.com
A vegetarian dining guide that includes an international search option, a monthly veggie restaurant contest, and the opportunity to purchase a VegDining card for discounts at participating vegetarian restaurants.

www.vegetarianteen.com
An online magazine with articles on vegetarian teen lifestyle, activism, nutrition, social issues, and more.

www.vegfamily.com
A comprehensive resource for raising vegan children, including pregnancy, vegan recipes, book reviews, product reviews, a message board, and more.

www.vegnews.com
An award-winning magazine that focuses on a vegetarian lifestyle featuring news, events, recipes, book reviews, the best veg products, travel tales, interviews, celebrity buzz, and more.

www.vegsoc.org
The Vegetarian Society is a registered charity committed to promoting the health, environmental, and animal welfare benefits of a vegetarian diet.

www.vegsource.com
Features over 10,000 vegetarian and vegan recipes, discussion boards, and information on nutritionists, medical doctors, experts, authors, articles, newsletter, and the vegetarian community.

www.vegtv.com
The site for Veg TV video production company, producing and streaming original content about vegetarian and vegan food, health, nutrition, and eco-travel.

www.vegweb.com
A vegetarian megasite with recipes, photos, articles, an online store, and more.

www.vrg.org
The Vegetarian Resource Group (VRG) is a nonprofit organization dedicated to educating the public on vegetarianism including information on health, nutrition, ecology, ethics, and world hunger.

Asian Specialty Ingredients

www.asianfoodgrocer.com
The Asian food online superstore!

www.AsiaRecipe.com
A comprehensive site from which you can learn about the history and folklore of Asian ingredients. Free recipes and an online store.

www.goldminenaturalfood.com
An online source for a vast selection of organic foods, raw foods, macrobiotic, vegan, gluten-free, Asian, gourmet, and specialty foods as well as natural cookware and home products.

www.indiablend.com
Online source for Indian ingredients.

www.PacificRimGourmet.com
A large selection of gourmet Asian ingredients, from oils and sauces to vegetables and fruit.

www.quickspice.com
For ingredients and equipment with an emphasis on Japanese and Chinese products.

www.TempleofThai.com and www.Importfood.com
For all of your Thai ingredients, equipment, and more.

Organic and Gardening Web Sites

www.avant-gardening.com
A site advocating organic gardening with information on composting, soil building, permaculture principles, botany, companion and intensive planting, and more.

www.biodynamics.com
The Biodynamic Farming and Gardening Association supports and promotes biodynamic farming, the oldest nonchemical agricultural movement.

www.earthflow.com
Earthflow is an all-natural approach to permaculture design, offering garden tours and training programs, including permaculture courses.

www.gefoodalert.org
GE Food Alert Campaign Center is a coalition of seven organizations committed to testing and labeling genetically engineered food.

www.ifoam.org
The International Federation of Organic Agriculture Movements (IFOAM) is the umbrella organization for hundreds of organic organizations worldwide.

www.foodsubs.com
An awesome site, the Cook's Thesaurus is a cooking encyclopedia that covers thousands of ingredients and kitchen tools. Entries include pictures, descriptions, synonyms, pronunciations, and suggested substitutions.

www.organicconsumers.org
The Organic Consumers Association is an online grassroots, nonprofit organization dealing with issues of food safety, industrial agriculture, genetic engineering, corporate accountability, and environmental sustainability.

www.organicgardening.com
Find out where to get your soil tested, manage pests without using chemicals, and read vegetable and flower growing guides.

www.ota.com
The Organic Trade Association (OTA) Web site will tell you anything you want to know about the term *organic*, from food to textiles to health-care products. The OTA's mission is to encourage global sustainability through promoting and protecting the growth of diverse organic trade.

www.permacultureactivist.net
The Permaculture Activist reports the work of grassroots landscape designers and social change artists from around the world.

www.seedsofchange.com
This site is now divided in two sections—one for seeds and gardening, the other an online store for organic food products.

www.wwoof.org
World-Wide Opportunities on Organic Farms (WWOOF) is an association helping those who wish to volunteer on organic farms internationally.

Environmental and Sustainability Web Sites

www.childrenoftheearth.org
Children of the Earth United is a children's environmental education site that educates the public on ecological concepts and aims to provide a forum for people to share knowledge and ideas.

www.conservation.org
Conservation International is involved in many conservation projects worldwide. On its site you can calculate your carbon footprint based on your living situation, car, travel habits, and diet.

www.dinegreen.com
The Green Restaurant Association (GRA) is a national nonprofit organization that provides a convenient way for all sectors of the restaurant industry, which represents 10 percent of the U.S. economy, to become more environmentally sustainable.

www.greenpeace.org

Greenpeace focuses on the most crucial worldwide threats to our planet's biodiversity and environment.

www.higean.org/kauai

GMO-Free Kauai is a grassroots organization created to raise awareness and educate the public about the health, economic, and environmental risks of genetically engineered and modified organisms. Hawaii, including the island of Kaua'i, is one of the top two states in the country for open-air GMO field testing.

www.nrdcwildplaces.org

The Natural Resources Defense Council (NRDC) is an environmental action group with over one million members working to safeguard the American continents' natural systems.

www.pirg.org

The Public Interest Research Group (PIRG) is an alliance of state-based, citizen-funded organizations that provide result-oriented activism to protect the environment, develop a fair marketplace, and encourage a responsive, democratic government. Look for your state's PIRG on the Web site.

www.ran.org

Rainforest Action Network is working to protect tropical rainforests around the world and the human rights of those living in and around those forests.

www.sierraclub.org

The Sierra Club is America's oldest, largest, and most influential grassroots environmental organization.

Eco-Friendly Products and Services

www.blendtec.com/

Blendtec's Fine Living Products include mixers, blenders, grain mills, and more. Their blender is a favorite in our household.

www.ecoproducts.com

Ecoproducts is the premier site for biodegradable and compostable food service products and environmentally friendly household supplies.

www.877juicer.com

This site carries way more than juicers, including everything kitchen-related, plus air purifiers, books, and articles.

www.foodfightgrocery.com

Food Fight! Grocery is an all-vegan convenience store located in Portland, Oregon, with an online market that emphasizes junk foods, imports, and fun stuff.

www.greenpeople.org

Green People provides a directory of eco-friendly products and services.

www.pureprescriptions.com

Pure prescriptions is an online superstore for high-quality nutritional products, complete with free consultations and a health library.

www.vitamix.com
Find the latest Vita-Mix blenders here on the official site, including factory-reconditioned models that still come with a seven-year warranty. For free shipping in the continental United States, enter code 06-002510.

Raw Food Lifestyle

www.sunfood.com
David Wolfe's Web site, Nature's First Law, provides the raw foodist with everything from food and supplements, to appliances, to books, and personals ads.

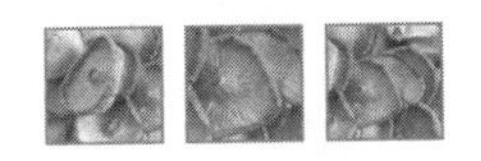

Glossary

Agave nectar a sweetener from the agave cactus, it ranges in color from golden to brown. Composed mainly of fructose and glucose, it has a low glycemic index and is about 1½ times sweeter than sugar.

Apple cider vinegar look for the raw variety, which preserves many of the apple's nutrients and is considered to have beneficial healing qualities.

Arame a species of kelp high in calcium, protein, iron, iodine, and other vitamins and minerals.

Arrowroot a powdered starch made from the root of the arrowroot plant. Used as a thickener in sauces, soups, and desserts. Dissolve arrowroot with an equal amount of cold water before adding to the mixture being thickened.

Barley malt syrup a sweetener that is roughly half as sweet as honey or sugar. Made from sprouted barley, it has a nutty caramel flavor.

Brown rice syrup a relatively neutral-flavored sweetener made from cultured brown rice. It is roughly half as sweet as sugar.

Buckwheat a triangular-shaped seed often considered a grain. It's not related to wheat and is entirely gluten-free. Raw groats are used in live food preparation. The roasted groat is called kasha.

Celtic sea salt unrefined, with a high mineral content, this light-gray salt is naturally harvested off the coast of France. It is one of the most highly regarded forms of salt.

Coconut oil although high in saturated fat, and therefore solid at room temperature, coconut oil is being studied for its healing potential.

Composting the natural biological process of breaking down food waste, grass trimmings, and leaves to create a nutrient-rich soil.

CSA Community-Supported Agriculture CSAs are generally small, local, organic farms where members buy in with labor, money, or both in exchange for a weekly selection of fresh produce from the farm.

Daikon literally translates as "large root," this white Japanese radish is spicy, crisp, and juicy.

Dulse an iron-rich sea vegetable that is a good source of vitamin B6, fluoride, and potassium. Use the flakes as a salt replacement, sprinkled on salads, soups, or steamed veggies. The whole pieces make for a nutritious snack.

Garbanzo beans also known as chickpeas, garbanzo beans are common in Indian as well as Central Asian and Middle Eastern dishes.

Genetically engineered and modified organism (GMO) a plant, animal, or microorganism that has had its genetic code altered, typically by introducing genes from another organism. This process gives the GMO characteristics that are not present in its original form.

Glycemic Index (GI) a scale demonstrating how quickly a food influences blood glucose levels. The lower the number, the slower blood glucose increases (due to a slower digestion time). Diabetics and persons with heart disease should eat low-GI foods.

Himalayan crystal salt considered one of the purist and least processed salts, it is more than 250 million years old, mined in the Himalayas by hand and carefully rinsed.

Hydrogenated fats fats created by synthetically adding hydrogen to the double bond of an unsaturated fat via a process called hydrogenation. It allows the fat to stay solid at room temperature and delays rancidity. Used to make margarine and shortening, these fats also occur naturally in small amounts in various animal products. Hydrogenation produces trans-fatty acids, which have been proven to increase the risk of coronary heart disease. *See* Trans-fatty acids.

Kaffir lime leaf the bay leaf of Southeast Asia, the kaffir lime leaf is added to stocks and soups and removed before serving. A must-have for Thai dishes.

Kelp brown algae that grows in large, dense underwater forests, some three stories high, in cold, clear waters. Growing as much as 2 feet per day, kelp is high in B vitamins, protein, iron, magnesium, and zinc and is a source of iodine.

Kombu a wide and flat seaweed, kombu is a good source of calcium, folate, and magnesium. We add it to beans while cooking to bring out the flavor of the bean and increase digestibility.

Lacto-ovo vegetarians vegetarians whose diet includes eggs and dairy products.

Lacto-vegetarians vegetarians whose diet includes dairy products but not eggs.

Lemongrass a grass popular in Thai and Vietnamese cuisine that imparts a lemony citrus flavor.

Live or living foods those raw foods that are soaked, sprouted, or cultured to enhance enzyme activity.

Maple syrup the boiled-down sap of sugar maple trees. It is rich in minerals such as manganese and zinc and contains fewer calories than honey. It is graded according to color and flavor. Grade A is the mildest and lightest, Grade C is the darkest and richest. Good for baking.

Mandoline a handy kitchen tool used to slice, julienne, or crinkle-cut harder vegetables quickly by hand.

Micro greens vegetables and herbs that are just past their sprouting stage. The small leaves and tender stems of young arugula, endive, and mizuna and many other plants pack a powerful burst of flavor and nutrients. Add some to your salad, wraps, or nori rolls.

Mirin a sweet and tangy Japanese rice cooking wine that many cooks use as a "secret ingredient" to add a unique flavor to a variety of dishes.

Miso a salty paste made by fermenting soybeans, grains, or other beans. Used in many recipes, including dips, dressings, sauces, spreads, and the traditional soup. Boiling miso destroys many of its beneficial nutrients.

Molasses this syrup is a liquid by-product of the sugar refining process. It contains many of the nutrients of the sugar cane plant and has a strong, somewhat bittersweet flavor.

Nama shoyu *nama* means "raw" or "unpasteurized"; *shoyu* is Japanese for "soy sauce." Nama shoyu is an unpasteurized condiment made from cultured soy beans and wheat.

Nori a highly nutritious red algae that's shredded, dried, and pressed like paper, providing calcium, iron, and other vitamins and minerals.

Nutritional yeast a plant-based culture consisting of up to 50 percent protein. The Red Star variety is a source of B vitamins including B12, is naturally low in sodium and fat, and is generally extracted from molasses.

Olive oil ranging in flavor from mild to strong; we recommend the organic extra-virgin cold-pressed variety, which is from the first pressing of the olives.

Organic farming a natural and environmentally friendly way to grow food without the use of chemical fertilizers and pesticides. Organic methods include, but are not limited to, crop rotation, integrated pest management, natural fertilizers, and composting.

Preventive medicine a healing modality devoted to health promotion and disease prevention. It advocates making diet and lifestyle changes to achieve maximum health and prevent illness.

Protein an important component of cells, tissues, organs, muscles, and bones. The current dietary guidelines recommend that healthy persons daily eat 0.8 g/kg body weight.

Quinoa an ancient Incan grain that is one of the highest plant sources of protein. It's also a source of calcium, iron, phosphorus, B vitamins, and vitamin E.

Raw foods foods that have not been cooked above a certain temperature, generally considered 116°F. *See* Live or living foods.

Saffron the hand-picked stigma or the saffron crocus flower, it's the most precious and expensive spice in the world. It imparts a bright orange-yellow color and an exotic flavor and aroma.

Sea salt made from evaporated sea water. Higher in minerals than commercially processed table salt. *See also* Celtic sea salt and Himalayan crystal salt.

Seitan originating in ancient China and sometimes referred to as "meat of wheat" or "Buddha food." It is wheat gluten dough that has been cooked in a broth with different types of seasonings.

Shoyu a traditional Japanese soy sauce that is made from fermented soybeans and wheat. It imparts a strong salty flavor. *See also* Soy sauce and Tamari.

Soy milk a popular soy-based milk with a nutty taste, this alternative to animal milk is made using cooked soybeans. There are many brands and many different flavored soymilks available.

Soy sauce a traditional Japanese condiment that is made from fermented soybeans and wheat. It imparts a strong salty flavor. *See also* Shoyu and Tamari.

Spelt a highly nutritious and ancient grain that is in the wheat family and yet is generally tolerated by those with wheat allergies. It has a slightly nutty flavor and may be used to replace whole-wheat flour in baked goods and pastas.

Spiralizer a kitchen tool that slices and shreds and allows you to create unique garnishes and continuous strands of "pasta" from vegetables such as zucchini or summer squash.

Standard American Diet (SAD) the eating habits of the "average" American. It generally refers to a low-fiber diet that is high in animal fats, processed and fast foods, and foods high in sugar, salt, and artificial ingredients.

Stevia leaf a member of the mint family originating in Paraguay, South America, Stevia is hundreds of times sweeter than sugar and is actually purported to benefit tooth health. For baking conversions, please visit www.steviashop.com/additional uses.php.

Sucanat is an abbreviation for "sugar cane natural," a granular sweetener that consists of evaporated sugar cane juice. It has approximately the same sweetness as sugar but retains most of the vitamins and minerals of the sugar cane.

Tamari a by-product of the miso making process, tamari can have some wheat in it but is also frequently marketed as a wheat-free variety of soy sauce. It is thicker,

darker, and has a stronger flavor than other soy sauces. *See also* Shoyu and Soy sauce.

Tamarind a tropical fruit widely used in drinks, sauces, and Pad Thai. The pulp has a sweet-and-sour flavor and is rich in B vitamins and calcium. It's popular in chutney in Indian cuisine and is used in drinks around the world.

Tempeh originally from Indonesia, tempeh consists of soybeans cultured in a rice culture, then cooked. Many different varieties are created by mixing the soybean with grains such as millet, wheat, or rice.

Tofu processed soybean curd with origins in ancient China. It is commercially sold in a number of different varieties, including extra-firm, firm, soft, and silken. Each variety lends itself to a particular type of food preparation.

Turbinado sugar a large crystal created as a by-product from the first pressing of sugar cane. Moister than refined sugar, it is roughly as sweet as brown sugar and retains some molasses content.

Trans-fatty acids produced during the hydrogenation process, this synthetic fat has been linked to heart disease. The use of trans-fats in restaurants has been banned in several countries as well as in New York City, Philadelphia, and several other U.S. cities.

Transition foods products or ingredients that assist us in switching from less healthful foods to healthier alternatives. While not necessarily the most healthful items themselves, they fill a role in satisfying cravings. It's not recommended to have these transition foods make up a large part of our diet.

Umeboshi plum a Japanese plum that's salted, pickled, and aged for many years. The paste imparts a tangy, salty flavor to many dishes and is also used as a spread in nori rolls.

Unsaturated fats mono- and poly-unsaturated fats that are liquid at room temperature. They're found in nuts, seeds, and foods such as avocadoes, olives, corn, and their oils.

Vegans people who follow a plant-based diet. They eat and live without using or consuming animal products.

Vegetarians people who do not eat meat, fish, or poultry. *See also* Lacto-ovo vegetarians; Lacto-vegetarians.

Wakame part of the kelp family, this green seaweed is popular in Asia and is used in soups, salads, and noodle dishes. It's high in calcium, niacin, thiamin, and other B vitamins.

Wasabi powder a ground horseradish root that's pungent and quite spicy. When combined with water, it forms a paste that is a traditional Japanese condiment.

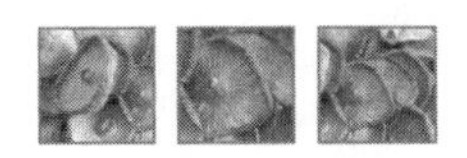

Index

INDEX

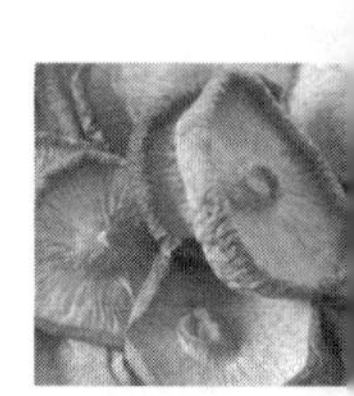

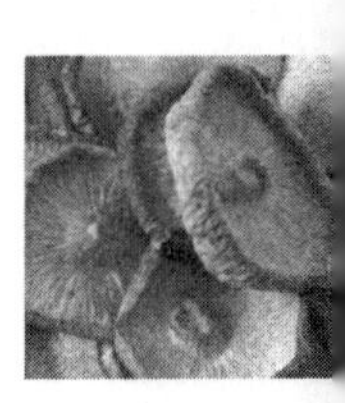